www.wadsworth.com

wadsworth.com is the World Wide Web site for Wadsworth Publishing Company and is your direct source to dozens of online resources.

At *wadsworth.com* you can find out about supplements, demonstration software, and student resources. You can also send e-mail to many of our authors and preview new publications and exciting new technologies.

wadsworth.com
Changing the way the world learns®

Becoming a Teacher in a Field-Based Setting

An Introduction to Education and Classrooms

Donna L. Wiseman
Northern Illinois University

Donna D. Cooner
Texas A&M University

Stephanie L. Knight
Texas A&M University

Wadsworth Publishing Company
I⊤P® An International Thomson Publishing Company

Belmont, CA • Albany, NY • Boston • Cincinnati • Johannesburg • London
Madrid • Melbourne • Mexico City • New York • Pacific Grove, CA
Scottsdale, AZ • Singapore • Tokyo • Toronto

Education Editor: Dianne Lindsay
Assistant Editor: Valerie Morrison
Editorial Assistant: Tangelique Williams
Marketing Manager: Becky Tollerson
Advertising Project Manager: Joe Fierst
Project Editor: Jennie Redwitz
Print Buyer: Barbara Britton
Permissions Editor: Bob Kauser

Production: Vicki Moran
Text Design: Vicki Moran
Text photo credits listed on page 283
Cover Design: Liz Harasymczuk
Cover Image: Ray Boudreau
Copy Editor: Darlene Bledsoe
Compositor: Publishing Support Services
Printer: Malloy Lithographing, Inc.

Printed in the United States of America
1 2 3 4 5 6 7 8 9 10

For more information contact Wadsworth Publishing Company, 10 Davis Drive,
Belmont, California 94002, or electronically at http://www.wadsworth.com

International Thomson Publishing Europe
Berkshire House
168-173 High Holborn
London, WC1V 7AA, United Kingdom

International Thomson Editores
Seneca, 53
Colonia Polanco
11560 México D.F. México

Nelson ITP, Australia
102 Dodds Street
South Melbourne
Victoria 3205 Australia

International Thomson Publishing Asia
60 Albert Street
#15-01 Albert Complex
Singapore 189969

Nelson Canada
1120 Birchmount Road
Scarborough, Ontario
Canada M1K 5G4

International Thomson Publishing Japan
Hirakawa-cho Kyowa Building, 3F
2-2-1 Hirakawa-cho, Chiyoda-ku
Tokyo 102 Japan

International Thomson Publishing Southern Africa
Building 18, Constantia Square
138 Sixteenth Road, P. O. Box 2459
Halfway House, 1685 South Africa

Library of Congress Cataloging-in-Publication Data
Wiseman, Donna L. (Donna Louise)
    Becoming a teacher in a field-based setting : an introduction to
education and classrooms / Donna L. Wiseman, Donna D. Cooner, Stephanie
L. Knight.
       p. cm.
    Includes bibliographical references and index.
    ISBN 0-534-50871-5
    1. Student teaching—United States—Handbooks, manuals, etc.
2. Teachers—Training of—United States—Handbooks, manuals, etc.
3. Education—Study and teaching (Higher)—United States—Handbooks,
manuals, etc. I. Cooner, Donna D. (Donna Danell) II. Knight,
Stephanie L. III. Title
LB2157.U5W57   1998   98-8094
370'.71—dc21

Contents

v

2

Surveying Educational History and Philosophy   28

3 Understanding Current Educational Context 49

4 Describing the Status of Contemporary Children 78

5

Interpreting Classroom Learning Theory   107

6 Establishing a Successful Classroom Environment 147

Preface

Teaching teachers, like teaching children, is not a morally neutral affair. It is the discharging and instilling of obligations, the primary one of which is discovery and growth in what can be termed the learning process . . . What we owe children, we owe teachers.

Sarason 1993; 135

Teaching in today's classrooms will be different from what you remember about your own early school experiences. The profession has changed quite dramatically, and teaching continues to acquire multiple and complex dimensions. You will need new and different skills than teachers of the present need. Some understandings will develop as you gain experiences. However, experience in the absence of reflection will not guarantee growth. Reflection is an important part of your development as an educator. Reflection can be both an individual and a shared process. Discussions with peers, teachers, mentors, university professors, and elementary and secondary school students will enable you to reflect upon your experiences through different lenses. As you mature as a teacher, reflecting on your experiences will allow you to effectively interface with colleagues and professionals who work with children and families, deliver instruction to diverse learners, use technology in classroom instruction, and create an environment of mutual trust between you and your future students.

The text is designed to introduce you to the education profession—its historical and current contexts, the complexities of teaching and learning, and the dynamics of a classroom. It assumes that what you learn about teaching during your university experience is only the first step in becoming a teacher. We cannot give you a set of skills to see you through your teaching career. Your needs as a beginning teacher are quite different from those of experienced teachers. The first steps of learning to teach are at times both exciting and daunting. As a beginning teacher you will need to realize that you are not the first to experience the insecurities and challenges of becoming a teacher.

One of the best places for you to learn about teaching is in a school environment. We are assuming that your preparation program includes several opportunities for you to work in schools and with students. The experiences you have in the schools are planned by university professors and classroom teachers through a partnership that has been formed between the school and the university. The school-university partnership that accompanies your teacher education program is an attempt to connect university- and school-based perspectives. Connecting the two perspectives is the best way to learn to teach—recognizing the contribution of university-sponsored research and theory while integrating the practical knowledge that teachers have gained from their own classroom experience (Zeichner, 1992). There will be times when theory and practice collide. The things you read in your textbook and talk about in class may not match what you are seeing in the classroom setting. When this happens it is important to talk about the differences and establish a balance between educational theory and classroom practice. Sometimes, educators don't understand the role of theory and feel that practice is the best way to learn to teach. To be a professional, you must understand both the theories and the practice of teaching.

It is important that you understand the ideas of teachers as you learn about becoming a teacher. The ideas in this text are accompanied by examples and descriptions written by beginning and experienced teachers. The "voices" sections of the chapters are designed to provide an element of "insider" account and are one way to provide a vehicle for the sound of teachers' voices (Shulman, 1992). The classroom narratives evolve from interviews and written responses provided by teachers who are currently dealing with issues discussed in the text. When appropriate, the views of children, parents, principals, and others will be included. Their stories provide clarification and interpretation for some of the topics presented in the text.

You will become a professional by observing, doing, inquiring, and reflecting on teaching and learning. Each chapter has suggested activities and guidelines for discussions with the classroom teachers in the school where you observe. This will cultivate working relationships between you and classroom teachers. The Field-Based Activities that are in each of the chapters will encourage you to become involved in reflecting upon what you see when you are in the classroom. Some of the activities will encourage development and collection of portfolio artifacts. You will select from the suggested activities—not all have to be completed. Your supervisor or university professor will help you select and personalize the activities. The portfolio activities are more than course requirements—they are designed to engage you in the important process of reflection and will serve as a representation of your growth in this important first phase of becoming a teacher.

References

Shulman, J. (1992). *Case methods in teacher education*. New York: Teachers College Press.

Zeichner, K. (1992). Rethinking the practicum in the professional development school partnership. *Journal of Teacher Education, 43*(4), 296–307.

Acknowledgments

We are particularly indebted to the many teachers and principals who collaborated with us as we have restructured our own roles to include a school-university perspective. All three of us have been inspired by the teachers who teach at South Knoll Elementary School, College Station, Texas. The teachers at this school made a commitment to preparing new teachers, and their school was transformed as a result of their efforts. Their ability to reflect on their own practice, continue their own professional development, and guide new teachers' first attempts at teaching produced one of the best examples of a Professional Development School that we have experienced thus far. They have taught us many new lessons about collaborating, teaching, and researching.

We owe a special debt of gratitude to Angela Vogeler at Northern Illinois University who patiently worked with our editorial scribbles and helped communication between the three of us go more smoothly.

We would like to thank the following reviewers for their suggestions: Ceola Ross Barber, The University of North Carolina at Greensboro; Nadine Bezuk, San Diego State University; Lynn Burlbaw, Texas A&M University; Jeri A. Carroll, Wichita State University; Linda K. Christian-Smith, University of Wisconsin–Oshkosh; Mary Dents, University of Minnesota; J. Gary Knowles, University of Michigan; Douglas MacIsaac, University of Northern Colorado; Carol Ann Mullen, Ontario Institute for Studies in Education; Barbara

Parramore, North Carolina State University; Sue Passmore, Texas Wesleyan University; Melvin J. Pedras, University of Idaho; Rita Saslow, University of Akron; Rita G. Seedorf, Eastern Washington University; and Betty Jo Simmons, Longwood College.

The Wadsworth editors and staff provided support and encouragement to help finish this project. Our ideas were first heard by Sabra Horne. Dianne Lindsay worked us through the finishing process. Valerie Morrison, a Wadsworth assistant editor, deserves a lot of credit for her unfailing humor and efficient guidance. Our thanks to to all of those people.

Donna L. Wiseman
Donna D. Cooner
Stephanie L. Knight

1
Developing a Personal View of Teaching

In this chapter
- Impact of Personal Biography on Teaching
- Reasons for Becoming a Teacher
- Characteristics of Good Teachers
- Teaching as a Lifelong Learning Process
- The Formal Steps of Learning to Teach
- Learning to Teach in a Field-Based Setting

remember every teacher I ever had. I say this not to boast about my memory but to illustrate just how powerfully my teachers influenced me. Some of them I knew quite well, particularly the ones in the elementary school, because of the intense relationship between elementary school teachers and their students in their self-contained classrooms and because they lived in my community and were a part of my life outside the classroom. Others I knew only as teachers. I had no idea what their lives were like outside the school or even if they had lives outside of school. The story of those I knew well could be the subject of a book unto itself. Memories of the others provoke a series of questions for me. Who were you really? What did you care about? What did you think of me? Did you even know who I am?

—Gloria Ladson-Billings, *The Dreamkeepers*

1

Good teachers touch learners' lives and captivate their students' attentions, motivating them to learn, and encouraging them to do their best. They can demonstrate passion about a content area while caring for and respecting their students. At the same time, teachers are capable of critiquing their schools and understanding the impact of state and local requirements on classroom instruction. Teachers interact with parents and community leaders from all walks of life. They play an important role in the community and know how to use the resources available to them to benefit their students. They are able to understand five-year-olds' explanations of important life events or adolescents' defense of their favorite rock music. In sum, they are lifelong learners who focus their varied skills and abilities on working with young learners.

The teaching profession is complex and challenging. To meet these challenges, future teachers need experiences that will help them acquire and later refine the required skills and abilities. The reflection encouraged in your formal teacher preparation will serve as a model for learning throughout your teaching career. This chapter will help you consider and answer questions such as the following:

- Why do you want to be a teacher?
- What experiences have shaped your ideas about teaching?
- What is a good teacher?
- How do teachers learn how to teach?

Impact of Personal Biography on Teaching

Teachers' past and present life experiences impact their attitudes and definitions of teaching and create important influences on their identities as teachers (Knowles, 1992). Personal—and professional—biography becomes a rich source of information that helps clarify teachers' dispositions and behaviors and accounts for some of their ability to be socialized into the world of teaching. Childhood experiences, early teacher role models, teaching experiences, and significant or important people (Crow, 1987; Knowles, 1992) make important contributions to an individual's definition of and approach to teaching.

Teachers explain that they have entered the profession because they want to positively impact young people's lives. Many believe that becoming a teacher is more than a career choice—it is a calling.

Childhood Experiences

Many teachers can recall when, as a child, they set up a school in their backyard and enlisted their brothers and sisters as students. While not every child who "plays" teacher in his or her early years becomes a teacher, it certainly indicates that teaching is something that we observe and know about early in our lives. These early observations and feelings about school and teaching contribute to the ways we think about teaching and what we do in our classrooms.

Even those childhood experiences that occur away from the classroom can become a part of how teachers identify their roles. Personality development, socialization patterns, and ways of interacting with others are some of the same traits developed during early experiences that ultimately become integral parts of teachers' identities. For example, our notion of intelligence as a factor that can change or not may develop in response to the way our parents and early teachers regard intelligence.

Family members provide a great deal of input in how you think about teaching. Those who grow up with parents who teach may be impacted by their parents' careers. If parents are teachers and talk about their work during family interactions, their philosophy and framework can easily become a part of their own children's philosophy. Dinnertime discussions about teaching and schools have the potential to remain with teachers throughout their career. Certainly, family attitudes toward teaching will impact a future teacher's way of thinking about schools.

In addition, family expectations and rules contribute to teacher identity. Behaviors learned as a child, as well as patterns of interaction and family values, can impact teaching behaviors. Parents and early childhood experiences influence future teachers in other ways as well. Parental expectations about work, learning, play, creativity, and other important issues are reflected in our teaching careers. Such personal attributes as work habits established as a young child stay with the adult teacher.

Role Models

Positive influences from teachers may provide a clear view of what it means to be a teacher. (The impact is even stronger if your parents were teachers.) As Kristen, a future teacher shares, "I have impressions in my mind of some of my favorite teachers; I want that same impression of myself in my students' minds." Obviously, favorite teachers can become significant in helping individuals become teachers. Teachers may recognize a particular talent and encourage their students to become teachers. School experiences also contribute to our perception of the teacher's roles. Even negative experiences with teachers can result in a clear conception of teaching based on what we do not want to be. If we did not have good experiences in the classroom, then we may have a different view of how to handle students. For example, those who had experiences in very structured schools may have difficulty developing spontaneous instructional patterns and open classroom responses. These early encounters with teachers continue to help us understand teaching. Studies of teachers' biographies demonstrate that positive school environments encourage positive role identification with teachers as well as positive preservice teacher behaviors (Knowles, 1992).

Teachers at the university also contribute to ideas about teaching. This influence is most powerful during the preservice stage of your career. Many of the experiences and interactions you have in your university coursework will begin to model your explicit views of teaching.

Teaching Experiences

Working with children in informal and formal learning environments also provides motivation for becoming a teacher. Experiences in church school, baby-sitting, and summer programs are ways future teachers discover that they have a special talent or preference for interacting with young learners.

Specific lessons are learned in these first encounters with teaching. Early teaching experiences provide frameworks for dealing with children, planning instruction, selecting strategies, and feeling comfortable in the classroom. Teachers' early experiences using small groups or discussion activities in church school might influence the use of some of the same techniques in their own classrooms. Tutoring experiences teach future teachers how to use one-on-one strategies effectively in classroom settings. Early experiences with teaching help individuals understand and use interpersonal skills related to teacher-student interactions.

Preservice teachers can easily relate to viewpoints and orientations to practices in classrooms that are like their images of teachers' work. You may find that you reflect on and consider your early experiences as you begin to learn to teach. Early experiences appear to be what new teachers rely on when faced with difficult experiences or important classroom decisions (Knowles, 1992). New teachers revert to behaviors they learned during previous teaching experiences. When your university professor talks about a certain strategy, such as cooperative grouping, it may remind you of times that you were involved in such a strategy. Early experiences can be used as a foundation for reflection. However, it is important to do more than remember the experiences. You also should question why a teacher used the strategy, how children responded, and how you might change or adapt your early experiences. Recognizing and analyzing your memories of early teaching or learning opportunities convert past experiences into strong influences on your response to current and future classroom events and teaching decisions.

The process of becoming a teacher starts long before you enter a formal university program. Many beliefs, attitudes about teaching, understanding about children and learning, and educational values are established by early life

FIELD-BASED ACTIVITY 1.1

Develop a biographical timeline that traces who or what influenced your decision to become a teacher. Form small work groups made up of classmates, and identify common themes and factors across the data. Categories can be established by writing group responses on three-by-five-inch cards and organizing them in themes that share similar features. After agreeing on common characteristics, the group can label and discuss each card grouping.

experiences. Your university preparation will provide you the opportunity to reflect and expand upon what it means to be an effective teacher in today's schools.

Reasons for Becoming a Teacher

The most compelling reason given for becoming a teacher involves the interpersonal interactions resulting from continuous contact with children and young people. Specifically, teachers mention that they like to work with children and youth, make a difference in their lives, and see the look of joy when a student finally "gets it" (Louis Harris & Associates, 1995). Reasons such as these are given by teachers who view teaching as a special mission in our society, consider teaching a valuable service and a way to make a lasting contribution to society. One teacher explained her career choice by saying, "I want to be a difference in somebody's life. I want to mean something . . . change something. I would choose teaching again in a minute if I had the chance. It's what I want to do."

Other reasons that influence people to become teachers include ease of entry, exit, and reentry into the profession, flexibility of time, and material benefits (Lortie, 1975; Louis Harris, 1995). The teaching career is accessible to individuals who start their careers in other fields and develop a second career. Parents enjoy the hours that parallel their children's hours, including the time

---

FIELD-BASED ACTIVITY 1.2

Either form a panel of teachers or professors working in your schools or interview your mentor and/or supervising teacher and ask about early influences on career decisions. Ask why they became teachers and remain in teaching. Work with your classmates and compile the responses. Using your notecards from Activity 1.1, compare the reasons of these experienced teachers with the categories generated. How do they compare? Prepare a chart, graph, or diagram that depicts differences between beginning teachers and experienced teachers. Compare your chart with material from this chapter, and see if your class has discovered findings similar to researchers in other settings.

---

off during holidays and in the summer. Satisfying salaries, job security, and benefits also attract individuals into teaching careers. Nevertheless, without fail, surveys continue to demonstrate that teachers who indicate that they are not likely to leave the profession give "love of teaching" as the reason they will continue (Louis Harris, 1995).

Perhaps due to the positive influences of family members, teaching often continues as a family tradition. One future teacher in five reports a mother or father who taught at one time or is still teaching. Parents serve as models and greatly impact decisions to become teachers. As one future teacher wrote, "I never had the opportunity to have my Dad as a teacher, but I have always heard wonderful things about him from his ex-students. . . . I guess you could say I am in the 'family' business."

Despite the statistics, some parents may not support their children's decisions to become teachers. Many beginning teachers report that family members tried to dissuade them from entering the teaching profession. Future teachers are often aware of the negative perceptions associated with a teaching career but not daunted by them. One future teacher admitted, "When I made it to college—graduating at the top of my high school class—my whole family said I shouldn't go into teaching. 'You're too smart to teach,' they said. 'You need to be a doctor or lawyer and make some money. I was the only one in my extended family to ever get a degree, so everyone was pushing me to do different things. I looked at business, but nothing excited me like teaching."

Characteristics of Good Teachers

Everyone has a vision of a good teacher or can tell a story of an exceptional teacher and her impact. Even as early as first grade, children have opinions on what makes a good teacher and produce delightful responses indicating what makes a good teacher (See Figure 1.1). But, what makes a good teacher may vary, depending on the perspective taken when descriptions are formed. A review of how young children define good teaching may provide a composite profile of what is honored and regarded as good teaching.

We may be more sophisticated than the first-graders when we describe what makes a good teacher, but it is possible to recognize their views in even the most academic presentation. The document that sets forth the national standards for teaching and establishes the fundamental requirements for proficient teaching as a broad grounding in the liberal arts and sciences; knowledge of the subjects to

Figure 1.1
First-Graders Describe a Good Teacher

These are excerpts of what first-graders wrote about what makes a good teacher. Their original spellings add to the charm of their descriptions.

A good teacher is nice, smart, and has good handwriting. And in order. And gets her stuff dun on time.

 —Zach, age 7

A good teacher is someone Who makes good disishons [decisions]. A good teacher is nice.

 —Manuel, age 8

A good teacher helps you lurn!

 —Elizabeth B., age 7

A good techer helps. A good techer has a plan. some techers giv you a good plan. A good good techer love all the cis [kids] in hr clas. A good techer givs you in st stuchins [instructions] all the time. a techer hast to have a room and qostivachin [positive action].

 —Beth Ann, age 7

I think that the qualities of being a good teacher is the importance of the children learning. You really feel good when you are a teacher. The main thing is to help the kids learn. I think being a teacher is a good job. you should try!

 —Dustin, age 8

Teachers sould have a good atutood [attitude] and be a little pushy. The teachers jobs are teaching math and siens [science] and arithmatick, acsedera acsedera [et cetera, et cetera]. A teacher wants to be a teacher because they jost wont to be by kids!

 —Stacy, age 8

---

be taught, of the skills to be developed, and of the curriculum and materials; knowledge of methods for teaching, learner development, skills in understanding the diverse needs of students, and ability to employ such knowledge in the interest of students (National Board for Professional Teaching Standards 1997). The national board further explains good teaching by describing five propositions necessary for good teaching

World Wide Web Site: You may learn more about the National Board for Professional Teaching Standards at: http://www.nbpts.org/

1. Commitment to Students and Their Learning

The basic assumption that teachers must possess is that all children can learn. In addition, teachers must be willing to act on that belief. Good teachers internalize knowledge about student development and learning processes. The work of social and cognitive scientists that apply to teaching are integrated with personal theories of learning and development. Good teachers recognize, accept, and rejoice in their students' differences. They demonstrate the ability and willingness to adapt teaching methodologies that take differences into account. An acceptance of differences and understanding of personal development and learning processes prods good teachers to provide opportunities for all their students to receive attention. To do so, teachers repress biases about ability differences, handicaps or disabilities, social or cultural backgrounds, language, race, religion, or gender. A good teacher constantly struggles to meet the needs of all students in personal and social learning, academics, interpersonal skills, and character development.

2. Knowledge of Subjects and How to Convey Content to Students

Good teachers are committed and enthused about the subject matter they present to their students. They have a general understanding how the content is organized and can integrate and connect related content areas. In addition to an understanding of the content, they also possess an understanding of the specialized knowledge of how to convey the subject to a student. In other words, it is not enough to know science—a teacher also must know how to present science content in an appropriate way to the learner. Use of materials and resources is also part of knowing the pedagogical content knowledge. Good teachers possess large repertoires of curriculum resources, teachers' guides, videotapes, computer software, and music recordings that can be used to teach their content. Various resources are used to generate multiple paths to knowledge.

Shulman (1987) describes knowledge of content in three different ways: (1) subject matter knowledge, (2) curriculum knowledge, and (3) pedagogical knowledge. Subject matter knowledge is a deep understanding of the content—for example, what a science major would know about plant phylum. Curriculum knowledge refers to a teacher's knowledge about what is to be taught, what materials are to be used in the classroom, and what students already know about the subject. Pedagogical knowledge refers to how subject matter can be presented to students—the strategies used by the teacher. Taken together, knowledge of these three types represent pedagogical content knowledge.

One of the most important contributions of this way of describing good teaching is the concept of pedagogical content knowledge. In other words good teachers are those who understand the content and also understand the best way to teach that content to whatever age students they teach. Often pedagogical content knowledge is discussed in relation to high school teachers. However, it is equally important to those who are going to be elementary teachers.

3. Ability to Manage and Monitor Student Learning

Good teachers have appropriately high expectations for all their students and see their job as facilitating students' learning. They are able to use a wide range of methods to meet instructional goals and help students learn based on their strengths and weaknesses. Teachers encourage student engagement by managing learning in varied arrangements including small groups, large groups, individuals, and pairs. This often requires that teachers control and manage behavior of students while at the same time encouraging social interaction and engagement. As teachers manage and monitor their students' learning, they are regularly assessing learning progress toward their principal objectives.

4. Ability to Think About Teaching and Learn from Experiences

Thinking about teaching includes understanding the decisions and actions that occur in classroom settings. The importance of decision making is one factor that makes teaching so complex. Good teachers must make difficult decisions that test their judgment, often while engaging in ongoing instruction. Part of the decision-making skill comes from what they know about teaching through their own experiences, but also results from the advice of others. In addition, they can draw on educational research and participate in teacher research to constantly improve their practice. Through the very act of teaching, teachers model what it is like to be an educated person and how one can practice lifelong learning.

5. Participation in Learning Communities

Even though much of their work is done in isolation with groups of young people, teachers are not solo performers. Good teachers contribute to school effectiveness by collaborating with their colleagues. They participate in the joint establishment of goals for learners, development of school curriculum, coordination of instruction, interpretation of state and local goals and objectives, and implementation of student services. Good teachers cooperate with their administrators, share their knowledge and skill with others, and participate in the ongoing development of strong school programs. In addition, teachers must work collaboratively with parents and take advantage of community resources.

The knowledge base about teaching and learning is growing steadily and provides an understanding about what it takes to be a good teacher. All the definitions of good teaching include certain common elements but may organize or emphasize different aspects of the teaching process. There are several ideas that can be taken from this review of effective teaching. First, as in any complex endeavor, there are multiple ways to be good or excellent. While it may not be easy to measure a good teacher, the processes that contribute to good teaching can be described. A review of these processes reveals the enormous responsibility of a good teacher. Often, these descriptions make teaching appear to be an almost impossible endeavor. Teaching will never be simple or easy, but skills acquired by beginning teachers can be refined through reflection on experience. Becoming a good teacher is a lifelong process.

As previously discussed, many aspects are involved in becoming a teacher. A teacher is molded by both formal and informal experiences in and out of classrooms. Various individuals and experiences contribute to the dynamic socialization and learning of future teachers. However, learning to be a *good* teacher results from conscious reflection on biographical events, professional training, personal experiences, reading, and other contextual contributions.

FIELD-BASED ACTIVITY 1.3

Work with your classmates and develop a questionnaire or interview designed to use with Pre K-12 students to discover what they think makes a good teacher. Individually, administer the survey to one or more classes or interview several students using your questionnaire. Bring your findings to class. In pairs or small work groups, compare students' models of good teaching with your text's descriptions of good teaching. Label and describe your findings. Develop a representation (picture, narrative, music, poetry, collage) of your summary of what it takes to be a good teacher and present it to your classmates.

Teaching as a Lifelong Learning Process

Good teachers are lifelong learners. A teacher's career is impacted by personal life experiences such as personal environment, family situation, positive life incidents, crises, individual dispositions, interests, and life stages. Becoming a teacher involves several years of formal preparation, but the concentrated university training that prepares a person to be a teacher is not the end of understanding about the profession. Successes and failures in the classroom, the adult development that occurs naturally through life experiences, and the continued formal learning that the profession offers contribute to the professional development of teachers. School regulations, management styles of supervisors, public trust of schools, societal expectations, professional organizations, and unions (Fessler & Christensen, 1992) add to a teachers' career development. As a result of life experiences, maturation, and normal development, teachers will progress through several stages of teaching. Certain characteristics and needs are identified with different phases of a teaching career.

The Preservice Years

Individuals who are involved in formal intensive university preparation are said to be in the preservice phase of their careers. Initial preparation offered by universities involves courses and field experiences planned by professional teacher educators. The characterization of the preservice stage and future stages of teaching careers can be described in many ways. Figure 1.2 illustrates one way for you to think about your future as a teacher.

Preservice teachers typically need to be socialized into the profession, become comfortable with the methods and processes of teaching and learning, develop instructional and interpersonal strategies to cope with the complexities of teaching, learn to work collaboratively in a professional setting, and understand the purposes of schools and how they work. Nevertheless, not all those in the preservice stage have exactly the same needs.

The period of life when you decide to enter the preservice stage of your career can make a great difference in how you learn and respond to university preparation. If you are a young adult, your family may provide financial support. Older students may have responsibility for families and for their own expenses. Depending on your age, you may be planning a marriage, raising young children, or caring for aging parents. Some of you may be entering the profession after several years in another career. You may have experienced responsibilities

Figure 1.2
The Teacher Career Cycle

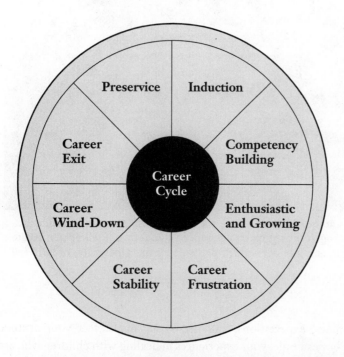

Source: Fessler, R. (1992). The teacher career cycle. In R. Fessler &
J. C. Christensen (Eds.), *The teacher career cycle: Understanding and guiding
the professional development of teachers*. Boston: Allyn & Bacon.

in workplaces that may or may not have been related to education. You may want
to teach because outside interests connected you with teaching. Working with
scouts, clubs, or providing child care may have provided you with experiences
that suggested teaching as a career.

Preservice experiences planned by universities often include several common elements, but may differ in the way that courses and experiences are delivered. Traditionally, courses and experiences have been provided on university
campuses. Increasingly, programs include courses and experiences that take
place in school settings. Preservice experiences have the potential to greatly
impact the way you think about teaching and the skills and abilities you acquire
at this stage of your career.

Relationships between future and experienced teachers are crucial when one is becoming a teacher. Teacher preparation programs are greatly enhanced when future teachers participate in school activities, plan lessons, and interact with students under the supervision of an experienced teacher.

Societal attitudes, expectations, and needs also may affect your attitude toward teaching. For example, your experiences in dealing with children who are poor, suffer emotional trauma, or speak different languages may impact how you approach teaching.

Beyond the Preservice Years

Classroom experiences as well as additional learning opportunities and personal development activities may result in different ways of thinking about teaching. One way to think about teachers' careers is to think about progressing through distinct stages (Fessler & Christensen, 1992). As with any suggestion of human development, these stages are not exact, but only a suggestion of what a person might expect during the progression of a career in teaching.

Induction

The induction stage occurs during the first few years of teaching and is the time when teachers are socialized into the profession. During this time, the new teacher works for acceptance and attempts to become comfortable with teaching on a day-to-day basis. This may be a time when the beginning teacher finds a location or situation where he or she "fits." Teachers may move from building to building or grade to grade until they find the situation where they feel most comfortable. The stress of beginning a new profession may be compounded by other events in individuals' lives (Head, Reiman, & Thies-Sprinthall, 1992). New teachers are usually adjusting from viewing themselves as a student to having a full-time job and getting to know a new community. They are dealing with issues related to personal relationships, finances, and activities outside of work. It is an exciting time for new professionals, albeit busy and stressful.

During this stage, many school districts provide support in the form of experienced mentor teachers to help induct a new teacher into the profession. Mentors provide new teachers with a support system as they begin their teaching by acting as peer coaches, helping with planning, sharing ideas, introducing school routines, judging appropriateness of teaching assignments, and explaining the context of specific teaching situations (Theis-Sprinthall, 1990). Mentors ease new teachers into the profession and increase the possibilities that they will stay in the teaching field for a longer period of time. This is an important role for an experienced teacher since 40–50 percent of new teachers leave teaching after seven years or less (Huling-Austin, 1989). New teachers who receive appropriate mentoring during their first year or two in the profession continue to learn, grow, and develop more positive attitudes toward the profession (Head, Reiman, & Thies-Sprinthall, 1992).

Competency Building

The competency building stage is an exciting time when teachers are growing and becoming more secure in their teaching processes. During this time a teacher begins to feel comfortable with teaching and seeks out new materials, methods, and strategies. Teachers may continue their professional development by attending workshops, conferences, and enrolling in graduate programs. This stage is characterized by a great deal of experimentation, innovation, and continued learning.

Enthusiasm

As teachers continue to work and gain experience, they begin to develop a high level of competency. The confidence resulting from positive experiences in a classroom leads to enthusiastic support of the teaching profession. Experienced enthusiastic teachers look forward to each day of teaching, enjoy interacting with students, and search for new ways to teach and improve their practice. They often become important contributors to the learning of others in their district and their school by sharing what works for them and designing innovations to be tried by others.

Stability

Experienced teachers achieve confidence and pride in their teaching and enter into a period of stability marked by increased expertise, leadership development, and student success. By this time, teachers have identified the strategies that are comfortable for them, understand their students, and can manage behavior and classroom activities effectively. They continue to refine and perfect teaching strategies and may become "experts" in a particular strategy, approach, or philosophy. This period may be marked by continuing professional education, education and experiences that lead to administration, or involvement in curriculum development and other projects. It is generally during this stage that teachers feel that they can contribute to the development and design of programs and experiences for new teachers by serving as mentors and supervisors in preservice programs.

Winding Down

There comes a time when teachers reach a certain age, develop other interests, or recognize that their life goals have made it necessary for them to move on to other jobs or situations. A spouse's retirement, a parent's illness, or other life events may cause an experienced teacher to consider retirement. Teachers who feel that it is nearly time for them to exit their careers may engage in reflection on different aspects of teaching. They begin to gather information to help them consider what their next career step will be. In the process, they may remember individual students and the stories that accompany their classroom experiences. Some teachers look forward to a career change or retirement, consider it a natural event, and begin to make plans for the future, whereas others struggle with leaving the profession. Depending on the action planned by a teacher who has decided to exit the profession, this stage may take several years or may occur only after a few months.

Career Exit

Teachers exit teaching careers with different plans and patterns. Some teachers leave teaching with the understanding that it may be only a few years while they are raising children, caring for parents, or exploring another career. Experienced teachers, not ready for retirement, may leave teaching to become a principal or an administrator in the central office. Teachers closer to retirement age avoid full retirement and look for opportunities for part-time teaching and other ways to ease out of the profession they love. Other teachers may close the doors on classrooms where they have spent many years and never return.

Frustration

As with most careers, almost all teachers suffer some level of frustration and disappointment during teaching. While stress may be expected, there are strategies that will help teachers overcome burnout and view their work with renewed attention, enthusiasm, and excitement. Returning to school, changing schools, or working on an innovation can renew and encourage an experienced teacher who is feeling less than positive about the profession. Overall, today's teachers maintain a positive attitude toward the teaching profession. Over three-quarters of teachers in a recent survey agree with the statement "I love to teach," and most would encourage a young person to pursue a career in teaching (Metropolitan Life Survey, 1995). Individuals who are just starting their teaching careers rate having a "satisfying job" as their top reason for entering teaching.

The career stages illustrate that teaching is dynamic and that anyone entering the profession can expect to go through periods of time where they experience different needs based on where they are in the career cycle. At this point, most of you are involved in the preservice stage of your career, and learning about teaching is your primary focus.

FIELD-BASED ACTIVITY 1.4

Choose a book or movie that features a practicing classroom teacher (e.g., *Dead Poet's Society, The River Is Wide, Stand and Deliver, Mr. Holland's Opus, Ferris Bueller's Day Off*). Briefly describe the teacher(s) portrayed. Can you place each teacher appearing in the book or movie in one of the career stages identified in the previous section? Do you see overlap across stages? Share your analysis with your classmates.

The Formal Steps of Learning to Teach

Informally, your first exposure to teaching may be working with children in the summer, church school, after-school tutoring, baby-sitting or various types of child care that involves untrained individuals. The first formal learning about teaching is usually embedded in the college experience when you enter a teacher preparation program during the last two years of undergraduate study or a year of intensive study after receiving a degree in a content field. The teacher preparation program should extend prior experiences, provide new experiences related to teaching, and give you opportunities to test your teaching ability, receive feedback, and learn to be an effective teacher.

Overview of Teacher Education

The preservice stage of teaching is guided by university curriculum. The goals of teacher preparation include the presentation of a connected and integrated professional program of (1) general and professional studies, (2) observations of practice, and (3) supervised teaching experience (Goodlad, 1990). Training is not a dramatic event in which a preservice teacher becomes as confident as an experienced teacher, but the beginning of a process that will be ongoing for many years. Preservice professional educational experiences should help you make the transition from being a university student to becoming a teacher. One of the major factors that happens during this transition is that you will become socialized into the profession.

Socialization into the profession means that teachers understand what they should know and be able to do in their profession. Early experiences with schools offer many examples and impressions about schools, teaching, and education. An important part of the socialization of preservice teachers is the opportunity to learn about schools through a guided sequence of activities introducing the culture of teaching. Preservice programs offer continuous framework for reflection and learning about teaching while experiencing the schooling process. Access to the instructional context of schools during this process is a key element. Formal preservice experiences should be carefully orchestrated between school and universities. Ideally, the contexts where preservice teachers are socialized are positive and represent the most current examples of teaching and learning. Occasionally, however, the schools may offer a preservice teacher a more negative aspect of school socialization. During your preservice experience, you may observe events and processes that are not the most beneficial for students and that do not fit with the theoretical frameworks discussed in your university classes. When you observe striking and contrasting events, your program should offer you the opportunity to talk with university professors and your school's teachers about what you are seeing.

A future teacher may take many courses in English and understand the content in that subject area very well. But knowing the content is not enough. Teacher education attempts to offer you a glimpse of some of the issues, questions, possible solutions, and strategies needed to move beyond content area proficiency. For example, teacher education helps future teachers learn about society at large—the social, political, and institutional connections that impact schools. Future teachers can benefit from an understanding of the connections between the organizational frameworks of schools and the historical and cultural roots that impact the schools. Future teachers learn about families, communities, and societies other than their own and how diversity enriches lives.

One of the striking features of teaching noted in earlier research on schools is the abruptness with which a person must take responsibility for a classroom (Lortie, 1975). Preservice teachers often move from positions of limited responsibility for students during their internship to sole responsibility during their first year of teaching, with little attention paid to the demands of the transition. School-university preparation provides a logical scaffolding as one becomes a teacher and provides needed support and structure. Increasingly, early field experiences that involve practicing teachers in development and implementation of the experiences are being offered.

Your university teacher education program will provide various types of activities designed to prepare you for and to induct you into the profession. This textbook and the course you are in right now will help you establish a framework for continued learning during your preservice program. Teacher education programs that are jointly developed and delivered by classroom teachers and university teacher educators provide an ideal opportunity to introduce you to the profession.

Linking Theory and Practice

One of the purposes of preservice education is to develop a scaffolding between content understanding of individuals and the study of pedagogy (Hilty, 1992). In order to develop stronger collaboration between the schools and universities, many teacher education programs have developed a partnership that provides high-quality preparation for new teachers. Partnerships that focus on teacher education may vary widely in their approach and arrangement. No two partnerships are the same—each has its own personality and character, reflecting the strength and uniqueness of the school's staff and the strengths and diversity of the university faculty. In field-based programs, at least a portion of your preservice coursework will be taught on the campus of a local school by a combination of school and university faculty. You will become familiar with the school and students, teachers, and parents from a wide range of cultural backgrounds. To take full advantage of the field-based setting, some of your class assignments will focus on meeting with teams of teachers, participating in varied field experiences, collecting data from teachers and students, and becoming comfortable with and using technology in instruction.

School-University Collaboration

Collaborative teacher education classes are not available at every university, but elements of school-university partnerships exist in most good programs. A collaborative teacher preparation program provides opportunities for university professors, public school teachers and administrators, university graduate and undergraduate students, public school students, and others to learn from one another.

The most complex collaboration between universities and schools has produced a concept called Professional Development Schools (PDS). PDS are schools in which a formal written agreement sets forth the methods in which the university and the schools work together. Any number of activities may be involved in the agreements, which tend to focus on (1) preparing new teachers, (2) improving preservice teacher preparation, (3) providing opportunities for experienced teachers to continue their learning, (4) changing the curriculum for young people so that they are able to achieve at the highest level possible, and 5) encouraging inquiry and research about teaching and learning. PDS may provide new models of teacher education and development by serving as exemplars of practice, builders of knowledge, and vehicles for communicating professional understandings among teacher educators, future teachers, and veteran teachers (Holmes Group, 1995; Darling-Hammond, 1994).

Partnerships between schools and universities in teacher education tend to provide opportunities for more exposure to schools and for a longer period of time. Future teachers become immersed in PDS and will often spend a full year in the schools. The preservice stage of a career may be completed entirely on a public school campus. By definition, there will be a substantial number of hours each week that the preservice teacher spends in the field. Public school teachers are usually involved in mentoring, teaching, or supervising a portion of the teacher preparation program.

For many who have experienced teacher education in PDS, it is difficult to think that teacher preparation would be done in any other manner. However, even after a decade of working for the establishment of PDS, there are only a few hundred across the United States. Many PDS have not been able to incorporate all of the characteristics traditionally associated with school-university partnerships (McIntire, 1995). Establishing partnerships is difficult since PDS involve combining the contrasting cultures of universities and public schools. Interestingly enough, these two settings often use different terms, rely on different funding sources, possess contrasting reward systems, and think about scheduling and workdays in very different ways (Knight, Wiseman, & Smith, 1992). Additionally, teachers and administrators worry that involvement in PDS activities may direct their attention away from students in their classroom when they concentrate on preservice experiences. Often, university faculty resist getting involved in partnership work since universities do not often reward them for their efforts (Winitzky, Stoddart, & O'Keefe, 1992).

The University and Public School Contributions

Despite the difficulties cited above, almost all the teachers and university professors who work in school-university partnerships share the common goal of effectively teaching young people in a school setting. They typically find common ground in their love of teaching and learning and in their concern for students and their learning. But aside from those commonalties, they bring different offerings to the preservice teachers.

University professors generally focus on research and theories about teaching and teacher preparation, learning theory, and content area learning. Although most of them were public school teachers at one time in their lives, they now focus on research and development of ideas associated with learning and teaching. Their schedules are flexible—they may write during the early morning hours, come into work late in the morning to advise and teach adult students and participate in university-based meetings, and teach graduate classes at night. They possess expertise in adult learning and spend a great deal of time writing, researching, and reading about education in general as well as their specific area of expertise. Areas of expertise may include diverse topics such as metacognitive strategies, mental imagery, children's literature, gender issues in education, social and cultural foundations of learning, and content area pedagogy. They are usually experts in a single area of educational expertise and receive promotion and tenure based on how they represent their knowledge in publications, presentations, and research activities. University professors also focus on the development of preservice and inservice teachers. They will use the knowledge associated with teacher education as they contribute to the blend of activities planned by schools and universities. They may become involved in presenting readings, theorists, and research findings connected to what is going on in the schools. Professors may work with teachers to develop research projects that help find answers to instructional issues in the classroom.

Teachers in schools focus on the young people that are in their classrooms. They possess expertise in such areas as child and adolescent development, classroom management, and motivational techniques related to teaching and learning. In addition, teachers typically have a wealth of practical knowledge about children and young people and the nature of teaching. They know what the state requires of teachers, techniques for organization, and management of classrooms. Their daily routine requires that they walk halls, bend over small desks, supervise lockers, stand on playgrounds, monitor busy hallways, and remain on their feet for long periods during a structured teaching schedule. They work from morning to midafternoon and have little time for any personal business during their workdays. If and when they do research, it focuses on classroom issues related to children and young people. They are rewarded by their students' achievements in the classroom, administrator and parental feedback, and other recognition programs in their district. Depending on whether they teach in elementary or secondary classrooms, they are usually experts in child/adolescent development as well as specific content areas, and they possess a large repertoire of knowledge linking content areas and day-to-day happenings.

The roles of practicing teachers in preparing future teachers are broad and varied. Experienced teachers serve as role models, provide mentorship, and share information and strategies. They can be crucial to the reflection and learning of future teachers as they plan, discuss, debate, and work together in the school setting.

In the PDS context, university teacher educators and Pre K–12 teachers exhibit different roles and responsibilities related to teacher education. Traditionally, university professors are responsible for planning the preservice teacher curriculum, participating in the delivery of the curriculum, and researching the results of what happens in preservice education. One of their major responsibilities is to increase the knowledge associated with teacher development and preparation and to integrate that new knowledge into the curriculum and experiences planned for preservice teachers. They are also expected to disseminate their findings to others in the field of teacher education.

Preservice teachers are heavily influenced by the teachers in the schools where they observe and where they complete their internships. When given a choice, preservice teachers admit to allegiance to their cooperating teachers and not their university connections (Hollingsworth, 1988). Preservice teachers are quickly caught up in the day-to-day activities of the schools and perceive that they need a great amount of knowledge related to practical aspects of teaching. Both the school teacher and the university professor have valuable experiences and knowledge to share with beginning teachers. Schools and university perspectives offer a preservice teacher a balanced view of education, and the roles of both are important to the beginning teacher.

Learning to Teach in a Field-Based Setting

The formal teacher education program will guide you as you enter the profession. You have different needs as a preservice teacher than you will have at any other phase of your career (see previous section, "The Career Cycle"). Learning to be a teacher in a school-university setting will provide you with the opportunity to learn where theory and practice are connected in relevant and meaningful ways. This experience is one of many of that will shape your beliefs, prepare you to interact with children and young people, and introduce instructional strategies.

Reflection in Teacher Education Programs

Preservice teacher activities should help a future teacher build an image of good teaching. This may be achieved by promoting good teaching, which is the product of research and theory, and by providing assisted learning from the range of experiences and involvement of future teachers (Johnston, 1994). Experience is not the only component required when building the image of a good teacher. Analysis and discussion of ongoing events as well as readings and writings featuring alternate perspectives will allow the future teacher to focus on a full range of experiences and promote effective learning from those experiences. The reflective processing of the experiences, coupled with research and theory are all important parts of the teacher education program.

Importance of Developing a Personal Philosophy

There is more to teaching than loving children, knowing content, and implementing instructional procedures. The decisions you will make in your future classrooms impact your future students and contribute to the reshaping of

Becoming a teacher is a lifelong learning process. Professional development activities that present new ideas and help teachers learn new skills and abilities are important at all stages of career development.

schools, families, universities, churches. Your actions and decisions are based on how you know and understand the world (Clark, 1995). Your own philosophy of life and way of thinking about education account for your unique teaching style, educational decision making, and interactions with young learners. Your beginning experiences should help you understand your teaching philosophy and how your beliefs impact your teaching.

Developing a personal philosophy of education involves clarifying educational issues, justifying educational decisions, interpreting educational data, and integrating that understanding into the educational process (Myers & Myers, 1995). Although your personal philosophy will influence much of what you do, your expectations for children and young people's learning is an important component of your beliefs. The development of a personal philosophy requires self-examination and honest comparison and consideration of what we are about as teachers. It is a continual process that involves seeking answers to hard questions over a long period of time.

PORTFOLIO REFLECTIONS AND EXHIBITS

Throughout each chapter you will complete a series of field-based activities. The activities will serve as the basis for a portfolio representation of learnings and understandings developed during the activities, readings, and discussions related to the chapters. For each chapter, you may choose one of the field-based activities suggested in the text or develop an alternate exhibit that represents what you have learned. Your responses to the activities or your exhibit can become part of your teaching portfolio or you may follow the alternate suggestion presented below.

Suggested Exhibit 1: Personal View of Teaching
A portfolio representation for this chapter might include:

1. A summary of all field-based activities (1.1–1.4) in this chapter including references to the text and other readings.

2. The identification of one field-based activity in this chapter that was most important to you.

3. A representation of your own decision to become a teacher. Consider the impact of your own biography on your choice to become a teacher. Use the different influences described in this chapter to guide the development of an autobiography of your career choice. Illustrate your childhood experiences, the teacher and family influences, and the teaching experiences that contributed to your decision to become a teacher. You can develop a portfolio representation of your biography in many ways. A narrative, poetry, music, artwork, or collage can represent your decision to become a teacher.

Related Readings

Clark, C. M. (1995). *Thoughtful teaching*. New York: Teachers College.
> *Dr. Clark believes that what teachers think, believe, and do will ultimately impact the learning of the young people in their classrooms. Teachers' personal and professional development, career paths, relations with their colleagues, working conditions, rewards, and the leadership in their schools—all impact the quality of instruction that they deliver. He describes teaching as a syntheses of reason and emotion, feeling and thinking.*

Fessler, R., & Christensen, J. (Eds.). (1992). *The teacher career cycle: Understanding and guiding the professional development of teachers*. Boston: Allyn & Bacon.
> *This entire text is devoted to describing the changes that occur throughout teachers' careers. This book makes the point that learning to teach does not end when one receives a degree and teachers change and have different needs throughout their careers.*

Jaolongo, M. R., & Isenberg, J. P. (1995). *Teachers' stories: From personal narrative to professional insight.* San Francisco: Jossey-Bass.

> *This is a themed collection of stories and anecdotes that will help you understand about teachers. Individual teachers tell stories about how they learn from their students, reflect upon their experiences, resolve conflict, and reflect upon their experiences. The authors of the book analyze individual stories and expand on the teachers' experiences.*

Lortie, D. C. (1975). *Schoolteacher: A sociological study.* Chicago: University of Chicago Press.

> *This is an older, classic study of why individuals become teachers and how they are socialized into the profession. Even though it was written over twenty years ago, there is still a great deal to be learned by studying the lives of teachers.*

Sarason, S. B. (1993). *You are thinking of teaching? Opportunities, problems, realities.* San Francisco: Jossey-Bass.

> *Dr. Sarason presents some of the opportunities, problems, and realities of the teaching profession. He presents teaching as a demanding, complex profession and attempts to help future teachers think about their choice of a teaching profession.*

References

Clark, C. (1995). *Thoughtful teaching.* New York: Teachers College Press.

Crow, N. A. (1987). Preservice teachers' biography: A case study. Paper presented at the Annual Meeting of the American Educational Research Association, Washington, D.C.

Darling-Hammond, L. (1994). *Professional development schools: Schools for developing a profession.* New York: Teachers College Press.

Fessler, R., & J. C. Christensen (Eds.) (1992). *The teacher career cycle: Understanding and guiding the professional development of teachers.* Boston: Allyn & Bacon.

Goodlad, J. I. (1990). *Teachers for our nation's schools.* San Francisco: Jossey-Bass.

Louis Harris & Associates (1995). *Metropolitan Life survey of the American teacher, 1984–1995: Old problems, new challenges.* New York: Louis Harris and Associates, Inc.

Head, F. A., Reiman, A. J., Thies-Sprinthall, L. (1992). The reality of mentoring: Complexity in its process and function. In T. M. Bey & C. T. Holmes (Eds.), *Mentoring: Contemporary principles and issues* (pp. 5–21). Reston, VA: Association of Teacher Educators.

Hilty, E. B. (1992). Teacher education: What is good teaching and how do we teach people to be good teachers? In J. Kincheloe and S. R. Steinberg (Eds.), *Thirteen questions: Reframing education's conversation* (pp. 103–113). New York: Peter Lang.

Hollingsworth, S. (1998). Making field-based programs work: A three-level approach to reading education. *Journal of Teacher Education, 39*(4), 28–36.

Holmes Group. (1995). *Tomorrow's schools of education.* East Lansing, MI: The Holmes Group.

Huling-Austin, L. L. (1989). Beginning teacher assistance programs: An overview. In L. Huling-Austin, S. J. Odell, P. Isshler, R. S. Kay, R. A. Edelfelt (Eds.),

Assisting the beginning teacher (pp. 3–18). Reston, VA: Association of Teacher Educators.

Johnston, S. (1994). Experience is the best teacher; Or is it? An analysis of the role of experience in learning to teach. *Journal of Teacher Education, 45*(3), 199–208.

Knight, S. K., Wiseman, D. L., & Smith, C. W. (1992). School-university partnerships: The reflectivity-activity dilemma. *Journal of Teacher Education, 43*(3), 269–277.

Knowles, J. G. (1992). Models for understanding, preservice and beginning teachers' biographies. In I. F. Goodson (Ed.), *Studying teachers' lives* (pp. 120–135). New York: Teachers College Press.

Lortie, D. C. (1975). *School teacher: A sociological study.* Chicago: University of Chicago Press.

McIntire, R. G. (1995). Characteristics of effective professional development schools. *Teacher Education and Practice, 11*(2), 36–49.

Myers, C. B., & Myers, L. K. (1995). *The professional educator: A new introduction to teaching and schools.* Belmont, CA: Wadsworth.

National Commission on Excellence in Education. (1983). *A nation at risk.* Washington, D.C.: U.S. Department of Education.

National Board for Professional Teaching Standards (1997). *What teachers should know and be able to do.* Detroit: National Board for Professional Teaching Standards.

Shulman, L. S. (1987). Knowledge and teaching: Foundations of the new reform. *Harvard Educational Review, 57*(1), 1–22.

Theis-Sprinthall , L. (1990). *Becoming a teacher educator: A curriculum guide.* Raleigh, NC: Department of Curriculum and Instruction, NCSU.

Winitzky, N., Stoddart, T., & O'Keefe, P. (1992). Great expectations: Emergent professional development schools. *Journal of Teacher Education, 43*(1), 3–18.

2
Surveying Educational History and Philosophy

In this chapter
- A Brief History of American Schools
- Philosophical Themes

P eople are asking what is the criterion of a teacher.

The first requisite and the last criterion of a teacher is to be a true follower of the Great Teacher, not so much in professing as in living . . . it means a right attitude toward the profession, toward each subject taught, toward the home, the community and the child. It means to possess knowledge and the ability to interpret it to right uses so that it becomes a power for good in the life of a child.

To be a teacher, many methods of approach are necessary in reaching the minds and hearts of growing boys and girls: these at the levels of the child's abilities to pursue and achieve. And when such happy team work is obtained the teacher continues to walk beside the developing mind and soul; pressing a little here, guiding, directing thoughtfully, prayerful, ever keeping the goal of a perfected character as the objective sought . . .

Someone had said to be educated meant to bring forth and train up all the faculties and powers of the mind and body to their highest possible use. To accomplish this makes it mandatory to live in such manner of thought and activity as will make the whole world better for our having lived in it.

—Sarah Gillespie Huftalen, "To Be a Teacher"*

When you are studying to be a teacher, you tend to want to focus on the here and now, learning how to deal with the children and young people in the classrooms where you are learning to teach. It may seem difficult to take time out and reflect on the past, but there are reasons for you to do just that. The foundations of teaching—philosophy and history—are with you in each classroom you enter. Little about teaching, learning, and children was discovered just yesterday. History can illuminate contemporary issues and provide insights into common problems. An understanding of history of education and how it connects with the present can help us interpret the present and perhaps help us avoid repetition of past mistakes. Cicero declared that "persons who are ignorant of history will remain forever children" (Power, 1991, p. ix), and educated future teachers have the responsibility to understand what their contribution will be to the continuum of education.

While knowledge of educational history places current educational issues in context, philosophy provides a tool for educational decision making. Philosophical beliefs impact the way that teachers make decisions, interact with children, and approach their careers. Traditionally, well-developed philosophies of education include statements about what education should and should not do; in other words, what the goals, content, and methods should or should not be. Analysis of the aims of education and the dispositions to be fostered in students, determination of the rationale for the dispositions, recommendations about the means of fostering the dispositions, and discussions of the line of argument used to support use of particular means provide a basis for discussing different philosophies (Frankena, 1974). In addition, these elements suggest guidelines

*From "To be a teacher," Sarah Gillespie Huftalen, Iowa, 1865–1955. In M. H. Cordier, *Schoolwomen of the prairie and plains* (pp. 175–209). Albuquerque: University of New Mexico Press, 1992.

for development of more personal definitions of the means and ends of education. As you develop your own philosophy of teaching, you may want to compare your beliefs about what educations should or should not do with philosophers (past and present).

This chapter will help you answer the following questions:

- How are educational history and philosophy interconnected?

- Are there ways to make ancient history and philosophy meaningful in today's classrooms?

- Who are the best-known philosophers in American education?

- What historical and philosophical roots can be linked to contemporary education?

A Brief History of American Schools

The Early 1600s

From the beginning of the settlement of North America during the first half of the 1600s, schools played an important role in establishing the new country. Thrust into their savage new world and working long hours on their new homesteads, busy pioneer parents looked toward schools as a way to transmit civilized behavior to their children (Perkinson, 1991). Settlers faced ambiguities related to learning and teaching. On the one hand, they wished to protect the culture they were developing in their new country; on the other, they were anxious to promote the intellectual, moral, and religious values they had inherited (Power, 1991).

What was happening in Europe had a major impact on early American education. During this period, John Calvin and Martin Luther were active reformers who believed that schools should serve many purposes, including teaching as many people as possible to read so that they could read and interpret the Bible. John Calvin's educational approach established mandatory and strict obedience to the church and a belief in God. He stressed civic training and strict discipline for all classes of the population. Luther articulated a plan for education in Germany. As part of the plan, he turned authority of education over to the mayors and aldermen of the cities to educate children of all classes. His theory cultivated future national educational control, and he connected the religious and civic purposes of education. The greatest legacy of this time was the concept of universal education for everyone, which became an important component in the American education system.

Later in Europe, the Age of Enlightenment (1700–1800) emphasized the power of the human mind. Philosophers such as John Locke and Jean-Jacques Rousseau believed that the way to a better life was through an educated mind, but philosophers differed greatly in their approaches. John Locke challenged both theological and humanistic conceptions of human nature and focused on the importance of the learners' experiences (Power, 1991). Locke believed that children began as a blank slate (Smith, 1979), a *tabula rasa*. They subsequently experienced events, developed simple ideas, and eventually replaced initial thoughts with more complex ideas based on experiences. The purpose of education, Locke thought, was to help children to experience a healthy, virtuous, and successful life.

On the other hand, Rousseau believed that education should conform to a child's individual needs and that young children learn by acting on natural impulses. "Society," he declared, "should reject any commission to teach persons or direct their scholastic course. Its role should be passive; nothing more than an environment wherein the natural impulses of autonomous persons can find full satisfaction" (Power, 1991, p. 202). He believed that all children were good and needed to be allowed to grow naturally. Although Locke and Rousseau held very different views of the role of education, they are considered the fathers of modern child psychology and their theories are the basis for much of modern-day child development. Their ideas spread to the colonies before the end of the eighteenth century and formed the basis of schooling, but it wasn't long before the new country produced thoughtful educators and uniquely American educational processes.

TEACHER'S CONTRACT.

It is Hereby Agreed, By and between School District No. *7 7*.... Township No. *13*...... Range No. *5*.....
County of... *Lincoln*........, Territory of Oklahoma, and... *Ephraim Wall*......................
the holder of a Territorial and County Certificate, this day in force, that said teacher is to teach, govern and conduct
the public schools of said district to the best of *his*...... ability, follow the course of study adopted by the District
Board, keep a register of the daily attendance and studies of each pupil belonging to the school, make all reports
required by law, and such other reports as may be desired by the County Superintendent of Public Instruction, and
endeavor to preserve in good condition and order the school house, grounds, furniture, apparatus, and such other district property as may come under the immediate supervision of said teacher, for a term of..... *7*.......... school
months, commencing on the.... *8*..........day of... *November*..................., A. D. 189*7*..
for the sum of... *Twenty seven*........Dollars per school month, to be paid at the end of each month;
PROVIDED, That in case said teacher shall be legally dismissed from school, or shall have h.*is*......certificate legally
annulled, by expiration or otherwise, then said teacher shall not be entitled to compensation from and after such dis-
missal or annullment: PROVIDED, FURTHER, That the wages of said teacher for the last month of the school term shall
not be paid unless said teacher shall have made the reports hereinbefore mentioned.

And the said school district hereby agrees to keep the school house in good repair, to provide the necessary fuel,
school register, and such other supplies as may be necessary.

IN WITNESS WHEREOF, We have hereunto subscribed our names, this. *13*..day of. *September*....
A. D. 189*7*..
.... *W. C. Yoder*....Director or Treasurer.
.... *Ephraim Wall*....Teacher.

ATTEST: *Henry Bergdorf*....Clerk or ~~Treasurer~~.

REMARKS:—This Contract shall be made out in duplicate, and one copy given to the teacher, and the other placed on file in the District Clerk's office. The
law does not authorize the Board of Directors to make a contract with a teacher, or to pay his salary, for any time during which his certificate is not in force.

Teaching has changed a great deal since the late 1890s. Individuals who were teachers may
have attended only eight years of grammar school, and the responsibilities outlined in this
contract were quite different than those of today's teachers.

Colonial Schools

Early American schools were established to provide young people with the
opportunity to study religion. Gradually, religious education began to give way
to the idea that the purpose of education was to provide knowledge that would
help future citizens uphold democracy. As the young government was established to rule itself, the role of education of all its citizens became more and
more important. Laws were passed requiring that everyone become literate and
that communities be responsible for establishing schools. As early as 1642,
Massachusetts had a compulsory education law that held parents responsible for
the education of their children (Perkinson, 1991). Other colonies replicated the

Becoming a Teacher in a Field-Based Setting

Massachusetts law. Even colonies that had no laws requiring schooling established schools and put schoolmasters in place to educate their children. The first laws passed in Massachusetts supporting compulsory education mandated that all children be instructed in reading, although it did not matter if that occurred at home, in school, or elsewhere. The Old Deluder Satan Act of 1647 required towns of fifty households or more to hire a schoolmaster capable of teaching reading and writing. Common elementary schools were established in Massachusetts to provide basic education in reading, writing, and math. Children usually attended the one-room schools from about ages five through fourteen.

Attitudes of elitism and who should be educated were transported from the European roots. During the early days of the colonies, education was based on the social class system (Timm, 1996). Those who were poor could not afford for their children to attend schools, and at first there was almost no educational opportunity offered poor children, children of slaves, and young girls. Slowly, educational opportunities became available to more and more children. Young women and a few boys attended the dame schools taught by women and held in private homes. The students would study reading, writing, religion, and the rudiments of arithmetic. Boys from higher socioeconomic status levels would continue in Latin grammar schools and learn from the classical system as they prepared for religious or civic careers. The Latin grammar schools were essentially the first secondary schools that prepared colonial boys for colleges—usually Harvard or Yale. A very small percentage of children attended the schools, and, of course, there was no need for girls to attend, because colleges of that time did not admit women.

During the colonial times, African Americans were treated as property and their education was limited to technical skills needed for the contribution to the economy of their owners (Timm, 1996). Some owners did provide opportunities for African Americans to learn to read the Bible, but this did not continue after the American Revolution. The Puritans provided a few of the slaves an opportunity to be tutored, but for the most part African Americans were left out of early colonial educational endeavors.

Contributions of Jefferson and Franklin

The ideas of Locke and Rousseau and the attitudes of the new country helped Thomas Jefferson (1743–1826) and Benjamin Franklin (1706–1790) frame the views of American education to focus on freedom of expression and universal public education. Franklin was a Puritan whose first writings, *Poor Richard's Almanac*, became popular reading of the colonists in the early 1800s. In addition to writing, Franklin was a scientist, inventor, philosopher, and educator. Franklin accepted Locke's philosophy of education but extended educational ideas to include all classes and those who had not been involved in the system thus far. As early as the 1760s, Franklin wrote that African Americans were equal to whites and appealed for better treatment of the American Indians.

Franklin supported the study of basic skills, classics, and religion and the development of high moral character, logical reasoning, integrity, and self-discipline (Smith, 1979). In an essay outlining the academy that he established, he called for a "well-stocked library (complete with maps, scientific instruments, and diagrams); a frugal diet and regular physical exercise for the scholars; training in such practical skills as penmanship, drawing, accounting, and gardening; and courses in arithmetic, geometry, astronomy, English grammar, and modern foreign languages" (McMannon, 1995, p. 17). Franklin's Puritan background influenced his ideas about school, and he wrote that spending too much time with the classics was wasteful and that the core of educational studies should be derived from what is useful and should meet the practical needs of the local communities. He viewed schools as a way to prepare young Americans for business or professions. One of Franklin's major contributions was his attempt to establish a permanent school, an academy, that would reflect stability (Perkinson, 1991). Imagine his disappointment when his academy eventually became a Latin grammar school, embodying many of the aristocratic and wasteful studies he abhorred.

Thomas Jefferson was educated in America and demonstrated great personal abilities in languages and literature. He was also highly talented in music and the arts and was an inventor, farmer, scientist, and architect. He was a student of Locke and Rousseau and believed that there should be a government-sponsored educational system so that all citizens could have equal educational opportunities (Smith, 1979). Jefferson envisioned schools as a way to produce future leaders for democratic society, and he believed that it was the government's responsibility to provide a system of education. He founded the University of Virginia based on this belief and worked to propose a system of schooling that would provide the most basic schooling to all children in the state. His plan, which was presented to his state legislature but was not successful, provided three years of elementary school. He envisioned an educational system designed to preserve the democracy through well-educated, capable leaders and citizens. Schools were to create a populace that would advance the common interest (McMannon, 1995) and protect the young democracy from tyranny or dictatorship.

The 1800s

In the beginning of the 1800s, schools refined the force that shaped American society, and connections between education and government became more explicit (Perkinson, 1991). Americans began to argue for an educational system that was common across the states, standardized in content and duration, and offered to all children equally. By 1860 almost all states had some form of public school system, and some of the ideas that we see in our schools today began to evolve.

The first schools were identified as common schools because they were designed for all children. The common schools of the early colonial times were impacted by ideas of educators in Europe and the United States. The famous Swiss educator Pestalozzi felt that men were neither good nor evil but shaped by their experiences (Button & Provenzo, 1989). He argued for child guidance based on caring, nurturing, and providing children opportunities to be actively involved in learning, as opposed to learning by rote memorization. Pestalozzi honored the role of mothers and believed that affection was the basis of obedience. A good teacher was like a good mother. He believed that women were well suited for teaching, especially because of their nurturing, caring attitudes and natural affinity for teaching, especially for young children (McMannon, 1995).

Other educators of the early 1800s began to establish characteristics of our educational system that are still in place. Horace Mann, crusading for common, or public, schools, proposed a state board to exercise control over public schools and insisted that the purpose of schooling was to educate the citizenry, not to focus on religion. He supported a practical curriculum aimed at developing moral character and effective citizenship. One of Mann's lasting contributions to the American educational system was to transfer Prussia's graded school levels to America. Classification of students was seen as advantageous over the one-room schoolhouses because it allowed the teacher the opportunity to address all lessons to one level.

The decades before the Civil War were almost all focused on elementary schooling. Schools provided free and universal elementary education to all children, particularly those who were poor, with the hopes that education would improve their lives. In 1820, fueled by the belief that democracy could not be totally run by those educated in common elementary schools, secondary schools began to emerge. Secondary schools were more comprehensive than the early Latin schools, which concentrated on classical education. History, bookkeeping, geometry, surveying, and algebra curriculum began to evolve from the first secondary schools.

Initially in the 1800s, a great deal of attention was given to common schools and secondary schools, but colleges began to gain attention. In particular, the evolution of state colleges was strong during the 1800s. Colleges began to add professional, technical and scientific curriculum to their curriculum of religion and social graces. By the mid-1880s an entire component of new learning emerged with the establishment of agricultural, industrial, mining, and engineering units. At first, colleges did not admit women, but women gained access to university in private schools, and examples of coeducation soon became representative in both colleges and universities. By the beginning of the 1900s nearly one-fourth of the students in college were women (Power, 1991).

The 1880s signified a growth in American school systems. Theories of teaching and learning began to grow. Nevertheless, education was still not available to all citizens. Secondary schools did not encourage attendance by women. When women enrolled, they were offered different experiences and less academic content than that offered to their male counterparts. Even though there was some movement to include African American students in formal educational experiences, children of slaves did not have equal access to education. In Boston during the early 1800s, African American parents began to establish separate school systems for their children and requested integrated educational systems. Abolitionists were in favor of education for African Americans, and a school opened to educate black Americans in Philadelphia in 1820. Education for slaves was still opposed in the South.

Some African Americans, albeit very limited numbers, had access to higher education during the 1880s. Oberlin College was one of the first universities to admit both black and white students (Timm, 1995). Soon, African American educators began taking leadership roles in the educational process. Booker T. Washington, who was born into slavery, was educated at Hampton Institute, and he founded Tuskegee Institute, a showplace that provided vocational training for blacks. He viewed Tuskegee as a way for blacks to win acceptance in the white world. His philosophy was to encourage educated blacks to do good work and win the approval of the white world by helping others.

A very different approach was taken by the educator W.E.B. Du Bois, who sought a liberal education for African Americans. He was born a freeman and, after becoming the first black Ph.D. in the United States, taught at Wilberforce College and Atlanta University before he took over the leadership of the newly formed National Association for the Advancement of Colored People (NAACP). His approach was much more aggressive than Washington's, and he advocated equal rights for African Americans in the United States. Du Bois viewed himself as an activist who fought for the rights of black Americans (Perkinson, 1991).

As late as 1860, Asian Americans were also prohibited from attending public school. As in the case of African Americans, Asian Americans began to establish segregated schools for their children. The first schools that taught in Chinese were in San Francisco in the 1870s. Even after a law was enacted to end Chinese immigration, the education of Chinese children continued. The Japanese did not begin to immigrate until the second half of the century, and their schools were established mainly in Honolulu. These Asian Americans predated and established the importance of education for the more recent immigrants from Vietnam, Laos, Cambodia, and Thailand.

American Indians were not treated fairly in the emerging educational system. The American settlers were intent on controlling the process for American Indian children and ignored family and tribal culture. President Monroe provided money to Protestant missionaries so they could establish schools for American Indians. They were to be educated so that they could understand Christianity. The missionaries tended to develop lessons and curriculum that attempted to teach the Native people to be subservient, to abandon their tribal ways, and to adopt the white culture. For the most part, Indians ignored the attempts to educate them in the way of the colonists and conveyed the message that their own learnings and way of doing things met their needs (Button & Provenzo, 1989). Indians recognized that the white man's education would cause them to surrender their own culture and lifestyle. They resisted the attempt to educate them in the white man's ways and in some cases ridiculed the process. Territorial schools for the Native Americans were closed during the Civil War and were replaced with Indian Boarding Schools. The boarding schools removed children from their homes and families and did not provide parents input in the educational processes of the children. Some schools focused on training Native Americans for manual labor associated with agricultural economy.

The Mexican War of 1854 brought the first Hispanics into the American educational system in the Southwest. Language instruction was one of the first concerns, and, almost immediately, laws were passed that recognized English as the language of instruction. In many states, legislation was designed to eliminate the Spanish language entirely. The discussions of language framed a bias against Mexican American students on the part of school officials. Many Mexican American parents avoided issues of language and cultural bias by sending their children to private Catholic schools.

While elementary and secondary schools were establishing policies dealing with race and culture that would remain for years, the higher education system was continuing to evolve with the help of the federal government. The Land Grant College Act of 1862 was the first federal aid to education and offered states a means to establish public colleges. States were given land that they were to sell in order to finance the building and establishment of new colleges. However, states did not always use the money as intended, and much of the money acquired by selling the property was used to build canals and bridges (Button & Provenzo, 1989). Normal schools were established to prepare elementary teachers, and universities developed programs to train secondary teachers. Two-year normal programs were open to students who were sixteen and wished to be teachers. Future teachers studied early forms of psychology and theories of teaching.

The 1800s marked many advances in the American educational system. Early educational processes established precedents, beliefs, and attitudes that can be seen in our current educational processes. At the end of the 1800s, schools were impacted by social and political changes in the nation (McMannon, 1995). Economic depression, political turmoil, and racial relations affected schooling in the country. Jobs became important resources, and schools were seen as one way to gain economic advantage. The most significant movement during the end of the century was free schooling, establishment of educational systems that began with the schooling of young children and continued throughout a university system, and the establishment of policies and governance systems to oversee the educational system.

The 1900s and the Progressive Era

As the new century began, the education system was reviewed and found guilty of providing ineffective educational experiences for children. Educators criticized the traditional curriculum, textbooks, and materials used in the schools during the 1800s (Button & Provenzo, 1989). Philosophies and purposes of education were questioned, and new ideas and theories began to emerge. Progress in government was connected to school reform. Progressives—those who identified the importance of linking progress and education—encouraged the adoption of a variety of educational strategies, some newly developed, others transported from abroad, and others reconstituted from the past.

The Progressive movement encouraged the schools to develop the new role as liberator, helping children realize their talents and potential so that they could make contributions to political life, enriching the quality of democracy (Perkinson, 1991). Progressive educators began to shift curriculum from subject-centered schools to child-centered schools, where students' interests were considered when planning educational experiences. Two American theorists-philosophers, Francis Parker (1837–1902) and John Dewey (1859–1952), criticized traditional education that was developed in the 1800s and became affiliated with new ways of thinking about education. Among other things, Parker advocated doing away with the old books and curriculum and bringing in current magazines, newspapers, and student accounts of their experiences.

Dewey developed a comprehensive American educational philosophy that was known as pragmatism. He based his theory on discovery in an environment that encouraged learning. He believed that a human's interaction with the environment was the basis for intellectual development (Tanner, 1997). Although often grouped with progressive educators such as Pestalozzi, Dewey resisted being known as a progressive educator and developed what he called a pragmatic philosophy. He considered change in education to be inevitable and that curriculum must constantly be reformed. He based his curriculum on problem-solving activity and experiences in natural settings. He joined the faculty at the University of Chicago and established on campus an experimental laboratory school where his teaching ideas could be practiced. The laboratory school is considered a forerunner to the recent school-university partnerships in which teachers and university professors collaborate.

World Wide Web Site: You may learn more about John Dewey at:
http://www.guam.net/home/bmarmie/dewey.html

The early 1900s were marked by the attempt to make an exact science of education (Button & Provenzo, 1989). This was brought on by developing research and testing techniques. Educational research would ultimately have a huge impact on schooling. One of the major changes came in preparing teachers. Increasing numbers of colleges were offering courses in pedagogy. Scholars and teachers began to build a community of educators who studied and practiced the best of teaching. Much of the first research developed around testing and measurements. The study of teaching and learning resulted in viewing

---

FIELD-BASED ACTIVITY 2.2

Imagine that you are a child in America in the early 1860s. Based on the readings, what kind of education would you receive? What family characteristics (e.g., race or ethnicity, gender, family economic level) would facilitate or hinder your access to education? As a class, tally the percentage of students in your class who would receive an education based on school attendance in America at that time. Ask those who would receive an education to explain what they would study and how they would be taught.

Now do the same for the early 1900s. How do the percentages change? Are the content and methods similar to that of the early 1800s?

In the early 1900s one-room schoolhouses were still common in rural communities, and teachers needed only one or two years of college to teach children of multiple ages.

curriculum construction as dependent on knowledge of subject specialties and child development.

Schools in the early twentieth century were sensitive to national and international events. Schools were greatly impacted by the Great Depression, and many, especially those in the South, became particularly impoverished. Teachers' salaries began to diminish and many teachers were laid off. The depression was followed by World War II, which changed the way that Americans thought about schools. Economy, labor, and the needs of the workforce began to influence what happened in our schools. The end of the war was followed by the baby boom, a large increase in birthrate, the children of which began to fill schools in the 1950s. Early technological advances were especially relevant to the history of education (Button & Provenzo, 1989). Technology began to revolutionize communication, change jobs and leisure time, and affect transportation and manufacturing. Education became one way for Americans to access the good life associated with improved technology. But not everyone had access to the good life, and as the century progressed, equality in the schools became a major issue.

By the 1960s Americans seemed less concerned with freedom than greatness. Government was growing larger and welfare was more prevalent. Taxpayers were asked to provide more and more resources for schools. When the former USSR sent Sputnik 1, the first artificial satellite, into space in 1957, Americans began to question the educational system and whether we had the high-quality schools that were held as a basic assumption of our society. This concern lead to the more recent reform efforts and the current educational system in which you are learning to teach (see Chapter 3).

Philosophical Themes

Educational history offers descriptions and stories that indicate change of venue, people, and contexts, but educational questions remain relatively constant. We can see that educators have constantly struggled with philosophical questions related to education: the purpose of education, the nature of the learner, the strategies associated with teaching, and the struggle between religion, basic education, and liberal approaches. Educational philosophies have evolved around the timeless struggles that are still present in current dialogues.

Philosophies form the basis for understanding purposes of education and help develop theories about what should be taught and how students learn. There are many ways to discuss the philosophies, but most philosophies can be traced to one of four major stances. Idealism and realism, two of the oldest philosophical positions, and pragmatism and existentialism, both newer philosophical systems, all impact educational thought (Myers & Myers, 1995). In most cases, philosophies do not reflect only one view, but represent an evolution of thinking that has guided decisions and theory building.

Idealism

The intellectual roots of educational philosophy can be traced back to ancient Greek and Roman history. Socrates (469–399 B.C.) made contributions to teaching and the value of knowledge (Power, 1991) by searching for basic meanings and truth and bringing others together to do the same. He attempted to educate social and political leaders by connecting knowledge and civic duty, and he used probing questions to explore the worth of human acts. Even in ancient times, those who questioned knowledge transmission and the existing power authorities were not popular. Socrates' questions disturbed the status quo and upset those who held and accepted common assumptions. His constant questions became unpopular because they were viewed as revolutionary and an affront to the authority of those in power. As a result, he was eventually tried for opposing those in power, found guilty, and forced to commit suicide by drinking poison. Socrates is best remembered for using a process of constant questioning, the Socratic method, in teaching. He was a master at creating a series of questions that helped his students develop an awareness of their own thought processes.

Socrates' philosophy and his teaching methodology are widely known to us through his student, friend, and constant companion, Plato (427–347 B.C.) (Power, 1991). Many feel that all educational philosophy originated with Plato's ideas. He developed and articulated a pattern of thought that suggests that societies and the character of society is highly dependent on the humans who control the processes. He was convinced that good citizenship and intellectual accomplishment were closely connected, that strong social structures were dependent on the education of citizens, although he had a clear preference for educating only the elite to provide leadership (Power, 1991). Plato's philosophy establishes that the purpose of education is to develop students' abilities so they can serve society (increase their social capacities). Plato is the founder of *idealism*, a philosophy that focuses on the spiritual and intellectual development of an individual.

Idealism includes ideas that go beyond the physical or concrete world. Idealists attempt to describe ideas, mind, consciousness, form, thought, energy, and other nonmaterial ideas. Ideals reside in the mind and reality is identified through the subconscious. Idealism reflects Plato's ideas and views education as necessary for an individual's freedom and limitless creative growth. Conservatism is valued in personal and social life.

Today's classrooms may reflect idealism in several different ways. Teachers are models in their own classrooms, and they encourage students to recognize and emulate the thoughts and actions of great people. The schools that reflect modern interpretations of idealism may focus on "back to basics," and the literature used in their classrooms reflect traditional classics. Translations of history and science focus on the Euro-American experiences and offer limited interpretations or perspectives. Many proponents of Christian and other current religious education movements draw on idealist philosophies to provide a rationale for the goals and content of education.

Realism

Aristotle (384–322 B.C.) studied in Plato's academy for seventeen years and introduced a novel educational philosophy—scientific empiricism—which became the basis for the philosophy known as realism. Aristotle felt that dialogue and questioning were too emotional and personal and failed to make good use of data. He considered the question methodology of Socrates and Plato a waste of valuable learning time because it depended too much on personal experiences. Instead, he encouraged learning to occur by writing and used descriptive prose as a teaching technique. His philosophy introduced the importance of habit and instruction, which he viewed as the basis of happiness.

Realism, antithetical to idealism, holds that objects and happenings exist regardless of how we perceive them. There is no dependence on our minds, but everything comes from nature and is subject to natural law. Scientific method is honored and each content area is precisely structured. Pestalozzi, Locke, Jefferson, and Mann were all realists. Learning and teaching are viewed as a science based on hard facts. Realists focus on skills of reasoning and believe that the major purpose of education is to promote thinking and understanding of subjects. The current drive for accountability is based on a philosophy of realism (Myers & Myers, 1995). Aristotle's emphasis on the virtues required and nurtured by the good life have strongly influenced contemporary advocates for character education (Noddings, 1997).

In today's classrooms, realism is often represented in science and environmental studies. Instruction reflecting a realist philosophy may focus on the environment and its influence on humans. There is a specific theory and truth applied to understanding the world. Teachers who maintain realism as a philosophy are usually subject-matter specialists who focus on reason and thinking.

Pragmatism

Pragmatism is a theory that constantly questions what is viewed as truth. John Dewey was a pragmatist who established experimental education and influenced notions of educational research. Knowledge is obtained and developed through experiences and interactions with the environment (Tanner, 1997). Humans become increasingly complex as they gain experiences and interact with the universe. Therefore, students need opportunities to act on their environment and undergo the consequences of that action. This experimentation goes beyond mere trial and error or mindless activity since it involves reflection on the connections between the action and its consequences.

From this perspective, education is defined as the reconstruction or reorganization of experiences (Dewey, 1916). A teacher who is a pragmatist will help students understand that what is known is changeable, that there are a number of ways to interpret events, and that there is no absolute truth. While Dewey, as noted previously, often avoided identification with popular notions of progressive education, he identified certain common principles shared by progressive schools.

Discovery learning and child-centered learning are terms that would be associated with the pragmatist philosophy. A pragmatist philosophy promotes inquiry and uses reflective thinking to solve problems. Classrooms reflecting the pragmatic philosophy may be child-centered, discovery-based, cooperative, and motivated by student interests.

Existentialism

Existentialism, a relatively recent philosophy emerging after World War I, focuses on the individual and interprets the world through feelings, anxiety, and choice. Existentialist thought establishes reality and humans as too complex and unpredictable to fit into a neatly predictable system. Truth is subjective. Based on the writings of some educational theorists who have primarily looked at the writings of Sartre, Nietzsche, Ortega, and Jaspers, existentialism has little to offer to educational philosophy and may even destroy education as it currently exists (Baker, 1974; Morris, 1963). However, Martin Burber (1957) has explicitly connected his general philosophy with an existentialist philosophy of education in his writings. From his perspective, teachers are in a position to impose their views of reality and truth on their students but choose instead to merely present their perspectives and allow students to develop their own views. Developing a capacity to love, appreciate, and respond emotionally are important elements of this philosophical stance. Values, arts, and multiple perceptions are used to explain events and interpret concepts. Terms such as self-actualization and self-realization are often associated with this view of existentialism.

A classroom of today that reflects an existentialist philosophy will focus on individuals and their perceptions of events. Students are encouraged to build meaning from their own experiences. A classroom interpretation of existentialism encourages students to accept responsibility for their actions and focuses on respecting ones own ideas as well as the ideas of others.

FIELD-BASED ACTIVITY 2.3

With your classmates, list as many past and present educational issues or controversies currently being debated as you can think of. Can you and your classmates identify educational disagreements that are clashes of basic philosophies? Ask teachers or administrators in your school to join the class discussion and review some of the major educational issues currently under discussion. What philosophies do you recognize during the discussion? Write a summary paragraph of the ideas you recognized during the discussion.

The country's attitudes toward racial and ethnic differences required many cultural and ethnic groups to establish their own schools. School segregation continued until the Civil Rights movements of the 1950s and 1960s.

While current educational systems have been influenced by the philosophers and educational philosophies previously described, many contemporary philosophies existing today display a "unique" outlook or focus. Nevertheless, there is a link between past and present philosophies. Philosophers from the past inform contemporary philosophies that impact today's schools directly. As a result, many contemporary philosophies are outgrowths of the four basic categories of philosophy.

FIELD-BASED ACTIVITY 2.4

Divide into small groups. Each group should choose one of the four philosophical approaches described in this section and prepare a vignette or concrete description of an activity in a classroom that exemplifies that particular approach. Have a representative from your group read your vignette to the rest of the class and ask them if they can identify the philosophical approach.

PORTFOLIO REFLECTIONS AND EXHIBITS

You may wish to prepare an exhibit that illustrates what you learned as you read and discussed the concepts in this chapter. Your responses to the activities or following suggestions provides you with some ideas that might contribute to professional portfolios.

Suggested Exhibit 2: Philosophy of a Preservice Teacher and Plans for Providing Appropriate Experiences

1. Review your response to Field-Based Activity 2.1. Use the response as the first step to identify your own philosophy of teaching. Prepare a demonstration of your philosophy. Write a poem, develop a collage, picture, essay, or identify a life story that helps you illustrate your perspectives on education. Make reference to the established history and philosophy presented in this text and other readings.

2. Share your philosophy and evaluations of experiences with your college professor and classroom teacher mentor. Allow them to provide you feedback.

Recently, a more critical stance has played a role in educational philosophy. Critical philosophers focus on how and why society and schools oppress some people and not others and on how political issues are impacted by oppression. Racism, sexism, religion, and economics form the basis of their critical analysis of curriculum, instructional strategies, and attitudes in the schools (Piner, 1998). They encourage teachers to question their classroom actions and to understand how teachers contribute to the success and failure of minority groups, women, and poverty groups in today's classrooms.

Over time, despite the influences of formal philosophy, most teachers develop their own versions of educational philosophy and theory, which are deeply rooted in what works in their classrooms. Understanding and reflecting on learning theories, teaching methodology, classroom management, and curriculum helps you understand your own philosophy of education. Teachers can learn about their philosophy through their own teaching experiences and by comparing their beliefs and actions to principles embodied in established educational philosophies.

Related Readings

Cuban, L. (1993). *How teachers taught: Constancy and change in American classrooms 1880–1990.*

    This book looks at the last century of American teaching and presents an interesting account of how elementary and secondary classrooms are impacted by history, sociology, and education. Cuban uses classroom observations of teachers teaching throughout the last 100 years to provide "snapshots" into classrooms. It is through this process that he identifies a remarkable continuity as well as instances of classroom change.

Kinchloe, J. L., & Steinberg, S. R. (1992). *Thirteen questions: Reframing education's conversations.* New York: Peter Lang.

    This is a series of philosophical essays that introduce important issues from differing perspectives. The voices in this book are often critical of existing practices and set out new solutions to some of our old problems. The chapter authors present information that is often omitted from the traditional discussions of educational history and philosophy.

Postman, N. (1997). *The end of education: Redefining the value of school.* New York: Alfred A. Knopf.

    Postman questions some of the assumptions and values that current educational practices are built on. He presents narratives and metaphors that help us consider different ways to think about schools.

Tanner, L. (1997). *Dewey's laboratory school: Lessons for today.* New York: Teachers College Press.

    Tanner explains how teachers developed and implemented curriculum in Dewey's laboratory school. She relates Dewey's teaching and learning philosophies to modern trends and issues. This book is a good introduction to Dewey and helps the reader make connections to Dewey and today's classrooms.

References

Baker, B. F. (1974). Existential philosophers on education. In J. Park (Ed.), *Selected readings in the philosophy of education* (4th ed., pp. 128–138). New York: Macmillan.

Burber, M. (1957). *Between man and man.* Boston: Beacon Press.

Button, H. W., & Provenzo, E. F. (1989). *History of education and culture in America.* Englewood Cliffs, NJ: Prentice Hall.

Dewey, J. (1916). *Democracy and education.* New York: Macmillan.

Frankena, W. K. (1974). Model for analyzing a philosophy of education. In J. Park (Ed.), *Selected readings in the philosophy of education* (4th ed., pp. 139–144). New York: Macmillan.

McMannon, T. J. (1995). *Morality, efficiency, and reform: An interpretation of history of American education.* Work in Progress Series, No. 5. Seattle: Institute for Educational Inquiry.

Myers, C. B., & Myers, L. K. (1995). *The professional educator: A new introduction to teaching and schools.* Belmont, CA: Wadsworth.

Morris, V. C. (1963). *Selected readings in the philosophy of education* (2nd ed., pp. 551–552). New York: Macmillan.

Noddings, N. (1997). Character education and community. In A. Molner (Ed.), *The constructions of children's character* (pp. 1–16). Chicago: NSSE and University of Chicago Press.

Perkinson, H. J. (1991). *The imperfect panacea: American faith in education 1865–1990.* New York: McGraw-Hill.

Piner, W. E. (Ed.). (1998). *Curriculum: Toward new identities.* New York: Garland.

Power, E. J. (1991). *A legacy of learning: A history of western education.* Albany: State University of New York Press.

Smith, S. (1979). *Ideas of the great educators.* New York: Barnes & Noble.

Tanner, D. (1997). *Dewey's laboratory school: Lessons for today.* New York: Teachers College Press.

Timm, J. T. (1996). *Four perspectives in multicultural education.* Belmont, CA: Wadsworth.

3
Understanding Current
Educational Context

In this chapter
- Twenty Years of Educational Reform: 1980–2000
- Reform Themes
- Success in a Time of Change
- Characteristics of Successful Programs
- The Case Against Change
- Laws That Change Educational Contexts

B*y several general measures, American secondary education, just like Tillson High School, has changed little since 1981. As a result of political pressure on school authorities students are taking moderately different patterns of courses from earlier ones, concentrating more on the established basic subjects (mathematics, English, science, and social studies) and less on electives with titles such as "Life Skills." . . .*

The past decades' hue and cry over the need for high school reform makes sense. The existing system doesn't work. What is far less clear and what there should be substantial argument about—is what should replace the schools we have today . . .

The prospect of fundamental changes in how education is institutionally delivered is as troublesome as it is inevitable . . . School reform at the end of this century is cast against a backdrop of extraordinary new influences, both philosophical and practical. Those responsible for the schools cannot pretend that these influences do not exist or are too paltry to deserve attention. On the contrary, they threaten to swamp the public school system as we know it, altering our assumptions about learning and teaching, about what a school in fact is and who has the right to control it. The danger that the educational system may continue to ignore these opportunities depresses Horace. The prospect of facing up to them, of seizing them in the service of substantial reform, however, gives Horace hope.

Getting people to change their minds about what school should be, even in a limited way, is a slow business, one requiring small but persistent steps . . .

—Theodore Sizer, *Horace's Hope**

Educators and the public seem to be preoccupied with making schools better. Citizens—not only educators but parents, corporate and other community members, banking and business people, and politicians—are all engaged in discussions about improving education. Different groups of individuals may have various educational agendas. Educators "reinvent" and develop new strategies for teaching and learning. Business, industry, social organizations, and educational institutions are developing new ways to work and need a workforce capable of adapting to new practices. New technologies require that we use different instructional tools. Organized groups often object to particular teaching approaches or new strategies. There are constant mandates, suggestions, and discussions that require educators to respond, consider, and change teaching and learning strategies. Schools and the teaching that goes on within the schools have been "scrutinized, criticized, eulogized, and 'reformed'" (Myers & Myers, 1995, p. 25). The calls for change have been intense during the past twenty years, and teachers who begin their careers during the twenty-first century are likely to experience continuous change. Some of the questions this chapter will answer include:

*Theodore Sizer, *Horace's Hope: What Works for the American High School* (pp. 16, 125, 127). New York: Houghton Mifflin, 1996.

Becoming a Teacher in a Field-Based Setting

- What are some recurring themes in current changes related to teaching and learning?
- What are some successful programs addressing changes in teaching and learning?
- How do you think reform movements will impact your teaching?
- What are some of the reasons that some people resist educational change?

Most would agree that the more complex requirements of our society—the rapid influx of technology, the diversity of our population, the increase of children in poverty, and the impact of drugs and violence—require that schools must change to meet new demands, but no one can be assured what direction changes and restructuring should take. The last twenty years provide an overview of some of the issues, challenges, and successes of educational reform.

Twenty Years of Educational Reform: 1980–2000

During the past twenty years school reform has taken several forms (Myers & Myers, 1995). In the early 1980s, several national reports warned that American schools were in trouble. One report that alarmed the nation about the status of schooling was *A Nation at Risk*, released in 1983. This report contributed to a national attitude of concerns for our schools that continues to impact education even as we approach the next century. It cited an alarming weakening and mediocrity of teaching and learning, suggested that the state of our schools would put the entire country at risk, and issued dire predictions about the future of our country. The report provided indicators such as lower standardized test scores, lower SAT scores, higher illiteracy rates, lower graduation requirements, and more students in remedial college courses (Myers & Myers, 1995) as examples that our educational system was not working. This document proved to be a major event in educational processes of our country. It framed many citizens' concerns and focused issues into a condensed set of statements. The report recommended (1) increased amount of content taught at schools, (2) higher standards and expectations for our students, (3) increased time for learning, (4) higher standards for teachers, and (5) increased leadership and fiscal support from elected officials.

Administrators and teachers work together to align curriculum with state and national standards.

The concerns of the public over the status of education as presented in *A Nation at Risk* prompted politicians to establish national goals designed to build a national commitment to education. The formulation of these goals began with the Republican era of President Reagan and continued into the Democratic administration of President Clinton. The original national efforts were outlined by the governors who worked to develop six national goals designed to guide educational reform. These goals (outlined in Table 3.1) are now known as "Goals 2000: Educate America" and were passed by Congress in 1994. (See Chapter 7 for additional discussion issues related to Goals 2000.)

For more information regarding the National Educational Goals, contact the following:

World Wide Web Sites: http://hp877.odedodea.edu:8001/dnatlgls.htm
http://www.ed.gov/legislation/ESEA/Guidance/app-c.html

Address: Department of Defense Education Activity (DoDEA)
4040 North Fairfax Street
Arlington, VA 22203-1635

Table 3.1
America's Educational Goals for the Year 2000

1. All children in America will start school ready to learn.

2. The high school graduation rate will increase to at least 90 percent.

3. American students will leave grades four, eight, and twelve having demonstrated competency in challenging subject matter including English, mathematics, science, history, and geography; and every school in America will ensure that all students learn to use their minds well, so they may be prepared for responsible citizenship, further learning, and productive employment in our modern economy.

4. U.S. students will be first in the world in science and mathematics achievement.

5. Every adult American will be literate and will possess the knowledge and skills necessary to compete in a global economy and exercise the rights and responsibilities of citizenship.

6. Every school in America will be free of drugs and violence and will offer a disciplined environment conducive to learning.

One solution developed to solve some of the problems identified in *A Nation at Risk* was large-scale governmental actions that introduced and mandated curriculum and competencies for children and teachers (Apple, 1996). Changes, such as longer school days, increased requirements for graduation from high school, higher standards for entrance into the teaching profession, and more testing for students and teachers, were implemented as a result of *A Nation at Risk* and similar reports.

Even before the first calls for reform settled, a second wave of change began and focused primarily at state level initiatives. Teaching processes became the focus of attention, and teacher and student testing as measures of accountability for student learning was the major outcome. Salaries of teachers were raised, leadership skills of principals and teachers were honed, and competencies for students and teachers were specified. Recommendations from the second round of educational reports occurring in the mid-to-late 1980s included a more subject-centered curriculum, back-to-basics approach, a greater focus on mathematics and science instruction, and a strong connection between testing, promotion, and graduation. The reports also called for alternative and flexible ways to educate teachers and included plans for merit pay, increased workloads, and longer school days.

The reform efforts of the 1980s were confusing and rather disjointed. On the one hand, there was an effort to control what teachers taught, while at the same time, recommendations suggested that decision-making processes should be decentralized and based in the school settings (Apple, 1996). A series of isolated innovations, including attempts to structure the teaching process into isolated behaviors and leadership training encouraging site-based decision making, came and went with regularity. In spite of the 1980 reform efforts, problems and concerns associated with educational change were not eradicated, but simply worsened. In reality, the reforms did little to change the content of instruction, failed to directly involve teachers in the reform process, and were unsuccessful in altering the practices related to teaching and learning that might bring about lasting change (Smith & O'Day, 1991). This period was extremely stressful for teachers who felt that they were neither involved in the change processes nor recognized for their efforts on students' behalf.

Toward the end of the 1980s and at the beginning of the 1990s, reform movements began to take on a different tone than earlier calls for change. Innovations became more comprehensive, and themes related to basic values and recognition of family (Hlebowitsh & Tellez, 1997) began to emerge. The development of standards for student achievement and teacher preparation became the focus of many reform movements. Change efforts attempted to connect requirements for student learning with teacher preparation and professional development of experienced teachers. There were also efforts to provide more educational choices to students and their parents, and schools worked to be more flexible.

The state educational agencies played an important role in facilitating educational change. One of the most comprehensive overall state change efforts was implemented by Kentucky. In 1990 the Kentucky Education Reform Act facilitated a complete rebuilding of the school system from scratch (Holland, 1997). The new school system was developed around three major areas: administration, curriculum, and finance. The changes included "establishing elected councils of educators and parents to run local schools, reorganizing the lower elementary grades into primary school classrooms that included children of different ages and abilities, and setting up a high-stakes accountability system that rewarded or sanctioned teachers and principals according to students' test scores" (Holland, 1997, p. 265). State officials report that as a result of the law more than 92 percent of the state's 1,400 schools improved student achievement between 1992 and 1996 (Rothman, 1997). But the law mandating the complicated changes is still hotly contested and most agree that it is not yet possible to determine whether improved student learning can be maintained.

During the second half of the 1990s, school reform activity has been widespread and extremely varied (Shields & Knapp, 1997). Even though there was evidence that students were taking more difficult courses and that the school dropout rate had stabilized, the SAT scores had not increased substantially, college professors were still complaining that students were not ready for university curriculum, and employers still believed that high school graduates were unprepared for the workplace (Jennings, 1995). After nearly twenty years of intense change effort, it is clear that attention to school reform is no guarantee of improved learning opportunities for children and young people. Calls for American education to reinvent itself are still heard. As the decade continues, the reform efforts focus on increasing flexibility and variety of educational opportunities. Educators are focusing on localized changes and encourage collaboration between parents, policy makers, state and national agencies, and communities (see Chapter 6). Changes in educational funding allowed the states to take control of the resources, and state governments encouraged local districts to allow students choice in where they attend schools. The most recent reforms attempt to link change efforts and become more comprehensive. The latest round of reforms also focused on students who were overlooked by the past reforms, and there is general agreement that special steps are needed to address the needs of poor and culturally diverse populations (Futrell, 1993).

Many believe that high educational expectations and accomplishments will be attainable only with the help of all concerned with the well-being of children. The recognition that educators alone cannot change the educational process has resulted in a clamor for collaboration between schools, universities, businesses, and social service agencies. Schools will have a better chance at succeeding when society values and supports children. As Goodlad (1992) stated, "Healthy nations have healthy schools, not the other way around." He goes on to explain that a large number of agencies and institutions must work together to develop an educational ecology that promotes improved lives for all segments of our society.

FIELD-BASED ACTIVITY 3.1

Pay attention to radio, television, and newspaper reports about education and note the nature of topics discussed. Are they primarily critical of education? Are they calls for change? Criticism of current practice? Reports of what's working or not working in education? Relate current issues to concerns and practices in your school setting. Share these with your classmates.

There have been some changes in the way that teachers teach, how children's learning is assessed, and how teachers, administrators, and others are held accountable for meeting the goals set forward by particular reform movements. But many believe that we must change the basic structures of our schools before we can make real differences. One fact has remained constant throughout the flurry of activity directed at improving our schools—the answers for questions relating to teaching, learning, and our schools are not easy. There is no secret formula—no panacea.

Reform Themes

When all the dust settled from the public's discussions about education during the 1980s and 1990s, a wide range of topics ranging from reforms in school funding to students' rights reforms emerged. Some of the most recurring themes include issues related to accountability, standards for students and teachers, school choice, professionalization of teaching, and equitable education for all students.

Accountability

Declining test scores, rising rates of illiteracy, and demands for greater accountability from schools have contributed to public interest in testing. Issues related to student test scores and criticism of what graduates seem to know and be able to do have prompted many American citizens and leaders to demand that successful students pass a series of standardized tests. The emphasis on testing as a way to hold schools accountable reflects the perspective that good teaching is measured by students' achievement (Clark, 1995). A movement toward the development of national tests is repeatedly discussed as a way to hold schools and teachers accountable for what they teach as well as one way to acquire comparative data. As a result of this emphasis, many states have developed curriculum requirements and companion standardized tests that are administered at predetermined intervals during primary and secondary schooling. Some calls for reform have developed when test scores of children and young people in one district or state are compared with the results of other locations. A constant comparison with Japanese achievement scores has been one result of this effort.

The testing movements suggest that there is general agreement among education professionals about just what should be taught to each and every student in our schools. However, the ideas associated with testing and the back-to-basics movements are highly debatable. What is meant and desired by the term "back-to-basics" and how basics should be measured can be very different. Some would argue that the definition of basics is rather static and has been the same for many years. Others may suggest that different learners may have different "basics" depending on their needs and their past experiences (Piner, 1992). For example, some people would include the infusion of "basic" African and African American knowledge (i.e., history, literature) in the school curriculum. Others disagree and say that the curriculum basics should come from traditional topics and approaches.

Despite some disagreement over the content and form of testing, few would argue the merits of evaluation in general. Teachers must assess what students know in order to plan for instruction. Testing allows the teacher to discover what concepts children understand and what experiences they need in order to continue effective learning. When teachers know their students, they are able to plan more effective, motivating activities and interactions. Continuous and long-range assessment identifies growth patterns and results from experiences.

Testing has always played a major role in education, but during the last few years, it has played a major role in what is being taught in the classroom. Testing of students' learning is more than an education issue and is a major influence on the teaching processes in modern classrooms. Teachers, curriculum, and educational practices are evaluated on the basis of students' performances on tests. This is particularly the case when standardized tests are used to measure the effectiveness of teaching. Every school uses standardized achievement tests to document students' achievement and growth over time. Tests are used for statistical, administrative, and political reasons and very few teachers accept the idea of measuring their students' growth and achievement with one test score. But those who administer and interpret test scores should realize that, at best, tests are a sampling of students abilities.

There are often subtle effects related to the reliance on standardized tests. Due to perceived pressures from administrators and parents, teachers may "teach to the test. " Some teachers are so concerned about their students' performances on the tests, they look to tests to guide the curricular and instructional decisions. Another danger of the tests is the role they may play in developing students' perceptions about their ability to learn. Teachers may expect less from students who do not perform well on a test.

Standardized tests are not in themselves a deterrent to learning if they are used with caution. Testing, or any other single effort, does not constitute an accountability and evaluation system. A school creates effective evaluation and assessment policies and procedures by using various tools that inform, contribute to decision making, and correct problems (Hlebowitsh & Tellez, 1997). When teachers know their students and use multiple methods to assess and evaluate learning, interpretation of school achievement will be more appropriate and improve instruction for all children. Regardless of how tests are used in the classroom, the results of testing are often a stated catalyst for change and reform in education. One must understand the contributions and potential dangers of standardized testing in order to truly understand reform and change movements in our schools.

Standards for Teaching and Learning

Standards are frameworks that focus on academic behaviors and assessments, and their purpose is to encourage high academic performance (Cohen, 1995). Goals 2000, the education goals that have guided three presidents, encourages the development of national standards. Similarly, state-based frameworks often reflect national standards, clearly stating the expectations for what teachers teach and students learn.

The Illinois Learning Standards (Illinois State Board of Education, 1997) are similar to other state standards that are developed to help design state assessment programs, guide school curriculum development, assess student progress, focus school improvement plans, and communicate the purpose and results of schooling to the community. The standards were developed with the input of teachers, administrators, parents, employers, community leaders, and representatives of higher education. Standards were developed in English language arts, mathematics, science, social science, physical development and health, fine arts, and foreign languages for early elementary, late elementary, middle/junior high school, early high school, and late high school (see Table 3.2 starting on page 60). As you can see from the excerpt of the English language arts standards in Table 3.2, the first state goal is that all students "read with understanding and fluency." The frameworks then present learning standards and the benchmarks that would indicate that appropriate student learning has occurred. Statewide achievement tests are being developed to assess the learning standards.

World Wide Web Site: You may learn more about the Illinois Standards at:
   http://www.isbe.state.il.us/ils/default.html

In addition to state efforts, many of the subject areas have developed or reevaluated existing standards during the past decade. Standards for specific content areas are emerging at national and state levels. Sometimes standards are

Becoming a Teacher in a Field-Based Setting

developed though collaborative efforts, linking the state and national efforts together, but more often, they are done separately without articulation between the two. During the 1990s, professional organizations such as National Council of Teachers of English, National Council of Teachers of Mathematics, and the National Science Foundation conducted a series of meetings, discussions, and studies that provide a basis for determining what should be taught to different ages of children. Specific goals and standards related to content areas taught in school have evolved from these national discussions.

The content area standards developed by some professional organizations generated concerns and disagreements from parents and other interested groups. The subject of social studies was particularly contentious and widely debated. Social studies educators interpreted standards from a broad perspective and accepted the history and culture of multiple perspectives as valid and desired. They presented an interpretation of social studies that recognized different perspectives based on gender, race, culture, and religion. For example, the history of the western United States settlements included the role of women in the wagon trains. Including diverse views of events from differing perspectives changes the stories and narratives associated with important events. Some educators and parents believe their schools should be focusing on traditional aspects of history and geography. In many cases, parental beliefs regarding the content and subject matter taught reflects their own experiences in schools. The resulting disagreements were reported on the national news and delayed the approval of the new standards in many settings.

World Wide Web Site: You may access professional organizations and learn more about their subject area standards at:

National Council for Teachers of English: http://www.ncte.org

National Council for Social Studies: http://www.ncss.org

National Council of Teachers of Mathematics: http://www.nctm.org

International Reading Association: http://www.reading.org

School Choice

In an effort to recognize parental opinions and desires, several changes regarding *school choice* became popular. Supporters of school choice believe that parents have the right to select the school that they wish their children to attend, that they should not have to send their children to the school that is in their neighborhood or school district. One of the ideas behind the popularity of school choice was the belief that schools could compete for students and make changes so that they could attract students by providing the best educational experiences

Table 3.2
Illinois Learning Standards/English Language Arts
State Goal 1: Read with understanding and fluency.

As a result of their schooling, students will be able to:

LEARNING STANDARD	EARLY ELEMENTARY	LATE ELEMENTARY
A. Apply word analysis and vocabulary skills to comprehend selections.	**1.A.1a** Apply word analysis skills (e.g., phonics, word patterns) to recognize new words. **1.A.1b** Comprehend unfamiliar words using context clues and prior knowledge; verify meanings with resource materials.	**1.A.2a** Read and comprehend unfamiliar words using root words, synonyms, antonyms, word origins and derivations. **1.A.2b** Clarify word meaning using context clues and a variety of resources including glossaries, dictionaries and thesauruses.
B. Apply reading strategies to improve understanding and fluency.	**1.B.1a** Establish purposes for reading, make predictions, connect important ideas, and link text to previous experiences and knowledge. **1.B.1b** Identify genres (forms and purposes) of fiction, nonfiction, poetry and electronic literary forms. **1.B.1c** Continuously check and clarify for understanding (e.g., reread, read ahead, use visual and context clues, ask questions, retell, use meaningful substitutions.) **1.B.1d** Read age-appropriate material aloud with fluency and accuracy.	**1.B.2a** Establish purposes for reading; survey materials; ask questions; make predictions; connect, clarify and extend ideas. **1.B.2b** Identify structure (e.g., description, compare/contrast, cause and effect, sequence) of nonfiction texts to improve comprehension. **1.B.2c** Continuously check and clarify for understanding (e.g., *in addition to previous skills*, clarify terminology, seek additional information.) **1.B.2d** Read age-appropriate material aloud with fluency and accuracy.

Becoming a Teacher in a Field-Based Setting

WHY THIS GOAL IS IMPORTANT: Reading is essential. It is the process by which people gain information and ideas from books, newspapers, manuals, letters, contracts, advertisements and a host of other materials. Using strategies for constructing meaning before, during and after reading will help students connect what they read now with what they have learned in the past. Students who read well and widely build a strong foundation for learning in all areas of life.

JUNIOR HIGH SCHOOL	EARLY HIGH SCHOOL	LATE HIGH SCHOOL
1.A.3a Apply knowledge of word origins and derivations to comprehend words used in specific content areas (e.g., scientific, political, literary, mathematical).	**1.A.4a** Expand knowledge of word origins and derivations and use idioms, analogies, metaphors and similes to extend vocabulary development.	**1.A.5a** Identify and analyze new terminology applying knowledge of word origins and derivations in a variety of practical settings.
1.A.3b Analyze the meaning of words and phrases in their context.	**1.A.4b** Compare the meaning of words and phrases and use analogies to explain the relationships among them.	**1.A.5b** Analyze the meaning of abstract concepts and the effects of particular word and phrase choices.
1.B.3a Preview reading materials, make predictions and relate reading to information from other sources.	**1.B.4a** Preview reading materials, clarify meaning, analyze overall themes and coherence, and relate reading with information from other sources.	**1.B.5a** Relate reading to prior knowledge and experience and make connections to related information.
1.B.3b Identify text structure and create a visual representation (e.g., graphic organizer, outline, drawing) to use while reading.	**1.B.4b** Analyze, interpret and compare a variety of texts for purpose, structure, content, detail and effect.	**1.B.5b** Analyze the defining characteristics and structures of a variety of complex literary genres and describe how genre affects the meaning and function of texts.
1.B.3c Continuously check and clarify for understanding (e.g., *in addition to previous skills*, draw comparisons to other readings).	**1.B.4c** Read age-appropriate material with fluency and accuracy.	**1.B.5c** Evaluate a variety of compositions for purpose, structure, content and details for use in school or at work.
1.B.3d Read age-appropriate material with fluency and accuracy.		**1.B.5d** Read age-appropriate material with fluency and accuracy.

Table 3.2 continues on page 62

Table 3.2, *continued*
Illinois Learning Standards/English Language Arts
State Goal 1: Read with understanding and fluency.

As a result of their schooling, students will be able to:

LEARNING STANDARD	EARLY ELEMENTARY	LATE ELEMENTARY
C. Comprehend a broad range of reading materials.	**1.C.1a** Use information to form questions and verify predictions.	**1.c.2a** Use information to form and refine questions and predictions.
	1.C.1b Identify important themes and topics.	**1.C.2b** Make and support infernces and form interpretations about main themes and topics.
	1.C.1c Mark comparisons across reading selections.	**1.C.2c** Compare and contrast the organization of selections.
	1.C.1d Summarize content of reading material using text organization (e.g., story, sequence).	**1.C.2d** Summarize and make generalizations from content and relate to purpose of material.
	1.C.1e Identify how authors and illustrators express their ideas in text and graphics (e.g., dialogue, conflict, shape, color, characters).	**1.C.2e** Explain how authors and illustrators use text and art to express their ideas (e.g., points of view, design, hues, metaphor).
	1.C.1f Use information presented in simple tables, maps and charts to form an interpretation.	**1.C.2f** Connect information presented in tables, maps and charts to printed or electronic text.

Note: Examples are designated by "e.g." and enclosed in parentheses. They are meant to guide the teacher as to the general intent of the standards and benchmarks, not to identify all possible items.

JUNIOR HIGH SCHOOL	EARLY HIGH SCHOOL	LATE HIGH SCHOOL
1.C.3a Use information to form, explain and support questions and predictions.	**1.C.4a** Use questions and predictions to guide reading.	**1.C.5a** Use questions and predictions to guide reading across complex materials.
1.C.3b Interpret and analyze entire narrative test using story elements, point of view and theme.	**1.C.4b** Explain and justify an interpretation of a text.	**1.C.5b** Analyze and defend an interpretation of text.
1.C.3c Compare, contrast and evaluate ideas and information from various sources and genres.	**1.C.4c** Interpret, evaluate and apply information from a variety of sources to other situations (e.g., academic, vocational, technical, personal).	**1.C.5c** Critically evaluate information from multiple sources.
1.C.3d Summarize and make generalizations from content and relate them to the purpose of the material.	**1.C.4d** Summarize and make generalizations from content and relate them to the purpose of the material.	**1.C.5d** Summarize and make generalizations from content and relate them to the purpose of the material.
1.C.3e Compare how authors and illustrators use text and art across materials to express their ideas (e.g., foreshadowing, flashbacks, color, strong verbs, language that inspires).	**1.C.4e** Analyze how authors and illustrators use text and art to express and emphasize their ideas (e.g., imagery, multiple points of view).	**1.C.5e** Evaluate how authors and illustrators use text and art across materials to express their ideas (e.g., complex dialogue, persuasive techniques).
1.C.3f Interpret tables that display textual information and data in visual formats.	**1.C.4f** Interpret tables, graphs and maps in conjunction with related text.	**1.C.5f** Use tables, graphs and maps to challenge arguments, defend conclusions and persuade others.

Source: Illinois State Board of Education (1997). *Illinois Learning Standards*. Springfield: Illinois State Board of Education.

possible. *Vouchers* were sometimes discussed as a way to increase the choices parents have in selecting schools. Tuition vouchers would be provided to parents so they could enroll their children in a school of their choice, whether it be public or private. Traditionally, students are required to attend schools in their districts, and the schools receive an amount based on school achievement. Traditionally, private schools are not provided with public educational funding. Since vouchers present a very different way of school funding, there is great difference of opinions about the value of voucher systems. Some educators argue that using vouchers would dramatically change the concept of public schooling, allowing private schools to intermingle with traditional public schools.

The development of alternatives to traditional public schooling, characterized by *charter schools*, was another innovation evolving from the desire to expand school choice. Charter schools are newly created, state-funded public schools offering a unique educational concept or theme. They may or may not exist within an existing school district. Museums, communities, businesses, individuals, teachers, and even for-profit organizations may develop a charter for a school. Charter schools can be established when a local school board or the state department of education approves an educational plan. The charters describe the finances, curriculum, organizations, and other logistical considerations. The students who attend charter schools must meet state assessment expectations, but administrators and teachers in the school may facilitate the learning in nontraditional ways. The first charter school was established in Minnesota in 1991, and by 1995 there were 150 charter schools throughout the country (Oliva, 1997).

There are many different charter school themes and arrangements. Charter schools often target low achievers or at-risk students and attempt to raise achievement by innovative and creative teaching and learning environments. Existing charter schools have evolved around traditional basic skills, home schooling, store-front programs, "distance learning," and computer-based learning (Oliva, 1997). They may encourage curriculum themes that focus on economics, bilingualism, or great books. Since the teachers and administrators are not held to state requirements and curriculums, charter schools are seen as a way to make changes in traditional methods of teaching and learning. This concept not only encourages innovation but is seen as a way to force traditional schools to change their approaches in order to compete and maintain their student populations.

World Wide Web Site: You may learn more about charter schools at:
  http://www.csr.syr.edu/index.html

Professionalization of Teaching

Several of the reform movements suggest that one of the problems with teaching is the lack of professionalism. Professionalism refers to teachers' ability to regulate their profession, the development and maintenance of a qualified teacher workforce, and continued professional development for experienced teachers. However, professionalism of teaching as addressed in the reform movements usually focuses on how to hold teachers accountable for what they do in the classroom. One answer to this concern is to develop standards and require testing to make sure teachers are meeting established standards. The standards movement has impacted teachers in two ways. Most states have developed tests that are connected to state standards for elementary and secondary students. Teachers are held accountable for helping their students meet standards established by local districts or individual states. Students take the tests each year, and the reports are used to evaluate the quality of teaching and learning that they have experienced.

Professionalism and standards also are connected in a second way. New standards or requirements for teaching may be adopted and result in the requirement of additional initial training and expanded requirements for maintaining certification. In many cases, teachers must pass statewide tests that reflect teaching standards before they are certified or licensed. Currently, state governments have had a great deal of control over the regulations that define who will teach and who will be licensed. State certification is usually guided by state standards of competence and establishes the labels and descriptions of professionalism accepted by the educational community in the state.

Another issue related to professionalism is set forth by those who feel teachers should have more freedom to make decisions and control their profession. Critics of the national standards movement feel that standards, assessment, and accountability, as it's being set forward in this country, actually reduce the professionalism of teachers by maintaining outside control of the profession through licensing and testing. Since teachers do not have a great deal of control over licensure and evaluation and testing, many argue that standards, testing, and accountability does not contribute to professionalism. Those who hold this view suggest that professionalism of teachers is dependent upon the amount of control teachers have over the establishment and maintenance of standards and testing.

While there are differences in opinion about national standards and the status of the profession of teaching, there is no doubt that teaching is moving toward a "higher, more complex demanding plane" (Myers & Myers, 1995, p. 616). The debates and consideration of teacher controls, standards establish-

Schools are required by law to modify teaching approaches and change the structure of school buildings so that all students, regardless of their physical differences, are able to experience equal access to learning.

ment, and how teachers are held accountable are necessary before the profession is perceived as credible and fully functioning. Defining a profession is an evolutionary process controlled by those in the profession and by some external events. Those of you who are currently becoming teachers will make a major contribution in the struggle toward professionalism that is ahead of the teaching profession.

Equitable Education for All Students

Student diversity and a wider range of economic stratification among the children in our country has forced the topic of educational equality into the forefront of educational issues. All students, including the poor, nonnative English speaking, and disabled, deserve quality education. Teachers must consider how issues of diversity affect the way children respond to schooling; recognize that differences influence learning; and take those differences into account when planning instruction. Teachers responsible for teaching children with the great range of differences should understand these differences and use their awareness to enhance instruction for all children.

One way to view equity issues relates directly to how teachers perceive the potential achievement of their students. Some students' learning difficulties attributed to differences arise from the teachers' expectations. Differences such as culture, race, family status, and socioeconomic backgrounds have historically been related to success or failure in schools. Often teachers believe, for example, that children who are poor or who speak English as a second language will not succeed in school. While life situations affect a child's achievement, it does not mean that they are doomed to failure. One of the first steps a teacher can take to eliminate learning difficulties is to accept the child and honor the differences. It is the very wise teacher who uses the differences to enrich the schooling experiences. A broader discussion of educational equity and equality is presented in Chapter 4.

Success in a Time of Change

With each wave of reform, the general public becomes a bit more cynical about school reform. Many believe that schools have changed little in the past hundred years (Cuban, 1984) and that they will continue as they have in the past, despite efforts to the contrary. Schools often appear to be resistant to change, and when change occurs it is very difficult, stressful, expensive, and time-consuming for all involved. Despite this pessimism, there are examples where educational reform has made a difference for children characterized with particularly difficult homes and educational situations. Three successful programs implemented by innovative educational leaders have led to improved conditions and provide us with models that provide success for all children.

Theodore Sizer: Essential Schools

Sizer takes on the mountain of issues and problems associated with secondary schools and has established a network of high school–university partnerships across the country to impact secondary school teaching and learning. Changes in high schools are made based on nine common principles that help the schools set clear and simple goals about intellectual skills and knowledge of their students. Schools that adopt his model establish a vision of integrated, comfortable, trusting environments that focus on collaboration (Sizer, 1992; 1996).

Schools following Sizer's model focus on helping all adolescents to master skills and use their minds as opposed to merely covering content. Teachers involve students in hard work and become the coaches as their students work to learn. There is no strict age grading, but students are judged successful on the basis of exhibitions or demonstrations of their learning. The essential schools attempt to utilize larger blocks of time for instruction than traditionally allowed and have attempted to get students in smaller, more manageable working groups so that instruction can be more personalized.

World Wide Web Site: You may learn more about the Coalition of Essential Schools at: http://essentialschools.org/

Robert Slavin: Success for All

Slavin determined that many of the instructional interventions designed to improve the attitudes and achievement of hard-to-teach students (i.e., pullout programs, special education, reduced class size, etc.) actually have had a detrimental effect on school achievement and attitudes (Slavin & Madden, 1989). As a result, he developed an intervention model that focused on helping the students before they dropped behind. His model focuses on instructional procedures and goals that are self-paced and utilize cooperative learning techniques (see Chapter 4). His first efforts focused on instructional methods in reading, writing, and language arts from kindergarten to grade six. Recently, he has added Roots and Wings (Slavin, Madden, & Wasik, 1996), a mathematics, social studies, and science curriculum, and Lee Commigo, a curriculum sequence appropriate for the Latino culture.

Teachers who work in schools that adopt the Success for All model believe that they are responsible for all students' success and that it is their responsibility to prevent students from falling behind. His model is responsive to individual needs of students and involves students in their own learning (Slavin & Madden, 1989). Slavin and his colleagues have conducted a great deal of research that shows that his program results in consistent, substantial effects with groups of students who experience the Success for All curriculum.

World Wide Web Site: You may learn more about Success for All and Roots and Wings at: http://successforall.com/

James Comer: School Power

Convinced that educational systems have failed black children (Haynes & Comer, 1990), James Comer developed a model for inner-city children that recognizes and addresses cultural heritage and diverse socioeconomic situations. Comer's model emphasizes nurturing for students who are identified as hard-to-teach. He acknowledges the importance of adults in children's lives, and his programs require a great deal of adult involvement. He believes that school governance teams are the most important structural component of a school and proposes new methods of school leadership. His schools are governed by teams of ten to fifteen representatives from all the adults who work with students in the schools, including teachers, counselors, principals, parents, and social. The team focuses on building strong relationships among children and adults. His model is characterized by a particularly strong parental involvement program, which involves parents and families in everything from school governance to curriculum planning. Instructional activities tend to focus on dual development of academics and social skills. His model consistently results in improved achievement scores and improved attitudes and behaviors for children who were not succeeding in traditional school organizations (Comer, 1994). He is currently expanding his model to include middle and high school.

World Wide Web Sites: You may learn more about James Comer at:
http://info.med.yale.edu/comer/
www.ncrel.org/cscd/newlead/lead12/1-2e.htm

Characteristics of Successful Programs

The studies of effective schools produced evidence that schools can make a difference even when children came from low socioeconomic settings, families who are in crisis, differing ethnic backgrounds, and other areas that don't match with traditional school organizations. These schools usually have a staff of enthusiastic and caring teachers who are knowledgeable in subject matter and pedagogy;

a cohesive curriculum plan that is integrated across all subjects in the curriculum; recognition of diversity in students' backgrounds, cultures, and talents; a high level of teacher and student engagement; and they encourage strong parental involvement (Smith & O'day, 1991). Crucial to each of the three programs briefly described above is the belief that all children can learn if expectations are high and meaningful.

Characteristics of successful programs can easily be transferred to most educational systems and offer some ideas about the ideal results of school reform. Most successful schools are small organizations with fewer students than the average enrollment usually expected in today's schools. Teachers work together to plan for teaching and learning. The vision, goals, and means of achieving the goals are clearly articulated and developed through continuous discussion and reflection. Teachers have professional development and planning time and are encouraged to collaborate and plan integrated approaches that consider language and cultural diversity. Caring for students is an important component of successful school reform. This is particularly true in Comer's model, for example, in which the importance of developing a supportive, caring relationships of the adults in the school is explicit (Rossi & Stringfield, 1995). Innovative learning strategies are incorporated to engage students in motivating and relevant activities. Most successful programs will present a "parent and family friendly" school where many different individuals are welcomed as a caring community (Minicucci et al., 1995).

The Case Against Change

Not everyone agrees that change is needed, and some believe that change efforts are expensive, time-consuming, and take away from the educational processes. Some even suggest that the call for reform is bogus and politically motivated. One major report from the Sandia National Laboratory (Carson, Huelskamp, & Woodall, 1993; Tanner, 1993) concludes that the nation's educational system does not need an overhaul. This report suggests that the data used as the foundation for reform rationales has been skewed to justify the need for change. Others, while calling for change, do not want new, innovative educational techniques implemented, but instead call for a return to the way they remember schools. Still others call for schools to do better at what they are already doing (Schlechty & Cole, 1991). The objections to changes in schools during the last few years have gone beyond the typical past disagreements about philosophy and use of successful strategies. They now carry a great deal of political weight and can be heard in the rhetoric of presidential speeches, new laws, federal budget debates, and church pulpits.

A great deal of the recent criticism of schools has originated from business, industry, and government. The criticism and increased involvement of businesses and government in education produces two schools of thought. On one side, criticisms coming from business and industry have claimed that our test scores are terribly low, that U.S. students are not performing well in international assessments, and that work habits of young people have deteriorated. On the other hand, Berliner and Biddle (1996) make a case that many of these beliefs are myths that have damaged public schools and that test results in the United States are holding steady in international assessments. They claim that "school bashing" has been a "popular sport" for years. This controversy is rooted in the belief by some that big business and government are too involved in schools and are involved for the wrong reasons. As Berliner and Biddle (1996) themselves admit, this argument is based on a fundamental difference in values and beliefs in what education is about.

World Wide Web Site: You may learn more about the Berliner/Biddle study at: http://seamonkey.ed.asu.edu/epaa

Many of the arguments against change are centered on a return to basics and encompass the restoration of traditional values of family, religion, and assimilation of immigrants through education. In President Reagan's 1984 State of the Union address, he urged Americans to return to traditional values in education. "Excellence must begin in our homes and neighborhood schools, where it's the responsibility of every parent and teacher and the right of every child . . . restore discipline to schools . . . encourage the teachers of new basics . . . and put our parents back in charge" (McGraw, 1984, p. 39). Later in 1989, strategists for the Christian Coalition established the "Contract with the American Family" and suggested support for educational issues such as the advocacy of school vouchers, discouragement of the teaching of history from a multicultural perspective, the elimination of the Department of Education, reduction in the arts in schools, and denial of and withholding of benefits for young unmarried mothers.

One particularly powerful group that opposes school change is known as the New Right. When the New Right discusses parental involvement in education, it means a strong control (Fege, 1993) and implementation of parental beliefs. A network of national, state, and local agencies was formed to promote the causes of the New Right and to attempt to influence a more conservative approach to education. On the local level, school board elections have been easy entry into impact on schools by proponents of the New Right.

Many decisions about education are made by the courts and legislative mandates. Decisions about highly debated issues such as school prayer and integration have been argued and ultimately decided in the Supreme Court.

Those who argue against change from this perspective want religion to be included in the curriculum and target multicultural curricula as being unpatriotic. Volatile issues such as the use of the Bible and prayer in schools, violence, sex education, and other controversies are tied up with discussions about school reform. These topics are often so hotly contested that solutions and mediations between opposing views are worked out in the nation's courts of law. A series of cases related to teaching curriculum based on the Old Testament has recently made its way through the court system, and its solution will undoubtedly impact our ideas about separation between church and state. This case is an example of how the court system is called upon to help make changes in our educational system.

Becoming a Teacher in a Field-Based Setting

Laws That Change Educational Contexts

There are times when the issues related to educational change emanate from our legislatures and court. The leaders of our country are elected by including specific educational beliefs in their election platforms. Several court cases in the modern-day courts have a tremendous impact on schooling in America. Federal and district courts commonly make rulings that affect teachers and students, and usually decisions are made about topics that are controversial and debatable.

Our laws and the courts have contributed to how our society thinks about minorities and their schooling. This is particularly true in issues related to segregation and integration, and over the years, the courts have occasionally reversed long-standing beliefs and practices. In 1896 the courts established "separate but equal" in the *Plessy* v. *Ferguson* case, which established segregation (Timm, 1996). The country supported and encouraged the building of segregated educational systems until the 1954 case of *Brown* v. *Board of Education* in which the Supreme Court ruling legally ended segregation. But the Court ruling alone was not enough to make significant changes in our society, and it wasn't until Congress passed the Civil Rights Act of 1964, which outlawed segregation in our schools, that the interactions between minorities and majorities changed forever.

Important cases dealing with language instruction have been reviewed by the Supreme Court. Often the Court is asked to deal with situations in which a state has proclaimed that English is the major language. Student entitlement to instruction in their first language during the time they are learning English is often at the center of the controversy. Often those who support teaching in English believe that everyone needs to speak English in order to bind our country together; others feel that it is their right to receive instruction and honor different languages. This debate is ongoing and will be discussed as our country's diversity continues to grow even more diverse.

Related to the language debates are issues related to the public education for illegal immigrant children. States and the federal government are in constant debate about using tax money to educate children who are in our country illegally. Texas and California have been the center of cases related to this issue. In 1980, the District Court of Southern Texas, after hearing several other related cases, ruled that illegal immigrant children's needs were no different than the needs of any other children and that they were entitled an education. In these cases, the court tends to view children as innocent bystanders who should not be punished because their parents were in this country illegally (Timm, 1996).

Issues of language differences and immigration are likely to be part of educational discussions for years to come. Teachers will need to stay abreast of the changing laws and policies related to these issues.

The 1974 legislation PL94-142, which specified criteria for special education funding, has had a wide, sweeping impact on the way that teachers teach and children learn. The very specific law requires that all handicapped learners be provided an "appropriate education" in the least restrictive environment and imposes specific responsibilities on the classroom teacher to assure that the letter of the law is met (Armstrong & Savage, 1997). You will find further discussion of this educational law in Chapter 4.

Church, state, education, and religion are often the focus of court cases and laws. Some of the famous church and state court cases focused on the debate between creationism and evolution in schools. John Scopes, a Tennessee teacher, was the defendant in one of the most watched and oft-quoted cases. Scopes was accused and convicted of teaching Darwinian theory in his high school. A legal technicality eventually freed him, and the law that made teaching evolution a crime was never enforced. Nevertheless, the debate has continued, and several evolution cases have been tried since that time.

Another topic finding its way into the courts deals with separation of church and state and has to do with the role of prayer in schools. In 1963 the case of *Abington Township* v. *Schempp* was brought to the courts by a family who argued against required prayer in the school on the basis that it violated their rights. In another case, Baltimore's Madeline Murray filed suit against the schools protesting daily prayers and Bible reading at school. In both of these cases, the court agreed that required religious exercises were in violation of the Constitution. The Supreme Court upheld the separation of church and schools as recently as 1990 when issues of prayer and school were argued. A moment of silence appears to be one compromise on this issue, and some rulings allow prayer at school functions and outside the regular school schedule. In 1990, the courts found that those who exercised their personal right to pray at graduation did not violate the First Amendment. Other court cases involving clashes between religion and schools involve the relationship between religion and compulsory school attendance. So far, the courts have ruled in various ways when families view that school attendance is in conflict with their religion. It usually depends on the context of the particular case; for example, some religious groups such as the Amish of Pennsylvania do not respond to compulsory school attendance laws.

There are many more court cases that affect education and your future profession. It would take an entire textbook to review important cases and their influence on teaching and learning. The important thing to remember is that teachers' work is affected by our country's court system and government regulations. Decisions made in the courts often require changes in teaching and in school policies.

There will always be calls to make changes in teaching and learning. Many changes related to education result from differing philosophical stances (see Chapter 2); others are brought on by new information and technologies. But the key factor of the reform movement is the classroom teacher (Hord, 1992). Teachers who are educated in ways that encourage them to support all students' learning will attempt changes in their classrooms that support their students' successes and achievement.

Related Readings

Dorsch, N. G. (1998). *Community, collaboration, and collegiality in school reform.* New York: SUNY Press.

> *This is the story of four teachers who are attempting to make changes in their own classrooms. The crisis and triumphs of their efforts to implement an interdisciplinary curriculum are described. This book offers important insights into what it is like for teachers during a time of school reform.*

Sizer, T. (1989). *Horace's compromise: The dilemma of the American high school.* Boston: Houghton Mifflin.

Sizer, T. (1992). *Horace's school: Redesigning the American high school.* Boston: Houghton Mifflin.

Sizer, T. (1996). *Horace's hope: What works for the American high school.* Boston: Houghton Mifflin.

Horace Smith, a fictional teacher, and other characters make Sizer's arguments and suggestions for changing American high schools informative, inspiring, and positive. The three books demonstrate successful educational changes.

Wasley, P. A. (1994). *Stirring the chalkdust.* New York: Teachers College Press.

In this book you can read about teachers who are involved in the changes that come about when Sizer's Coalition of Essential Schools processes are put in place. Secondary teachers who are working to change the way they teach write about the rewards and challenges of change. The book also presents a description of the most common changes teachers are making.

References

Apple, M. W. (1996). *Cultural politics and education.* New York: Teachers College Press.

Armstrong, D. G., & Savage, T. V. (1997). *Teaching in the secondary school: An introduction* (4th ed.). Columbus, OH: Merrill/Prentice Hall.

Berliner, D. C., & Biddle, B. J. (1996). *The manufactured crisis: Myths, fraud, and the attack on America's public schools.* Addison-Wesley.

Carson, C. C., Huelskamp, R. M., & Woodall, T. D. (1993). Perspectives on education in America. *Journal of Educational Research, 86*(5), 259–310.

Clark, C. (1995). *Thoughtful teaching.* New York: Teachers College Press.

Cohen , D. (1995). What standards for national standards? *Phi Delta Kappan, 76* (10), 751–757.

Comer, J. (1994). Home, school and academic learning. In J. I. Goodlad & P. Keating (Eds.), *Access to knowledge* (pp. 23–42). New York: College Board.

Cuban, L. (1984). *How teachers taught.* New York: Teachers College Press.

Fege, A. F. (1993). A tug of war over tolerance. *Educational Leadership, 51*(4), 22–23.

Futrell, M. H. (1993). K–12 Educational reform: A view from the trenches. *Educational Record,* 7–14.

Goodlad, J. I. (1992). On taking school reform seriously. *Phi Delta Kappan, 74*(3), 232–238.

Haynes, N., and Comer, J. (1990). Helping black children succeed: The significance of some social factors. In K. Lomotey (Ed.), *Going to school: The African American experience* (pp. 103–113). Albany: State University of New York Press.

Hlebowitsh, P., & Tellez, K. (1997). *American education: Purpose and promise.* Belmont, CA: Wadsworth.

Holland, H. (1997). KERA: A tale of one teacher. *Phi Delta Kappan, 79*(4), 264–271.

Hord, S. M. (1992). *Facilitative leadership: The imperative for change.* Austin: Southwest Educational Development Laboratory.

Illinois State Board of Education (1997). *Illinois Learning Standards.* Springfield: Illinois State Board of Education.

Jennings, J. (1995). School reform based on what is taught and learned. *Phi Delta Kappan, 76*(10), 765-769.

McGraw, O. (1984). Reclaiming traditional values in education: The implications for educational research. *Educational Leadership, 38*(1), 30–42.

McMannon, T. J. (1995). *Morality, efficiency, and reform: An interpretation of history of American education.* Work in Progress Series, No. 5. Seattle: Institute for Educational Inquiry.

Minicucci, C., Berman, P., McLaughlin, B., McLeod, B., Nelson, B., & Woodworth, K. (1995). School reform and student diversity. *Phi Delta Kappan,* 77 (1), 77–80.

Myers, C. B., & Myers, L. K. (1995). *The professional educator: A new introduction to teaching and schools.* Belmont, CA: Wadsworth.

Oliva, P. F. (1997). *Developing the curriculum* (4th ed.). New York: Longman.

Piner, W. F. (1992). The curriculum. In J. L. Kincheloe & S. R. Steinberg (Eds.), *Thirteen questions: Reframing education's conversation* (pp. 31–38.) New York: Peter Lang.

Rossi, R. J., & Stringfield, S. (1995). What we must do for students placed at risk. *Phi Delta Kappan.,* 77(1), 73–77.

Rothman, R. (1997). KERA: A tale of one school. *Phi Delta Kappan,* 79(4), 272–275.

Shields, P. M., & Knapp, M. S. (1997). The promise and limits of school-based reform: A national snapshot. *Phi Delta Kappan,* 79(4), 288–294.

Sizer, T. (1992). *Horace's school: Redesigning the American school.* Boston: Houghton Mifflin.

Sizer, T. (1996). *Horace's hope: What works for the American high school.* Boston: Houghton Mifflin.

Slavin, R. E., & Madden, N. A. (1989). *Effective programs for students at risk.* Boston: Allyn & Bacon.

Slavin, R. E., Madden, N. A., & Wasik, B. (1996). *Success for all: A summary of research.* Baltimore: Johns Hopkins University.

Smith, M. S., & O'Day, J. (1991). Systemic school reform. In S. Fuhrman & B. Malen (Eds.), *The politics of curriculum and testing* (pp. 116–133). Philadelphia: Falmer Press.

Tanner, D. (1993). A nation truly at risk. *Phi Delta Kappan,* 75(4), 288–297.

Timm, J. T. (1996). *Four perspectives in multicultural education.* Belmont, CA: Wadsworth.

4

Describing the Status of Contemporary Children

In this chapter
- Equity
- Social Challenges
- Health-Related Issues
- Providing Equal Educational Access to Learning

My own teachers encouraged me and demanded nothing less than excellence. They made me feel smart and I responded. But there was still something wrong with my education. There were lots of smart kids in my elementary school, but they weren't all as economically stable as I was—I came from a working-class family with a father who was a laborer and a mother who was a clerk. I remember one girl in particular; her name was Portia. She was the smartest person I had ever met. She could sum a column of numbers with lightning speed. She could reason beyond her years. But she almost never came to school with her hair combed. Her teeth had not seen a toothbrush in years and she often smelled of urine. I liked her because she was smart and had a great sense of humor. It did not bother me that her house was dark, smelled funny, and had furniture that looked like the kind of stuff people set out curbside to be collected with the trash.

I lost track of Portia after elementary school. She did not attend the junior high school where I went to across town. The last time I saw her was in eleventh grade. Portia was pregnant and had dropped out of school. As smart as I believed I was, I knew I was not as smart as Portia. So why wasn't she on the fast track to college? Why had she been passed over in the academic shuffle?

—Gloria Ladson-Billings, *The Dreamkeepers*

Teaching is a human relations profession, and teachers enjoy working and being with children and young people. As pointed out in Chapter 1, working with children is a major reason why people become teachers in the first place. Successful teaching involves a great deal of understanding of interpersonal relationships, and an ability to adapt social expertise to interactions with children and young people. Good teachers relate to their students and place a high priority on maintaining environments where children can succeed academically and socially. In order to accomplish this difficult task, a teacher must not only understand children and tolerate differences but also be willing to accept a wide range of ways of looking at the world. Successful teachers understand the impact of different backgrounds, behaviors, learning rates, and attitudes on learning.

Most of the students entering colleges and universities to become teachers are predominantly white, female, and middle class—yet the children they are to teach are becoming more and more diverse. Minority students are now the majority in all but two of the twenty-five largest cities in the United States. Nevertheless, fewer than 15 percent of teachers are from minority groups (Delpit, 1995). This mismatch can lead to misunderstandings about the responses and reactions of students in today's classrooms. Teachers can misread acting-out behavior, silences, and verbosity when children's backgrounds are not considered. Effective teachers must have a good understanding of what it is like to be a child or young adult in contemporary society and then use that knowledge to react, interact, and respond to their students.

To be an effective teacher in today's classrooms, you must stop and reflect on your own cultural belief system and on teaching in a culturally diverse classroom. Many of your students will have experiences that are very different from your own, but differing experiences can add a richness to the classroom. This

The children in today's classrooms represent a wide range of cultural, ethnic, and religious diversity. Elementary children's representations of their own faces illustrate the diversity that today's teachers will find in their classrooms.

self-reflection can move you toward a better understanding of how you will react to students and situations in the classroom. Accepting all the cultures of our society is a first step to understanding the differences among children. Teachers need to understand how their own cultural background contributes to what happens in classrooms and affects classroom climate, teaching strategies, and student's attitudes. Gaining a multicultural perspective is a complex task that requires examination of your own biases and beliefs about different cultures. To enhance your understanding of students today, this chapter will focus on the following questions:

- Do all children have the same opportunities to succeed in school?

- What are some of the major social issues impacting the lives of today's children?

- What are some of the contrasts between your educational experiences and those of children who are educated in low-income areas?

- What can you learn from children and young people who have backgrounds different from your own?

Equity

One of the fundamental goals of the American education system is to educate all children. Despite all our attention toward this goal, disparities in measured opportunities to learn are many times greater in our country than in other countries (Darling-Hammond & Ancess, 1995). The United States has attempted to educate a wide range of students in public schools for a very long time. Our schools have traditionally provided good experiences and opportunities for some, but they have delivered greatly different experiences to others. Providing vastly different experiences for children results in a group of people in our country who consistently have fewer opportunities than others.

Many factors contribute to the social dilemma of educational inequity. Differences in school funding, the number of children who live in poverty in a given school district, different levels of excellence in teacher training and teaching, and troubled schools and families make the inequities in education of children and youth major issues in today's society. In order to provide access to understanding social and technical knowledge, educators must strive to provide equity. Equity is not the same as equality. Equality means that all children are treated the same, regardless of the starting point. Equity means that resources are supplied based on need. In order to meet the goal of educating all children, those children who have more needs will require more.

While many issues related to equity, such as resource equalization, are beyond the teachers' influence, classrooms can provide the flexibility, respect, responsiveness, and rigor that encourages students to achieve (Darling-Hammond & Ancess, 1995). Structures that focus on individuals and make the best of their talents, interests, and past experiences can help educators ensure equity for all students.

Teachers in America's schools have never before faced classrooms of learners so varied in abilities, language, social class, and race. Many classrooms include a wide variety of cultures and languages, making the classrooms of today far more diverse than most societies in the world. Yet the expectation of our society remains the same. Teach all children. Teaching all children—with all their differences—requires teachers to develop an equitable classroom climate where all are valued and all are respected.

The changing demographics of today's classrooms will have profound effects on new teachers entering the workforce. Our schools have not seen so many immigrants enter their doors since the beginning of the twentieth century. Combined with a low birthrate from native citizens, the faces in our nation's schools are changing dramatically and having a profound impact on educational needs. It is estimated that as many as 5 million children of immigrants will be entering the pre K-12 education system in the 1990s (Huelskamp, 1991). More than 150 languages are spoken in schools across the country, and some large school districts are already reporting close to that number of languages within their schools alone.

Not only are the language and ethnicity of children changing, but so are the families in which they live. Teachers are encountering more children from single-parent homes, more from homes in which both parents work, and more who don't have a home at all. Almost one-third of the nation's homeless are families (Mihaly, 1991), leaving anywhere from 225,000 to 500,000 of America's children without a home (Kelly, 1993). As a result, teachers are recognizing an increased need to address not only the academic needs of their students, but also their social needs.

The learning needs of today's students are varied and complex. In order to best meet the needs of all the students in the classroom, teachers must understand how instruction and learning are influenced by social, economic, historical, and cultural factors (Ogbu, 1992). Without this vital knowledge, and with the majority of past experience based within one cultural group, teachers may unknowingly limit the potential achievement for students by prejudicial or ethnocentric practices in the classroom (Zeichner, 1993).

FIELD-BASED ACTIVITY 4.1

Describe your cultural background and that of your family. Include a description of the community where you grew up. Take a walk or a drive through your students' neighborhoods. Compare and contrast the community where you grew up and the ones where your students live. Identify cultural and community factors that should be considered by teachers.

VOICE OF A TEACHER

I was a young, white teacher from a middle-class background teaching in a largely poor, minority school. It was located downtown, right between a mental hospital and a funeral home. I knew most of the children in my classroom were from poor families, but it was the winter holidays of my first year of teaching before it became a reality. I had received a donated Christmas tree from a local business to decorate our room for a unit on winter traditions from around the world. It was a big, beautiful pine that almost reached the top of the ceiling of my kindergarten room. The day school let out for the winter break, I selected a student to take the tree home—a student who had indicated he did not have and would want the Christmas tree. William was delighted when he was chosen. Part of a large family, all of William's older brothers and sisters came down to the kindergarten building after school to help carry the tree down the street to the house. I carefully packaged the ornaments and lights to go with the tree, telling William he could bring them back when he returned to school after the holidays, but each time I turned around I would discover the tree lights carefully wrapped and lying back on my desk. Finally, after I put them back in the bag for the third time, Curtis, the older brother had to speak up.

"We can't take these," he said, pulling them out of the sack once again.

"Sure you can," I smiled at him.

"They won't light up," he said slowly, looking at the floor. "There ain't no electricity."

"Oh," I said, and took the lights from his hands for the last time.

I watched that small band of children drag the huge tree off down the downtown street until they disappeared from sight over the railroad tracks. William was last, following along behind carrying the bag of ornaments and trailing a long gold snake of tinsel in his wake.

The lights stayed behind with me. As I watched, I thought about the house I would be going home to and how different we lived. I thought about how dark it would be in that place they were going to, but mostly I thought about how much responsibility I had to be holding the only light they had in their lives.

Poverty

Since 1974, children have been the poorest of all Americans. More than one in five children in America now live in poverty. Research has shown that children who live in poverty are much more likely to do poorly in academic areas (Orland, 1990). In fact, a poor child is about twice as likely to be a low-achieving student in the classroom. Almost one fourth of the students in an average classroom will live below the poverty level. The longer children live in poverty, the more likely they are to have academic problems (Orland, 1990).

Most of these poor children attend poor schools that reflect the economic condition of society. Schools located in poor communities are often staffed with less-experienced teachers who practice grouping students by their presumed learning potential. The neighborhood schools of the poor are underfunded and poorly maintained, resulting in an educational class structure promoting unequal educational opportunities based on income alone. Students in poor schools have less access to science and mathematics knowledge, fewer available curriculum resources, fewer engaging learning activities, and fewer qualified teachers (Oakes, 1990).

Children, even those who are not poor, who attend schools that have a high percentage of students living in poverty are much more likely to be low achievers in school. In fact, a student who is not poor but who attends a poor school is even more likely to be a low achiever than the poor student in the same school (Orland, 1990).

Teachers in today's classrooms confront poverty in the faces of their students every day. Yet most teachers will come from a middle-class background with few life experiences to prepare them for the reality of true poverty. Their belief system can be clouded with many myths and misconceptions about children living in poverty. Consider the following:

- *Myth #1: Poor families are unemployed.* Surprisingly, almost 60 percent of all poor children under age six live in families where one or both parents work, and almost one-third of these families include an adult with a full-time job who still cannot earn enough money to raise the family's income above the poverty line. Close to 40 percent of all poor families with children under six are supported exclusively by their own earnings (Knitzer & Aber, 1995), even though the money they earn is not enough to bring them out of poverty. This is not so surprising when you consider that a full-time minimum wage job only brings home about $7,000 to $8,000 a year, keeping a family of three $2,500 below the poverty line.

- *Myth #2: Poor children are children of color.* Poverty is color-blind. Two-thirds of America's poor are white. Although the rate of poverty is higher with minorities, with almost half of all black children and over a third of Hispanic children living in poverty, 42 percent of children living in poverty under age six are white. This makes the poverty rate in America for white youth the highest in the western industrialized countries (Kammeman & Kahn, 1994).

- *Myth #3: Poor children live in big cities.* Poverty for young children occurs in all locations, with the poverty rate for children living in urban areas only slightly higher than for children living in rural areas. Living in rural areas can make some things more difficult for families and children. Children and young people in rural areas often face isolation and other barriers from health and human support systems that might be more readily available in the cities.

- *Myth #4: Poor children come from mostly single-parent homes.* While statistics may show that many poor children live in single-parent homes, almost half of

America's poor children and young people live in homes with both parents. In single-parent homes headed by a woman, there is a 50 percent chance that the family lives in poverty. Those numbers are even higher in single-parent homes headed by women of color (Reed & Sautter, 1990). The average annual income for single-parent homes headed by females is just over $11,000, but the average for married couples with children is above $36,000 (Hodgkinson, 1993).

- *Myth #5: Poor families are on public assistance.* In reality, most poor families earn more money than they receive from welfare (Sherman, 1994). Only about half of the poor families in America actually receive public assistance, and one-third of those families earn income to supplement the assistance they receive.

Teachers' behaviors are impacted by some beliefs that may indeed be myths. Just because children are poor does not mean that they do not have people who care about them, or just because they are from single-parent homes does not mean that they do not have strong family support systems. Crucial differences in teacher expectations and the provisions of equal access to learning can be greatly influenced by questioning long-standing beliefs about children and young people's circumstances. Value judgments about children and young people are often based on teachers' own experiences, which may vary greatly from their students' experiences and values.

In many cases, children who enter the classroom from a middle-class background have learned values at home that are closely aligned with the values shared by the teacher and the school in general. The middle-class child is entering a familiar culture with a shared belief system of social skills, behaviors, and attitudes that teachers find acceptable (Campbell, 1996). Children who come from backgrounds different from the teachers may hold an entirely different set of values, speak different languages, and worship different gods.

Children of poverty often come to school with a limited knowledge of the language of school (Villegas, 1991). Not only is the verbal language of the school unknown to many poor students with limited or nonstandard English, but the shared language of story and literature is also often missing. They enter a strange world of books and speech drastically different from their world of experience. This strange new world is complicated further by a high mobility rate. As caretakers lose jobs and housing, children are moved from school to school, unable to form attachments to either the people or the culture of the school. These children often reflect the depression, anger, and antisocial problems of their primary caretakers, leading to a strong sense of failure in even the earliest years of school (Natriello, McDill, & Pallas, 1990).

Race and ethnicity, gender, and family structure are all related to the probability of living in poverty. Children living in poverty are also more likely to die in infancy and early childhood, have serious illness, become pregnant during

Recent immigrants provide classroom diversity of an international nature. Teachers are constantly challenged to relate learning to the many diverse backgrounds and languages of our newest citizens.

their teen years, or drop out of school (Kirst, 1993). Nevertheless, living in poverty does not automatically mean children will have problems in school.

Many children overcome great obstacles to succeed in spite of their income level. Teachers who enter the classroom with preconceived ideas about children's ability based on income will present an even larger obstacle to poor students. A teacher's belief that children from low socioeconomic levels cannot learn as well as their classmates can be translated by the teacher, sometimes unknowingly, into everyday classroom practices.

Grouping procedures, questioning strategies, and even curriculum choices are all based on a teacher's beliefs about students' capabilities for learning. Teachers who believe students from low socioeconomic groups are not able to excel in school may use expectant voice prompting, less interaction, and differential activities and questions. Students internalize the teacher's lower expectations into their own self-assessment, and the teacher's belief system becomes the students' beliefs as well.

World Wide Web Site: You may learn more about the Children's Defense Fund at: http://www.childrensdefense.org

Race/Ethnicity

Teachers, no matter what their ethnicity, are critical to the success of students. Teacher expectations constantly influence classroom interactions and student achievement. Everything in the classroom is filtered through the teacher. Teachers design the curriculum and learning strategies for the classroom, drawing on their own background and experiences in every teaching decision. Teachers, therefore, must constantly reflect on their teaching habits to discern any prejudicial barriers keeping all students from succeeding. In spite of the fact many teachers lack a frame of reference in dealing with their racially different students, it is possible for all children to learn regardless of the teacher's race/ethnicity (Gay, 1993).

By the twenty-first century, the U.S. Department of Education predicts that one out of three students will be Hispanic, African American, or Asian. The changes and resulting diversity in our population is clearly observable in our children. Children who come to schools with incredible differences in language, experience, and culture present a huge challenge for teachers. Because these children are at risk of failing to succeed in the European-dominated culture of the schools, it becomes the vital job of the schools to overcome these risks (Hodgkinson, 1993).

According to Ogbu (1990), the United States contains two different types of minority groups—immigrant or voluntary minorities and involuntary minorities. Immigrant minorities come to the United States looking for economic gain, more personal freedom, and an overall better lifestyle. In the past, Germany, Italy, Ireland, the United Kingdom, the Soviet Union, Canada, and Sweden were the nations sending the most immigrants to America. Our nation has always strongly represented primarily European cultures, but the growing population of immigrants from other regions of the world is changing our makeup. We are no longer a nation of Europeans.

Immigrants now arrive primarily from Mexico, the Philippines, Korea, China, Taiwan, India, and Cuba. These countries bring to the United States a wide variety of languages, foods, cultures, and even religions far different than the European culture that formerly dominated our schools. For example, there were more Moslems than Episcopalians in the United States in 1991 (Hodgkinson, 1993). Although this growing population encounters many barriers to success in the school system, many of these immigrants maintain their own cultural identity and do not identify academic success with assimilation into the dominant white culture of the school. Even when faced with overwhelming economic, social, and language barriers, many immigrants believe that American schools provide a better educational opportunity than what they had experienced in their homelands (Ogbu, 1990).

Involuntary minorities were brought to America not by choice but by slavery or dominance (Ogbu, 1990). Such minorities—including African Americans and Hispanic Americans—resent both the loss of freedom and the barriers to success they encounter within our society. These groups experience prejudice, segregation, and exclusion from the mainstream of American life. Involuntary minorities view the barriers they face as permanent and insurmountable, not just a temporary situation that can be overcome with hard work and education. Instead of comparing their current way of life to a previous experience in a foreign "homeland," involuntary minorities compare their status in society to that of white Americans. The resulting frustration and resentment lead to a distrust of white Americans and the public schools. Success in school is identified with assimilation into the white culture and with a loss of cultural identity.

Minority parents want their children to succeed in school, just like any other parent, but many doubt the schools will provide equal educational access or that the resulting education will provide increased economic or social opportunities. This mistrust of the system is often translated to even the youngest children entering the school.

Mistrust in the system is rooted in a long history of inequities within the school system. Traditionally schools have not succeeded in providing equal opportunities for students from minority backgrounds. Minority children are more likely to be placed in special education classes, with African American students three times as likely as whites to be placed in classes for the educable mentally retarded (Children's Defense Fund, 1987). They are also more likely to be placed in lower-level academic classes, to be expelled from school, and to drop out of school all together.

Most minority students are not at risk of failure in school because of learning or developmental problems. The problems they experience in school are a direct result of the distance between the schools and the diverse students, families, and communities they serve. "There is a mismatch between what these children know and can do and what is expected of them by schools that are organized to accommodate and reinforce white, middle-class values, beliefs, and behavior. The social world of the school operates by different rules from the ones these children and their families know and use" (Bowman, 1994 p. 219).

In addition to all the other barriers to success that minority students face, they will have few opportunities to interact with teachers of color. Even though one-third of the classroom population will be comprised of children from minority groups, little representation of their background and culture will be seen in the teaching staffs of the schools, with only 13 percent of America's teachers coming from an ethnic or racial minority group. The increasing gap between the cultural backgrounds of teachers and students is critical. Teachers' decisions in the classroom are strongly influenced by their own background and by former teachers. With little or no diversity in the teaching profession, the traditional white culture continues to form the basis for most teaching decisions—even though the educational needs of the growing number of students from different cultural backgrounds are not being met through traditional methods. The problem is further complicated as fewer and fewer students observe role models in the teaching profession that might inspire them to enter the profession in the future.

In order for teachers to teach students from diverse cultures, they must be sensitive to similarities and differences between themselves and their students. They must create a classroom environment, built from the past experiences of all members, with a new social system (Bowman, 1989). While it may be difficult for teachers to understand learning needs from different backgrounds than their own, if the classroom environment is built on the foundational belief that all children can learn—all children can succeed.

FIELD-BASED ACTIVITY 4.2

This exercise can help you define cultural differences among students. Take a class photo of your students. Locate, or reflect on, a class photo from a classroom you were a student in at approximately the same age. What similarities do you see? What differences? What experiences have you had in your past that might help you relate to today's students?

Gender

Today's schools have different expectations for boys and girls (Kohl & Witty, 1996). These differing expectations lead to different school experiences that ultimately guide career choices and perpetuate economic differences between men and women. Girls will often choose to take fewer science and mathematics classes in school, usually completing only the minimum required for graduation. Girls are also more likely to be found in introductory or lower-level courses than in advanced courses (Tavris, 1992; Pipher, 1994).

Even though women now earn half of the bachelor's and master's degrees awarded in the United States, they remain drastically underrepresented in fields with strong mathematics and technical requirements, opting instead for majors in traditionally female-dominated careers with lower status and less pay (Tavris, 1992). The impact is also seen in the workplace with women currently representing less than 5 percent of the engineers and scientists in America.

Women make up the only group of students who enter school ahead—with higher achievement than men in all academic subjects—and lose ground throughout the school years. How do schools perpetuate unequal opportunities for boys and girls? And what can teachers do to equalize the educational settings for boys and girls? School structure and teacher-student interactions are two important factors that relate to differences in achievement between boys and girls.

The average female student in the classroom is simply ignored—not scolded; not praised—with high-achieving females receiving the least attention of all students (Sadker & Sadker, 1986). Even though girls traditionally learn verbal and math skills, and develop small motor skills quicker and much earlier than their male classmates, schools are structured around the development of male students. The introduction of material—such as when students learn to write in cursive or read chapter books or learn long division—is traditionally based on the readiness of the boys in the classroom. Girls, waiting to be challenged, can become bored. Girls also learn to hold back their answers and wait quietly for boys to reach their level of understanding (Tavris, 1992; Pipher, 1994).

The structure of the traditional coeducational school can also hinder the achievement of girls (Shakeshaft, 1986). Boys are provided a better education through the structure of a coeducational school, which provides an equal academic background and also provides an additional curriculum in social skills. Women, however, do better in single-sex schools—exhibiting higher self-esteem, becoming more involved in academic life, and expanding their participation in social and leadership areas. Yet most public schools are coeducational, despite the fact that girls may succeed better in single-sex schools.

In a study conducted by Sadker and Sadker (1993), researchers collected data in over a hundred classrooms in five different states to look at teachers' interactions with students. Even though the sample represented diverse students and teachers from diverse settings, all had one common characteristic—the persuasiveness of sex bias. Researchers discovered that students in the same classrooms with the same teachers were experiencing very different educational opportunities.

Sadker and Sadker (1986; 1993) found that boys received significantly more responses from teachers than did girls—especially in the area of redemption comments (responses intended to help a student correct a wrong response); praise (positive reactions to a student's response); and criticism (specific teacher response indicating the answer is incorrect). Boys were also able to gain the teacher's attention by calling out responses. In fact, boys in elementary and secondary schools were eight times as likely to call out responses in class, demanding the teacher's attention and response. In comparison, when girls called out responses, teachers corrected the response with a behavioral comment to remind the girls to raise their hand and wait to be called on—delegating girls to a role of passive observers of the academic interactions in the classroom.

A more recent study completed by the American Association of University Women (1992) supported almost all the findings of the earlier Sadker and Sadker study. The AAUW study pointed out that boys' failure is attributed to external factors and success is attributed to ability, whereas girls experience almost the opposite attitudes. The AAUW report explains that as children go through school, boys feel better about themselves and girls' self-esteem declines.

Teaching approaches can offset girls' and boys' reactions to classroom instruction. "The most valuable resource in a classroom is the teacher's attention. If the teacher is giving more of that valuable resource to one group, it should come as no surprise if that group shows greater educational gains. The only real surprise is that it has taken us so long to see the problem" (Sadker & Sadker, 1986, p. 514).

World Wide Web Site: You may learn more about the American Association of University Women at: http://www.aauw.org

Disabilities

Children with handicapping conditions and learning impairments are entitled to the same educational opportunities as other children. "Special education" is individualized instruction designed to meet the needs of students with disabilities (Blackhurst & Burdine, 1993). Public law 94-142 and the Americans with Disabilities Act (ADA) of 1990 states that people with disabilities should be educated in the least restrictive environment and allowed to live, work, and attend school in settings that provide the greatest possible amount of freedom and contact with people who do not have disabilities. With the support of this legislation, special needs students are no longer being separated from regular students but are included in regular classroom settings and in all the activities of the school. This trend toward inclusion has emphasized the growing need for schools to create educational programs that meet individual needs. "Students who have special education needs are only some of the many students who require carefully designed interventions and support to enhance their learning and life situation" (York & Reynolds, 1996, p. 821).

Regular classroom placement of a disabled student can have a great impact on the classroom and the teacher. Administrative and family support are important (Villa & Thousand, 1990) to the successful placement of such students. Learning specialists (Margolis & McCabe, 1989) can also help ease the transition and provide needed support for the classroom teacher. Teachers must be trained in practices and methods that support learning for special education students and must often learn to work together with special education personnel to team-teach classes with special needs students.

Social Challenges

Poverty, violence, family, and health interact in every community, and those interactions have profound effects on the children. The schools that serve these communities are impacted every day by the resulting consequences. When children leave school at the end of the day, they go home to many different environments. All home environments, whether positive or negative, effect the classroom the next day. Some children may go to bed hearing the sounds of gunshots in their neighborhood. Others may spend most of the time away from school in front of a television set. Still others may be abused or left alone for most of the time outside of school.

Children enter school with overwhelming concerns about the world in which they live, unable to concentrate and often unable to see any connections to the world of school. In order to address academic needs, teachers must also recognize the social issues that come to school with the student—issues that play an important role in the classroom. Teachers must understand the concerns of today's child in order to successfully select strategies for the success and empowerment of their students.

Violence

Neighborhoods and communities no longer provide a safe environment for children as they grow into adults. The murder rate for children under the age of 19 has quadrupled in the last decade. Homicide is now the leading cause of death for black teenagers, and it doesn't always occur outside the protection of the school. Twenty percent of high school students now claim to be carrying a weapon of some kind to school on a regular basis (Bennett, 1995). The Children's Defense Fund estimates that 135,000 children bring guns to school on a daily basis and that the sophistication of these guns often exceeds the firepower of the police assigned to protect the school.

Not only are children the victims of violent crimes, but they are also responsible for committing crimes. Juvenile arrests have increased dramatically, making children the fastest-growing criminal population in the United States. Seventy percent of these juvenile offenders will be released from the justice system and commit crimes again (Bennett, 1995).

Children growing up in communities full of crime and violence may be faced with the sound of gunfire on a daily basis. Their safety may be threatened on a daily basis by gangs and drug dealers. All of this impacts their state of mind in the classroom, leaving them preoccupied during the day and struggling to stay awake.

Child Abuse

Teachers are faced with the sad reality of child abuse in classrooms every day and are often the first adults involved in reporting abuse. The responsibility weighs heavy. Along with the many incidents of child abuse reported in the media, thousands more go reported only by a classroom teacher. Reporting suspected child abuse is a necessary, although difficult, responsibility in the classroom. (U.S. Department of Health and Human Services, Child Bureau, 1997). Teachers worry about the child's safety when reporting the abuse and are often discour-

VOICE OF A TEACHER

When I saw the marks on my student I felt sick at my stomach. It was the all-too-clear red out-line of an extension cord that covered his four-year-old back.

I did everything by the book—just as I had been instructed to do in a workshop on report-ing child abuse. The nurse took pictures for documentation. The principal called in Child Protective Services, and the counselor spent most of the morning talking with the student. But things were not going to work out as smoothly as the workshop had described.

After lunch, we learned the parents had somehow been informed of our actions and were on the way up to school to take the child out of school. Child Protective Services were nowhere in sight.

"Keep all your students inside and lock the classroom door," the principal told me. "Don't come out until I personally say it is safe."

I did as I was told, locking my classroom of prekindergarten students inside and trying to go on about the day as though nothing was happening outside in the hallway. The children painted red and yellow spring flowers on manila paper, oblivious to the drama taking place right outside the door. I wasn't so lucky. I couldn't keep my eyes from the windows beside our locked door.

Outside in the hall a six-foot man in mirrored sunglasses towered over my five-foot-two inch principal. She stood her ground between that angry man and our classroom full of chil-dren with amazing courage. She and I both knew what this man was capable of—we'd seen it on the back of his young son.

Her mouth moved and his mouth moved. I couldn't hear what she was saying, but I hoped it was the right words—words to keep him from hitting her . . . words to keep him from pulling out a gun and killing us all . . . words to make him go away. I never thought that being an educator might someday cost me my life, but I thought about it a lot that day.

The father did go away. Eventually. The police came and took the child and an older sis-ter away into protective custody. I can still remember the look on that child's face as we put him in the police car. The student came back the next week—back in the same home with the same father and back to my classroom.

Two weeks after that, he came into my classroom one morning with a black eye . . .

aged at the lack of easy solutions to a complex problem. Teachers must also con-tinue to teach the victims, in spite of the circumstances, and to help them suc-ceed in the classroom.

The abuse can be physical, psychological, or sexual. It can be an isolated incident or occur repeatedly over long periods of time. Teachers are in the posi-tion to be the first to recognize the abuse and take action. They must overcome their own fears and find the courage to report suspicions of child abuse to the proper authorities.

Becoming a Teacher in a Field-Based Setting

VOICE OF A TEACHER

Billy came up to me at recess one day, obviously upset.

"They won't play with me," the tearful kindergartner wailed.

"Who won't play with you?" It was a complaint I had heard many times during my twelve years of teaching kindergarten, but one we were usually able to solve in a short period of time.

"Juan and Arthur." Billy wiped the tears away and sat down beside me on the bench. "They say I can't join."

"Join what?" I said concerned.

"The gang." He lifted his hands and waved them in the air in front of my face. "I don't know how to do the sign."

It was a shock—five-year-olds making the sign of a local gang who called the intersection in front of our school their address. Looking down at the wistful expression on the small boy beside me, I realized something worse. Billy wanted more than anything to be a member of that gang and I didn't know what to offer him in its place.

Gang Activity

Students of all ages have a strong need to belong. Just like fraternities and sororities, gangs are organizations that meet a young person's need to belong to a group. Unlike that associated with some other social organizations, gang life can also lead to crime, drugs, and violence. Gangs, like schools, are in the business of teaching children. Gangs teach students role relationships and communication styles, and young people learn the rules of the gang quickly in order to be accepted by their peers. Youth gangs can also meet needs for safety, status, and a sense of belonging (National Crime Prevention Council, 1990). If the school and family do not offer positive alternatives, the gangs can offer incentives, com-

---

FIELD-BASED ACTIVITY 4.3

Watch the local news and collect articles that have to do with the area of your community where your children live. Collect articles that illustrate violence and/or abuse in their community and those that describe or explain fine arts events, musical presentations, or other cultural affairs. How many of these events have impacted your students? Develop a map that illustrates where in the community the violence occurs, and then indicate where many of the cultural events occur. Does this provide you any additional information about your students' environment?

---

munication, and motivation to reinforce disrespect for many school norms (Campbell, 1996).

World Wide Web Site: You may learn more about violence in schools at:
National Alliance for Safe Schools: http://www.safeschools.org/
National School Safety Center: http://nssc1.org/
National Center for Education Statistics:
 http://nces.ed.gov/pubs98/violence/index.html
Eric Clearing House on Urban Education:
 http://eric-web.tc.columbia.edu/digents/dig115.html

Changes in Family Life

Family life in America is changing. In 1965 more than 60 percent of Americans lived in a traditional family unit with a working father and a mother who stayed at home to provide child care and manage the house. Today only 10 percent of the families in the United States fall into that category. This country has the highest divorce rate in the world. The Internal Revenue Service now recognizes thirteen different variations of the family—including dual-career families, single-parent families, and step-families. Most children no longer have an adult at home whose primary responsibility is to supervise and care for the children.

One of the strongest predictors of educational success for students is the educational background of the parent. Recently, when nine-year-old students were tested for achievement in reading, math, and science, dramatic differences were discovered when comparing the educational level of the parents. Twenty-two percent of students whose parents had some college coursework had a high level of comprehension, while only 6 percent of the students whose parents were high school dropouts were able to read at the same level (Barton & Coley, 1991).

Single Parents Four out of ten children in the United States are living without a father in the home. Children in single-parent homes are twice as likely to drop out of high school and, even if they stay in school, tend to have lower grades and poorer attendance than those children who come from a two-parent family home (Bennett, 1995). By some predictions, only 30 percent of white children and 6 percent of African American children born in 1980 will be living with both parents by the time they reach the age of eighteen. By the end of this century, researchers predict that 40 percent of all births and 80 percent of minority births will be by unmarried women.

Working Parents More and more children have both mothers and fathers joining the workforce. In 1970 only 32 percent of mothers of preschoolers worked outside the home, but by 1990, 58 percent of mothers with preschool-age children were in the workforce. Single parents and parents who both work outside the home are away during the day with a work schedule that often doesn't match the school's hours. Between the time school lets out and the time parents return from work, children are often left at home alone—unsupervised by any responsible adult for several hours. Forty-two percent of all American kids between the ages of five and nine are home alone often or at least occasionally, and up to 10 million children in the United States are latchkey children, spending most afternoons alone (Willwerth, 1993).

When parents are at home, children compete with hectic schedules for a very limited amount of time. One study of a thousand adolescents found that they spend only about five minutes a day exclusively with a father and about twenty minutes a day with their mothers (Csikszentmihalyi & Larson, 1984).

Communities, which once felt a collective responsibility for the children, are growing more uncaring and even dangerous. Children not only have to face negative peer pressure from other children but must also cope with untrustworthy adults who would prey on their innocence. The result is a large majority of children and adolescents who spend a significant amount of time alone, or with peers, unsupervised by any responsible adult.

Unsupervised time after school hours can be time spent on illegal and even dangerous activities. It is also a time when adolescents experiment with sexual activity (Zelnik & Kantner, 1977). Adolescents who are left alone unsupervised are also more likely to engage in substance abuse. In one study, unsupervised eighth-graders, left alone for more than eleven hours a week, were twice as likely to experiment with drugs than those who were supervised by adults (Richardson et al., 1989).

FIELD-BASED ACTIVITY 4.4

Find out where your students go after school. Who cares for them after school? What do they do when they leave the school grounds. If they go to an organized activity such as Boys Clubs or Girls Clubs or after-school programs, spend a few afternoons with them. Be ready to share with your class what you have discovered. Discuss how this may impact their ability to succeed at school.

Health-Related Issues

Not all American children have access to proper health care. Poor children are more likely to experience health-related problems than other children. Those children growing up in poverty are also often the children with no health benefits. The United States is the only major industrialized nation in the world with no system of health care, and since we also pay more for health care than most nations of the world, most poor families are unable to afford the expense. According to the Children's Defense Fund (1987), one-third of uninsured Americans are children, and the majority of these children are from low-income families unable to afford the cost of health care without insurance.

One-fourth of all the babies born in America receive inadequate prenatal care. Infant mortality rates in the United States are higher than in twenty-one other developed nations. Nearly 40,000 babies die in America each year before reaching their first birthday. In 1992 almost half of all two-year-olds had not been fully immunized against preventable childhood diseases (Children's Defense Fund, 1994), and in a 1991 survey 21 percent of American children had not seen a doctor in the past year (Plante, 1993). Health conditions, just like economic and family situations, strongly influence a child's readiness to learn.

AIDS

In 1981 the Center for Disease Control (CDC) reported 164 AIDS-related deaths. By 1994 the CDC reported that 270,870 people had died of the disease and estimated that over 1 million Americans were carrying the virus (HIV or HIV-1). One of the greatest groups at risk for infection is teenagers. Believing themselves invincible, teenagers often engage in high-risk behaviors such as unprotected sex and drug use. In a one-year period from January 31, 1989, to February 1, 1990, the CDC reported a 40 percent increase in the number of AIDS cases reported by teens thirteen to nineteen years old. AIDS is currently the sixth leading cause of death among young people fifteen to twenty-four years of age. Other studies estimate that 1 in 100 teens in Miami and New York have the AIDS virus and 0.3 in 100 teens in rural areas are infected (Alali, 1995). These statistics grow even more alarming when considering that approximately 30 percent of young adolescents report having sexual intercourse by age fifteen, with six in ten reporting that they do not use any contraception (Planned Parenthood Federation of America, 1986).

World Wide Web Site: You may access and learn more about the CDC National
AIDS Clearinghouse at: http://www.cdcnac.org/nachome.html

Teenage Pregnancy

In the past thirty years, the number of children born to unmarried teenagers has
increased by 200 percent. Approximately 1 million teenage girls become pregnant each year, with most of these births occurring outside of marriage. In 1990,
31 percent of eighth- and tenth-grade females dropped out of school because
they were pregnant (National Educational Goals Panel, 1992). Children of
unmarried teenage mothers are four times more likely to be poor and remain
poor for a longer period of time (National Commission on Children, 1991).
Babies born to teenage mothers are more likely to be born prematurely, have a
low birth weight, and need expensive neonatal intensive care. They are at risk of
cerebral palsy, epilepsy, mental retardation, and other handicaps. How does all
this affect the classroom? Children of teenage mothers have higher school
dropout rates and lower academic achievement rates and are more frequently
retained than those born to women in their twenties (Schorr & Schorr, 1988).

Nutritional Deficits

Poor nutrition during any period of childhood can have harmful effects on the
cognitive development of children (Tufts University School of Nutrition
Statement on the Link Between Nutrition and Cognitive Development in
Children, 1993). Nutritional deficits impact the behavior of children, their
school performance, and their overall learning development. Even relatively
short-term deficiencies can effect a child's behavior. A shortage of iron in a
child's diet, for example, can have a direct impact on the child's attention span
and memory, and yet an estimated one-fourth of all low-income children in the
United States currently suffer from anemia. Poor children, who attend school
hungry, are often tired and uninterested in school and perform significantly
lower on standardized tests than children who are not hungry. Poor nutrition, in
addition to environmental factors associated with poverty, can permanently
inhibit physical growth, brain development, and cognitive functioning. The
longer a child's nutritional needs go unmet, the greater the chance for overall
learning deficits.

Drug Abuse

Even before birth, a child is affected by the mother's social community context and family. Poor parents are more likely to be uninsured and unable to afford proper treatment for addictions they may suffer. Although substance abuse occurs within all groups and social classes, there is a higher rate of abuse among minorities and low-income populations. There is a lack of available services to poor families, with most programs and treatment centers targeting the middle- and upper-class insured substance abusers (Orland, 1994).

The behavior of an addicted parent can have serious consequences for the child. Pregnant women who abuse alcohol and other drugs impact the development of the child they carry. Fetal alcohol syndrome (FAS) is fast becoming a major concern for educators as children already severely effected by drugs in the home enter schools. Children born to alcoholic mothers have smaller head diameters, lower birth weight, and, in those children with fully developed FAS, damage to the central nervous system (Landesman-Dwyer, 1982). FAS, however, could be the most preventable form of mental retardation and birth defects, because it could be avoided if the mother could abstain from alcohol during pregnancy. Children are also born addicted to other substances such as crack and heroin, which impair their development and impact the classrooms they will enter.

By the time children reach early adolescence many have made alcohol and other drugs a part of their life. In a recent survey, 77 percent of eighth-graders reported having used alcohol, with 26 percent saying they had five or more drinks within the past two weeks (Carnegie, 1992).

Teachers can help identify children from alcoholic or substance abuse homes by watching for behavioral problems in the classroom that may indicate abuse at home (Edwards & Zander, 1985). Children from an alcoholic or substance abuse home can change drastically in personal appearance and health from day to day and exhibit poor attendance and tardiness. They may also exhibit wide ranges of academic performance—one day performing well on academic tasks and the next unable to complete even the simplest assignment. These children may be over-concerned with pleasing adults and are often afraid of parent-teacher interactions.

FIELD BASED ACTIVITY 4.5

In small groups of your classmates, build a scenario of your concerns as you were growing up. Talk to your class or interview students about their concerns. Find out what worries them. Visit with students who are at a different age than those in your classroom. Ask them the same questions. Compare your childhood concerns with those of today's students. Are there differences? Did your students list other concerns not discussed in the text?

VOICE OF A TEACHER

I didn't want Edward in my classroom. I already had more students in my class than any other teacher in the grade level. But even more important, Edward was being put into my room for a reason. The new teacher down the hall couldn't control him. Edward was constantly disrupting the classroom and parents were complaining daily in the principal's office about his violent behavior with other students.

So Edward came to me because, as my principal explained, "You can handle him."

After that first day I wasn't so sure. The son of an abusive prison guard, he was a big kid. Bigger than any of the other boys in the room. He walked into the room with a swagger and then proceeded to "shoot the finger" at my back as soon as I turned around to write on the chalkboard. When I began to speak, he stood and sauntered over to the pencil sharpener—grinding away with a cocky smile—while I tried to talk over the noise.

The rest of the class was astonished at his behavior. It was completely alien to the classroom environment we had spent the last three months working so hard to establish, but I knew some students would soon follow his lead. I had to make him a part of the class quickly.

It was obvious he was a natural-born leader so that's where I began. I highlighted his leadership abilities in every possible activity. I asked him to mentor a much younger child with severe behavior problems in a lower grade. He immediately rose to the occasion and proved to be a natural teacher, although surprisingly tough on discipline. I appointed him the hall monitor and he ruled the line of students like a tough drill sergeant—pacing up and down the line—watching for any small infraction of the hallway rules. He was just as exacting on academic tasks. When appointed the leader of his table, I knew the group assignment would be completed.

I'll never forget his face on the last day of school when I announced his name as the most improved student.

Edward broke out in a smile that spread ear to ear and proudly swaggered up to the front of the room, accompanied by the loud applause of his classmates. A positive classroom leader, he had earned their respect and admiration. He had also earned mine.

Providing Equal Educational Access to Learning

Even with all the problems confronting America's children, schools can make a difference. Many schools are beginning to work with communities and parents to provide a safe, nurturing environment for all children. Effective schools are learning to reach out into the community and become a center of learning for all members.

Parent and community involvement and support in schools contributes to students' successful school achievement. When parents are involved, their children earn higher grades and test scores and they stay in school longer. The performance of all children in the school tends to improve when parents are involved in a variety of ways at school. The more the relationship between families and school approaches a comprehensive, well-planned partnership, the higher the student achievement (Berla & Henderson, 1994). Strong communi-

VOICE OF A TEACHER

I left the shopping mall one night and was surprised to see a group of six or seven young men standing by my car in the parking lot. It was near closing time and the parking lot was otherwise deserted.

I nervously noted the gang colors worn by several in the group, and considered turning around to go back into the store, but I could see the store manager locking the doors from the inside. I swallowed hard and began walking toward my car, trying to look confident and unafraid, eyes focused straight ahead. When I was about ten feet from the car, one of the young men who looked about seventeen stepped out in front of me. I had to stop. I looked up, way up, into his scowling face at least two feet above my head.

"Mrs. Wilson, don't you recognize me?" I was startled and looked closer at the young face. "It's me. Chris Jackson."

I could hardly believe it. "I would never have recognized you in a million years, Chris. You don't exactly look like the third-grader I remember."

His face broke out in a huge grin.

"You look just the same," he said, laughing.

I wasn't sure if it was a compliment or not, but I took it as one. We stood and talked for a while—mostly about the third grade. It was amazing how many details Chris remembered about that year. When I asked him about his current activities, he was quick to change the subject.

"You better get on home now. It can be pretty dangerous in this parking lot after dark," he said, taking the large shopping bag out of my arms.

Then, turning toward the rest of the boys, he called out, "Hey, I'll be back. I'm gonna walk my teacher out to her car."

On the way home I wondered about all my other third-graders spread out all over the city—maybe even the world. Where were they now? Who had they become? Did they remember the year they spent in third grade?

Would they still call me teacher?

ty support and involvement is necessary for schools to begin to address the variety of problems and needs facing the children they serve. A comprehensive discussion of parent and family involvement can be found in Chapter 5.

Successful teachers who are effective with a wide range of differences in students are self-reflective about their own attitudes, beliefs, and actions. They constantly work to recognize and eliminate teacher expectations based on race, class, and/or sex. Effective teachers provide diversity in instructional activities and classroom environment.

Many children come to our classrooms each day with all the indicators associated with failure, overwhelming problems that threaten to distract them from learning, and yet they succeed and even excel in an academic setting. Many children from a wide variety of backgrounds and cultures experience few problems

Becoming a Teacher in a Field-Based Setting

Every Day in the USA

- Every day 2,989 children see their parents divorced. One-quarter of the divorced mothers with court orders for child support in 1985 received nothing.

- Every day in 3.4 million families with children, at least one adult goes to work, yet these families are still poor.

- Every day up to 2 million children are left alone while their parents work. Care for one child costs almost half of the income of a parent working full-time, year-round, at the minimum wage.

- Every day more than 12 million children wake up poor.

- Every day 27 American children die from the effects of poverty.

- Every day 135,000 children bring guns to school. Every day 10 children die from guns, and 30 are wounded.

- Every day 100,000 American children are homeless. One-third of homeless shelter residents are children and families.

- Every day 105 American babies die before reaching their first birthday.

Source: *Outside the Dream: Child Poverty in America.* Aperture: Children's Defense Fund 1991, 20 East 23rd Street, New York, NY 10010.

----

with learning within the school context. Within the walls of your classroom, you will meet examples of all of these young people—students with problems to overcome and students who learn easily and quickly—but the mission will be the same. Teach all children. "Suffice it to say that *all* children must be prepared for responsible participation as citizens and for critical dialogue in the human conversation, and that the pedagogy and stewardship of teachers must embrace *all* children and young people and the whole of the schools' moral functioning in a social and political democracy" (Goodlad, 1990, p. 186).

PORTFOLIO REFLECTIONS AND EXHIBITS

Choose one of the field-based activities suggested in the text or develop an exhibit that represents what your have learned during the readings and discussions accompanying this chapter. Your response to the activities or your exhibit can become part of your teaching portfolio.

Related Readings

Kotlowitz, A. (1991). *There are no children here.* New York: Anchor Books.

> *This is another book about the plight of poor children in our country. The setting of this narrative is the projects of Chicago. The reader becomes acquainted with Lafayette and Pharoah and the other children in the neighborhood. This book was made into a TV movie starring Oprah Winfrey.*

Kozol, J. (1991). *Savage inequalities: Children in American schools.* New York: HarperCollins.

Kozol, J. (1995). *Amazing grace.* New York: Crown.

> *Both of Kozol's books are sobering descriptions of poor children's lives. In Savage Inequalities, he describes the results of limited resources on several inner-city school districts. Amazing Grace describes the day-to-day lives of some of the poorest children in our country. Neither of these are particularly uplifting, but both present some realities that middle-class Americans need to understand.*

References

Alali, A. (1995). *HIV and AIDS in the public schools: A handbook for curriculum development, teacher education, and the placement of affected students, with a directory of resources.* Jefferson, NC: McFarland.

American Association of University Women (1992). *How schools shortchange girls.* Washington, DC: American Association of University Women Educational Foundation.

Barton, P., & Coley, R. (1991). *Performance at the top: From elementary through graduate school.* Princeton, NJ: Educational Testing Service.

Berla, N., & Henderson, A. T. (1994). *A new generation of evidence: The family is critical to student achievement.* Washington, DC: National Committee for Citizens in Education. (Distributed by the center for Law and Education, 1875 Connecticut Avenue, N.W., Suite 510, Washington, DC 20009.)

Bennett, W. (1995). What to do about the children. *Commentary, 99*(3), 22–28.

Blackhurst, A., & Burdine, W. (Eds.). (1993). *An introduction to special education* (3rd ed.). New York: HarperCollins.

Bowman, B. (1989). Self-reflection as an element of professionalism. *Teachers College Record, 90,* 444–451.

Bowman, B. (1994). The challenge of diversity. *Phi Delta Kappan, 76*(3), 218–225.

Campbell, D. (1996). *Choosing democracy: A practical guide to multicultural education.* Englewood Cliffs, NJ: Prentice Hall.

Carnegie Corporation of New York. (1992). *A matter of time: Risk and opportunity in the nonschool hours.* New York: Carnegie.

Children's Defense Fund. (1987). *A children's defense budget: An analysis of the FY/87 federal budget and children.* Washington, DC: Author.

Children's Defense Fund. (1994). *CDF report.* Washington, DC: Author.

Csikszentmihalyi, M., & Larson, R. (1984). *Being adolescent: Conflict and growth in the teenage years* (p. 73). New York: Basic Books.

Darling-Hammond, L., & Ancess, J. (1995). Democracy and access to education. In R. Soder (Ed.), *Democracy, education, and the schools* (pp. 151–181). San Francisco: Jossey-Bass.

Delpit, L. (1995). *Other people's children: Cultural conflict in the classroom.* New York: The New Press.

Edwards, D., & Zander, T. (1985, December). Children of alcoholics: Background and strategies for the counselor. *Elementary School Guidance and Counseling, 20*(2), 121–128.

Gay, G. (1993). Building cultural bridges: A bold proposal for teacher education. *Education and Urban Society, 25*(3), 285–299.

Goodlad, J. (1990). *Teachers for our nation's schools.* San Francisco: Jossey-Bass.

Hodgkinson, H. (1993). American education: The good, the bad, and the task. *Phi Delta Kappan, 74*(8), 620–632.

Huelskamp, R. (1991). Perspectives on education in America. *Phi Delta Kappan, 74*(9), 718–721.

Kammerman, S., & Kahn, A. (1994). *A welcome for every child: Care education and family support for infants and toddlers in Europe.* Arlington, VA: Zero to three/National Center for Infant Programs.

Kelly, D. (1993). A haven for homeless students. *USA Today,* Tuesday, March 9, p. 10.

Kirst, (1993). Strengths and weaknesses of American education. *Phi Delta Kappan, 74*(8), 613–618.

Knitzer, J., & Aber, L. (1995). Young children in poverty: Facing the facts. *American Journal of Orthopsychiatry, 65*(2), 212–230.

Kohl, P. L., & Witty, E. P. (1996). Equity challenges. In J. Silula (Ed.), *Handbook of research on teacher education* (2nd ed., pp. 837–866). New York: Macmillan.

Landesman-Dwyer, S. (1982). Maternal drinking and pregnancy outcome. *Applied Research in Mental Retardation, 3,* 241–257.

Margolis, H., & McCabe, P. (1989). Easing the adjustment to mainstreaming programs. *Educational Digest, 55*(4), 58–61.

Mihaly, L. (1991). *Homeless families: Failed policies and young victims.* Washington, DC: Children's Defense Fund.

National Commission on Children (1991). *Beyond rhetoric: A new American agenda for children and families.* Washington, DC: National Commission on Children.

National Crime Prevention Council. (1990). *Changing perspectives: Youth as resources.* Washington, DC: Author.

National Education Goals Panel (1991). *The national education goals report: Building a nation of learners.* Washington, DC: U.S. Government Printing Office.

Natriello, G., McDill, E., & Pallas, A. (1990). *Schooling disadvantaged children: Racing against catastrophe.* New York: Teachers College Press.

Oakes, J. (1990). *Multiplying inequalities: The effects of race, social class, and tracking on opportunities to learn mathematics and science.* Santa Monica: Rand.

Ogbu, J. (1990). *Overcoming racial barriers to equal access.* In *Access to knowledge: An agenda for our nation's schools* (pp. 59–90). J. Goodlad & P. Keating. New York: The College Board.

Ogbu, J. (1992). Understanding cultural diversity and learning. *Educational Researcher, 21*(8), 5–14.

Orland, M. E. (1994). Demographics of disadvantage: Intensity of childhood poverty and its relationship to educational achievement. In J. I. Goodlad & P. Keating (Eds.), *Access to knowledge: The continuing agenda for our nation's schools* (pp. 43–58). New York: The College Board.

Pipher, M. (1994). *Reviving Ophelia: Saving the selves of adolescent girls.* New York: Ballantine Books.

Planned Parenthood Federation of America. (1986). *American teens speak: Sex myths, TV, and birth control.* (The Planned Parenthood poll by Louis Harris and Associates). New York: Author.

Plante, K. L. (1993), February). The competitiveness and production of tomorrow's workforce: Compelling reasons for investing in healthy children. (Fact sheet prepared for participants in children as capital corporate health policy retreat). Washington, DC: American Academy of Pediatrics & Washington Business Group on Health.

Reed, D. & Sautter, T. (1990). Children of poverty: The status of 12 million young Americans. *Phi Delta Kappan, 71*(9), 764–770.

Richardson, J. L., Dwyer, K., Hansen, W. B., Dent, C., Johnson, C. A., Sussman, S.Y., Brannon, B., & Flag, B. (1989). Substance use among eighth-grade students who take care of themselves after school. *Pediatrics, 84*(3), 556–566.

Sadker, D., & Sadker, M. (1993). *Failing at fairness.* New York: Scribner.

Sadker, M., & Sadker, D. (1986). Sexism in the classroom: From grade school to graduate school. *Phi Delta Kappan, 67*(7), 512–515.

Schorr, L. B., & Schorr, D. (1988). *Within our reach: Breaking the cycle of disadvantage.* New York: Anchor Press.

Shakeshaft, C. (1986). A gender at risk. *Phi Delta Kappan, 67*(7), 499–503.

Sherman, A. (1994). *Wasting America's future: The Children's Defense Fund report on the costs of child poverty.* Boston: Beacon Press.

Tavris, C. (1992). *Mismeasurement of women.* New York: Simon & Schuster.

Tufts University School of Nutrition Policy. (1993). Statements on the link between nutrition and cognitive development in children. Boston, MA: Tufts University School of Nutrition Policy.

Villa, R., & Thousand, J. (1990). Administrative supports to promote inclusive schooling. In W. Stainback & J. K. Stainback (Eds.), *Support networks for inclusive schooling: Independent, integrated education* (pp. 201–218). Baltimore: Paul H. Brookes Publishing Co.

Villegas, A. M. (1991). *Culturally responsive pedagogy for the 1990s and beyond* (Trends and Issues Paper No. 6). Washington, DC: ERIC Clearinghouse on Teacher Education.

Willwerth, J. (1993). "Hello? I'm home alone . . ." *Time,* March 1, pp. 46–47.

York, J., & Reynolds, M. (1996). Special education and inclusion. In J. Sikula (Ed.), *Handbook of research on teacher education* (2nd ed., pp 820–836). New York: Macmillan.

Zeichner, K. (1993, April). *Educating teachers for cultural diversity and learning.* Paper presented at the Annual Meeting of the American Educational Research Association, Atlanta.

Zelnik, M., & Kantner, J. F. (1977). Sexual and contraceptive experience of young unmarried women in the United States, 1997 and 1971. *Family Planning Perspectives, 9,* 55–71.

5
Interpreting Classroom Learning Theory

In this chapter
- Learning as Behavior
- Learning as Cognition
- Learning as Constructivism
- Putting It All Together: Using Behavioral, Cognitive, and Constructivist Theories

Chris should have pointed her station wagon north, toward a greener town where children scored high on Basic Skills Tests in rough proportion to their parents' incomes and years of schooling. But on most of those spring mornings she was eager to get to her room. When she thought of this class now she saw that many were performing very well, better than ever. It was a good class, all in all . . .

She'd come hurrying across the parking lot at a quarter to eight always a few minutes behind, overballasted and listing slightly under her bookbag, eyes on the front door. The top math group discovered geometry—first of all, at her direction, in the many angles they'd noticed in the room during daydreamy times: the joints in the metal trim around chalkboards, the intersecting lines of their classmates' legs under desks. The low group had finally finished with division. She had adminis-

tered a final review test to make sure and when she had gone over the last of the papers in the Teachers' Room, Chris had smiled and said, "I haven't changed Henrietta's attitude. I haven't changed Manny's. They're still going to be as obnoxious as the day is long. But they know long division."

Every child worked, even Robert. Some sat in circles of twos and threes, their voices mingling as they read each other their rough drafts. Others bent over their desks, writing assiduously . . . Chris thought she saw signs of new progress in grammar, syntax, and consecutive thinking.

—Tracy Kidder, *Among Schoolchildren*

You have probably frequently heard statements such as "teachers are born, not made." While the phrase is true to some extent, it implies that teaching is an art rather than a science. Some teachers seem to have natural abilities and personality traits that cannot be taught—at least not during the relatively brief period of preservice teacher education. Thinking of teaching as solely an art implies that people must be born with the ability to reach and teach children and adolescents or they will not become good teachers. Does this mean you should abandon your desire to teach if you feel that you don't "instinctively" know what to do when you're working with children?

Fortunately, we know that there are skills and knowledge that contribute to good teaching that we can pass on to novice teachers. The skills and knowledge form the scientific basis of the art of teaching (Gage, 1984) and often differentiate merely good teachers from great ones. Expert teachers draw on this knowledge when planning, making decisions, and implementing instruction. Although we cannot directly teach some of the dispositions associated with our notion of good teachers, such as caring, enthusiasm, or empathy, we can provide experiences for you in which you may be more likely to develop them. Part of the value of your field-based program lies in the opportunity you have to interact with teachers who possess these qualities.

A large part of the science of teaching is knowledge about the way humans learn—how they process information, what motivates them to learn, and how learning and motivation change over time and with experience. Understanding

Future teachers are often surprised about the long hours spent planning lessons and activities and by the effort it takes to provide feedback and evaluate students' responses.

how learning takes place helps teachers plan instruction and experiences for students that match their particular needs. Knowledge about how factors such as the type of task students perform, interactions with other people, and how attitudes and feelings influence learning enables teachers to reflect about teaching successes and failures. Knowing how previous experiences and learning impact new learning allows us to tailor our instruction for individuals of different ability levels who may come from different cultures or conditions or speak different languages than we do. While we teach groups in the classroom setting, individuals learn. Understanding how individual differences relate to human learning makes us better teachers.

As you continue through your program, you will need more and more of this knowledge about human learning to assist you in planning and implementing instruction, managing groups, and recognizing and addressing individual problems of learning. You may have already taken classes in educational psychology, learning theory, or child and adolescent theory, or you may be planning to study these as you continue in your program. The intent of this chapter is not to replace those courses, but to challenge you to think about teaching decisions in relation to what we know about how students learn. Typically, experts in teaching and learning have operated in isolation of each other, resulting in difficulty in applying or even seeing the utility of psychological theory for teaching (Alexander & Knight, 1993). Aside from the educational psychology textbooks provided in courses and often seen by students as unrelated to the real world of classrooms, few teacher education texts draw explicitly on psychological learning theory as a basis for instructional decision making. We have chosen a very limited selection of content in this area to demonstrate how knowledge of learning processes might inform your teaching and to provide a basis for observing and analyzing the classes you see in your field-based program. However, you should not think of this as material you need to "memorize." Use the information to focus your observations and discussions with teachers and your peers. If you are familiar with the content, the application of it in classrooms should make it more personally meaningful. If much of the content of this chapter is new to you, you may want to consider it as a framework for helping you think about teaching and learning during this course and to familiarize yourself with the information you will study in more depth at a later time. The reference section at the end of the chapter lists a number of books and articles about learning and teaching that will be valuable to you as you increase your own scientific basis for the art of teaching.

Meanwhile, the following questions will help you focus on the important information in the chapter as you read:

- What do I need to know about how humans learn in general in order to plan and implement effective instruction for my students?

- What do I need to know about how different conditions outside of the learner and characteristics and traits within the learner influence learning?

- What do the different theories of learning look like when they are used in a classroom?

FIELD-BASED ACTIVITY 5.1

Think of a learning experience you've had that was particularly powerful. Be prepared to describe the event to one of your classmates. What did you learn? How did you learn it? What were the conditions (the presence or absence of other people, the amount of time it took)? What made it so effective? Now do the same thing for an experience that was not effective for you. What were you supposed to have learned? Describe the event. List the characteristics of successful and not so successful learning experiences. Share the list with the rest of your class. Keep these two experiences in mind as you continue to read.

Becoming a Teacher in a Field-Based Setting

- How can I combine the different definitions of learning in my teaching so that students learn in meaningful ways?

What we know about learning and its relationship to effective teaching cannot possibly be contained or even summarized in a single chapter in an introductory textbook for students in a field-based program. As discussed previously, many of the learning theory courses take place in university classrooms with little contact with schools, students, or teachers. Also, the theories often seem to contradict each other and you may be left feeling more confused than enlightened. When you read the following sections about different approaches to how students learn, think about your own learning experiences. Do you learn some kinds of information best through more direct methods such as lecture or demonstration? Are there other kinds of learning that you have to experience rather than be told?

Since you have an opportunity through this course to make learning theories meaningful through observation and application, we have reduced and simplified the amount of information in this chapter. The following sections discuss learning from three perspectives that have been useful to educators as they design and implement instruction. Neither theory alone will explain all types of learning in all kinds of situations for every learner. The term "learning" has different meanings for different people and for different tasks. However, reflecting on the different theories of learning while planning or troubleshooting and determining when to apply a particular aspect of a theory becomes part of the art of teaching that you will refine with experience.

Learning as Behavior

At first, Javier was doing well in geometry class. Then he got confused and failed a test. Now Javier has difficulty even completing a quiz because his hands shake so badly he can't hold a pencil. His teacher has decided to give him his next test orally after school.

Students in Ms. Gordon's class receive a construction paper "happy face" every time they move quietly from their reading group into center activities. When they have ten or more happy faces they can trade them for something in the class "store," such as a sticker or school supplies.

A group of four students completes one of Mrs. Smith's learning centers and carefully puts away all materials. As they are doing this, Mrs. Smith says aloud: "Joe, Amy, Juan, and Alicia all get a 'scratch 'n sniff' sticker because they have returned their center materials to the proper places."

What do all these scenes have in common? They all contain examples of the application of different types of behavioral learning theory in elementary or secondary classes. Behavioral learning theory has exerted considerable influence on American educational practices for almost half a century. You will recognize many of the applications from your own school experiences and will see others as you observe in classrooms.

Behaviorism is not a single theory. There are various types of behavioral learning theory and multiple theorists associated with the approach. Many of the distinctions among the different theorists, while important to other theorists and researchers, do not significantly affect the application of the approach in educational settings. For this reason, we will focus on elements that all behavioral theories share and how these common elements apply to the classroom. In the case where differences in theory result in different implications for teaching, as in the differences between observational learning theory and operant conditioning, we highlight and discuss differences as well.

From a behavioral perspective, learning is a lasting change in observable behavior that occurs as a result of experience. Notice that the definition specifies lasting change. Random or unintentional behaviors do not indicate that learning has taken place. For example, if a student completes a multiple-choice test using a predictable pattern of responses unrelated to the content of the questions (e.g., alternating a, b, c, or d for each answer), and gets 25 percent of the answers correct, we cannot say that she or he has learned 25 percent of the material.

All behavioral theories also share an emphasis on observable, measurable behavior. A student may know the answers to all the questions on a test but may not respond to the test. Since we have not observed the behaviors, we cannot say learning has occurred. According to strict behaviorists, experience that results in learning comes from interactions with the external environment. Changes due to internal mechanisms, such as those attributed to development, would not constitute learning. From a behavioral perspective, learning occurs because the connection between a stimulus (something in the environment) and the response (a behavior) has been strengthened. Learning is conditioning (recognizing relationships or associations between stimuli) and dependent on reinforcement (something that strengthens the connection) of the stimulus with the response. While all behaviorists share these principles, they sometimes differ on the type and role of reinforcement in conditioning and the stimuli and responses of interest.

Classical Conditioning

The example of Javier at the beginning of this section is illustrative of a type of behavioral theory known as classical conditioning. Pavlov was a brilliant physician who won a Nobel Prize based on his work on digestion. However, his observations on the salivation of dogs in the absence of food initiated research that changed the direction of psychology at the time. Pavlov noticed that caretakers of the dogs he used in experiments rang a bell just before they gave them their food. The dogs eventually began to salivate in anticipation of food even when caretakers rang the bell and did not provide food. Pavlov theorized that the food served as a stimulus that naturally prompted a physiological response, in this case salivation. However, with repeated presentations of the food (unconditioned stimulus) and the bell (conditioned stimulus) together (contiguity of stimuli), dogs began to associate the ringing of the bell with presentation of food and reacted to the seemingly dissimilar stimulus in the same manner. The unconditioned response of salivation in reaction to food then occurred as the conditioned response of salivation in reaction to the bell. Furthermore, salivation also occurred for sounds that were similar to the ringing of a bell, such as the sound of a tone or buzzer (generalization). Further research revealed that dogs could be taught to differentiate between similar stimuli (a buzzer or bell) depending on their association with food (discrimination). While association of food with a stimulus strengthened the response, removal of the food from the stimulus resulted in a gradual weakening of the reaction (extinction).

Although this theory focuses on reflexive behavior, usually emotional and physiological responses to stimuli, it does have some applications to our work with children in classrooms. Javier's uncontrollable shaking of his hands when confronted with his geometry test is related to this theory. Javier's intense anxiety in response to his first failure on a particular geometry quiz now occurs when he attempts any geometry test. The unconditioned stimulus—in this case, the failure—has become closely related to the conditioned stimulus, the testing situation. The emotional anxiety that failure elicits, seen in his shaking hands, now occurs in a test-taking situation. The teacher is attempting to help him succeed, associating test-taking with a less stressful reaction, so he will no longer associate the two occurrences.

FIELD-BASED ACTIVITY 5.2

Modern advertisements are consistent with classical conditioning principles. For example, when we see an Olympic participant win a gold medal in an event, what kind of emotional response does it evoke in us? Respect? Pride? Awe? A general feeling of well-being? What happens when we repeatedly see that award-winning athlete's picture on a box of cereal? Collect other examples of advertisements that might affect school-age children and share them with your class.

Operant Conditioning

Whereas classical conditioning has only limited application in the classroom since it primarily deals with involuntary reactions, B. F. Skinner's concept of operant conditioning has widespread application. Operant conditioning provides the framework for many of the basic skill development models, classroom discipline approaches, special education interventions, and computer-assisted instruction models that we use in schools. Since Skinner was particularly interested in the application of his theory to education, he became actively involved in the translation of his work into practice (see e.g., Skinner, 1954, 1958, 1968).

Operant conditioning focuses on voluntary behavior used in operating on the environment. From this perspective, the stimulus is something in the environment and the response is the behavioral reaction. Learning occurs when the connections between the environmental stimulus and voluntary behavior become strengthened through reinforcement. Reinforcement, defined as any consequence of the voluntary behavior that strengthens, or increases, the behavioral response to the stimulus, is contingent on performance of the behavior. Whereas other behaviorists waited for animals to learn through exploration, using the theory passively to explain behavior (e.g., Thorndike, 1913), Skinner actively manipulated the environment to obtain specific kinds of learning. Through the basic mechanisms of positive reinforcement, negative reinforcement, extinction and punishment, he experimented with increasing or decreasing behaviors (Skinner, 1963, 1969).

Positive reinforcement involves receiving something desired as a consequence of operating in some way on the environment. Behavior increases since the reinforcement is contingent on performance of the behavior. Skinner's research on cats and pigeons indicated that this mechanism is perhaps the most effective way of increasing desired behavior. However, the key to effective positive reinforcement includes consideration of the degree of desirability of the reinforcer, or its potency, as well as issues of satiation, or "too much of a good thing." While primary reinforcers, such as food, water, shelter, physical comfort, and affection are powerful motivators, they may not always have the desired outcome or may not be feasible in instructional settings. Food works best when people or animals are hungry. However, we may have ethical problems with withholding food to increase the potency of a reinforcer! Similarly, chocolate may be a child's favorite food, but children may soon tire of a steady diet of chocolate, reducing its potency as a reinforcer.

Secondary reinforcers are objects, gestures, or events that acquire the status of a primary reinforcer through association with that reinforcer. In classrooms, teachers use some primary reinforcements (candy, snacks, hugs), but they usually use secondary reinforcers such as praise or grades. In order to make sure that a reinforcer is desirable to students and to guard against satiation, teachers also may use systems that enable students to choose their own rewards. They reward students for desired behavior with objects, or tokens, which appear to have little or no value but which can be "traded" by the student for a variety of desirable objects or experiences. The example at the beginning of this section of Ms. Gordon and the construction paper happy faces is representative of this type of token system using positive reinforcers.

Negative reinforcement, another mechanism to increase behaviors, involves removing something undesired. The removal of something unpleasant or unwanted, such as electric shock, is contingent on performance of desired behaviors, such as pushing a lever. An animal subjected to electric shock will push a lever as frequently as needed to avoid the shock. Likewise, an American history teacher might promise a class that if students do their homework all week, they won't have any homework over the weekend. Students who view weekend homework as something to be avoided will do homework during the week. As with positive reinforcement, student perceptions of the degree of unpleasantness of objects or experiences determine the effectiveness of the negative reinforcer. Students who enjoy doing homework or students who never do homework anyway will not respond as desired. Another difficulty with this approach lies in reinforcing the notion that something like homework, which research indicates results in increased learning for students (Wang, Haertel, & Walberg, 1993), is something students should avoid. Therefore, teachers should carefully consider the unintended consequences of negative reinforcement.

A variation of negative reinforcement called the Premack principle (Premack, 1965) has been particularly useful in classrooms. In this approach, students agree to do a less desired behavior so that they will also be able to do a more desired one. For example, a band instructor may tell students that if they do a good job playing one of the classical tunes they are learning, they can also play a modern one of their choice. While playing the classical tune may not be

FIELD-BASED ACTIVITY 5.3

What kinds of reinforcers do you see teachers in your building using? Ask your teacher how she or he uses reinforcement in the classroom. How do students respond? Share in your discussions what you are seeing and compare the different methods of positive or negative reinforcement used in your school.

entirely undesirable, playing the modern song may certainly be more popular with students.

While positive and negative reinforcement increase behaviors, Skinner determined that other mechanisms decrease behavior. Extinction, or reinforcement removal, eventually extinguishes behavior. For example, students who shout out answers to questions rather than raising their hand eventually should stop shouting out if the teacher does not acknowledge the contributions. However, the classroom is more complex than the laboratories where many of these experiments occurred. Students may continue to shout out if classmates provide reinforcement by acknowledging the answers or by noticing the aggressive behavior. Although the teacher has removed reinforcement, other students provide reinforcement. Ignoring the inappropriate behavior, enlisting the cooperation of the class in also doing so, and providing positive reinforcement when the students raise their hand may all be needed to solve the problem.

Punishment, in the form of painful or undesirable consequences, also decreases behavior. Punishment can be of two types: presentation punishment, which involves receiving something not desired, or removal punishment, which consists of removing something desired. Teachers or administrators who administer corporal punishment are engaging in presentation punishment. A secondary teacher who refuses to allow a student to attend a sixth-period pep rally because she or he arrived late for class three days in a row is using removal punishment. An elementary teacher might place a misbehaving student in time-out, in other words, remove the student from participation with the rest of the class, as removal punishment. The premise for time-out is that the student sees participation in class as a desirable event and will decrease the incidents that resulted in the time-out.

While negative reinforcement may be confused with punishment, the important difference lies in the consequences of the particular action. Both negative reinforcement and presentation punishment involve an undesirable object or event. However, the intent of negative reinforcement is to encourage students to perform in a certain way in order to remove or avoid something undesirable. Reinforcement is contingent on performance of certain behaviors. Conversely, the intent of presentation punishment is to discourage certain behavior of students by providing a negative consequence or taking away a pleasant one. If the student behaves in a certain way, something unpleasant happens as a result.

Removal punishment, on the other hand, differs from both negative reinforcement and presentation punishment since it involves loss of a desirable object or experience. However, teachers may have difficulty determining or controlling something that is desirable to students. One particular kind of removal punishment, response cost, works in conjunction with a positive reinforcement system to remove previously awarded reinforcers when behavior is inappropriate. As adults, we might recognize this approach in fines imposed for traffic violations or library book late returns. Using the example of Ms. Gordon given at the beginning of the section, students in her class might have to forfeit a "happy face" each time they fail to properly return materials.

Some of the examples of types of reinforcement may seem difficult to classify. For example, time-out could be considered negative reinforcement if the teacher makes removal of time-out contingent on some behavior (e.g., student calms down, stops crying, and muttering angrily). The intent of this section is not for you to be able to label examples but to consider the examples in relation to teaching. The label merely provides a cue to help you reflect on the purposes and consequences of your actions and those of your students. With that proviso, can you figure out whether the following example is negative reinforcement, removal punishment, or presentation punishment?

> *Each third-grade student in Ms. Gordon's class starts the day with three Popsicle sticks. Each time a student misbehaves, she takes one of the Popsicle sticks away. If a student loses all three Popsicle sticks in one day, the student has to remain after school with Ms. Gordon.*

Will Ms. Gordon's actions increase or decrease the misbehavior of students? Are the popsicle sticks representative of something desired or undesired? What is the consequence of misbehavior? Is it pleasant or unpleasant? How would this be different if Ms. Gordon did not use the popsicle sticks and just had students remain with her after school when they misbehaved? Would one approach be better than the other?

While some kinds of punishment can be very effective in decreasing undesirable behaviors, the side effects of punishment often make it less than effective for teachers. Punishment does not deal with the reasons or desires associated with misbehavior and may only suppress the behavior for as long as the punishment is in place. Students may expend more effort in "not getting caught" than in behaving appropriately and may continue to engage in negative behaviors when the teacher is "not looking." Even if the student wants to engage in appropriate behavior, punishment rarely provides any indication of what students should do or why the behavior is inappropriate, and it may cause resentment, particularly when physical punishment is used, which leads to further problems. The form of punishment used also has unintended consequences. Giving extra schoolwork as punishment conveys that schoolwork is undesirable. While this may stem certain kinds of negative behavior, it will not increase the kinds of positive behavior encouraged in most classes!

Certain patterns or schedules of reinforcement are more effective for some purposes than for others. Reinforcement schedules can be either continuous, which means that a desired response receives reinforcement every time it occurs, or intermittent, which involves reinforcement of desired responses periodically. Continuous reinforcement schedules are most effective for encouraging the development of new skills or knowledge. For example, an algebra teacher may demonstrate the steps involved in solving simultaneous equations and have students work with her. After each step, the teacher praises students liberally for correctly executing the step with her. This serves to give students feedback about their performance and strengthen correct performance at an early stage of skill learning. The opportunity for strengthening of incorrect performance is less likely since the task has been broken down into small parts and students receive feedback about performance on each part before continuing to the next part.

On the other hand, after students have advanced somewhat in their skill development, an intermittent schedule becomes more effective. Two types of intermittent schedules exist: ratio and interval. Ratio-intermittent schedules depend on the number of times a response occurs and can be either fixed or variable. Fixed-ratio schedules provide reinforcement after a certain number of desired responses. For example, our algebra teacher might announce to the class that as soon as they've correctly done five problems in a row, they can start on their homework assignment, with the possibility of finishing it by the end of class. A variable-ratio reinforcement schedule still relies on a certain number of correct responses prior to reinforcement, but that number varies in a way that is difficult for students to predict. In this schedule, students might have to finish only two problems on some days prior to beginning homework, five on others, or the entire set on others. The intent of the teacher would be to keep them working steadily because they never know how many problems they will have to have before they can start their homework.

Intermittent interval schedules are time, rather than number, dependent and can also be either fixed or interval. The same algebra teacher featured above might announce that he will take up all worksheets on Friday each week for a grade, setting a fixed interval for reinforcement. The danger inherent in this schedule is that students will wait until just prior to the time for reinforcement to do their work. Teachers, if they are not aware of the consequences of employing fixed-interval reinforcement schedules (or even not aware that that is what they are using), may complain that students "wait until the last minute to do their work." Students, however, are responding in a manner consistent with the reinforcement schedule the teacher has chosen. To obtain different responses, another type of schedule should be used.

A variable-interval schedule is also time dependent, but reinforcement occurs at varying, rather than fixed, intervals. The teacher using this schedule would take up worksheets for a grade at different times during the week. If the grade on these assignments is important to students, then students will keep up with daily work, not knowing when the teacher may choose to grade them. If the teacher wants students to spread their effort out evenly over a period of time, rather than waiting until just prior to reinforcement, a variable interval schedule is more effective. In general, variable reinforcement schedules, in particular variable ratio schedules, are more effective at sustaining student effort during tasks.

Look at the following example and try to determine what kind of schedule is being used:

A Spanish teacher uses a deck of cards with students' names on them as a strategy for calling on all students. She goes through the deck one-by-one to make sure everyone has an opportunity to speak.

What are the advantages and disadvantages of this schedule? Would another schedule be more effective? If so, what could the teacher do so that she can still use the deck of cards but employ a different reinforcement schedule?

Understanding and being able to use reinforcement schedules provides teachers with a means of managing individual and class behavior (see Chapter 6). Teachers can also use four processes associated with operant conditioning—shaping, chaining, cueing, and fading—to understand how students acquire complex skills and to design instruction to help them learn skills. *Shaping* involves the reinforcement of successive approximations of a desired behavior until students can produce the behavior. For example, if a teacher wants a student to write a paragraph, the teacher might initially reward the child for even taking out paper and pencil. As students move closer to mastering the target behavior, the teacher eliminates rewards for the approximate behaviors. How would you use shaping to solve the following problem?

FIELD-BASED ACTIVITY 5.4

Ask teachers or observe in their class to determine how they deal with collecting and grading homework or seatwork. What kind of reinforcement schedule do you think they are using? Do you think it is effective? Why or why not?

Teaching is more than standing in front of a classroom. Children learn from observing teachers and modeling is an important teaching stategy.

Mr. Smith usually gives his sixth-grade students math assignments in class to provide an opportunity for guided practice. When given an assignment of ten problems containing fractions, Avery put his head down on his desk and moaned, "I can't do this!"

Chaining involves the integration of the component skills of a complex skill or task. Behavioral theory dictates that complex behaviors be broken down into their component parts so that each part can be taught and reinforced. To shape behavior, teachers must first understand the smaller steps or component skills that comprise a more complex behavior and then break the task down for students. However, in order to accomplish integrated performance of the behavior, rather than performance of a series of component skills, the components must ultimately be linked. A common mistake in classrooms is the conviction that if we teach the subcomponents to students, they will automatically be able to integrate them.

Cueing and *fading* also play important roles in the teaching and learning of complex skills. Skinner found that pigeons could learn when to perform behaviors by discriminating certain cues in the environment. Reinforcement occurred in the presence of some cues but not others. For example, Skinner's pigeons "danced" in the presence of some kinds of light sources but not in others. Similarly, a red light at an intersection cues us to put on the brakes; a green light cues us to press the gas pedal. Likewise, students in classrooms are cued to appropriate behavior by teachers' direct statements ("Remember, no talking while another student is reading"), physical presence or movements (walking up and down the aisles during seatwork cues students to work on assignments), nonverbal expressions (frowns or raised eyebrows), or other signals (flipping the lights on and off to signal a change of activities). While teachers often use cues purposively, they are sometimes unaware of the cues they give or the way students interpret them. For example, teachers may want students to engage in deep processing of the text they are reading but may not give them adequate time to do so. The amount of time given becomes a cue that students use to judge whether they should read at a surface level or for deeper meaning (Knight et al., 1989; Knight, 1990).

One of the ultimate goals of schooling is to enable students to become independent learners. Fading is one process that can be used to accomplish this goal. If students perform academically only in the presence of certain teacher-controlled cues, they will not perform when the teacher is no longer present. Therefore, controlling cues need to be gradually withdrawn, while at the same time continuing to reinforce the behavior. For example, a teacher who cues students to engage in interactive discussion of readings by standing in front of the whole group and asking thought-provoking questions about the text might gradually diminish her presence as the cue by having other students take over the role of "teacher" (see e.g., Palincsar & Brown, 1984).

Observational Learning

Operant conditioning has provided teachers with an understanding of many classroom behaviors and with mechanisms for changing student behaviors. Nevertheless, the theory fails to account for learning in the absence of direct experience. We know that some students learn behaviors that were not directly reinforced. Bandura (1982) proposes a variant of conditioning that explains this phenomenon. From his perspective, students learn new behaviors or continue to perform existing behaviors through vicarious conditioning. They watch others and observe the consequences of their behavior. The example at the beginning of this section of the scratch 'n sniff stickers awarded to a group of students is an attempt by the teacher to obtain similar behavior by others in the classroom. The four students receive positive reinforcement from the teacher. The remaining students have observed this and are likely to perform similarly if they also have hopes of obtaining stickers.

Depending on the status of the model and the conditions of reinforcement, modeling serves to (1) focus attention on behavior or aspects of behavior, (2) change inhibitions that observers might have about performing certain behaviors, and (3) arouse emotions. Students may learn from models directly by attempting to imitate a model's behavior, as when a kindergarten student makes a "b" sound after the teacher demonstrates the sound. Students may also learn in less direct ways. Symbolic modeling refers to the imitation of behaviors displayed by fictional characters in books, movies, or television. While this may be harmless, as when teens dress like popular TV personalities, some educators fear that televised violence may prompt aggressive behavior on the part of students. Students may also develop behaviors by synthesis, or combination, of parts of observed behaviors. For example, teens may combine movements they have seen two different rock stars use to create a new dance step. Abstract modeling is even more complex and involves extraction of rules or patterns from observing different examples. For example, by observing the speech patterns of the teacher or the models on tape, students taking Spanish may learn that adjectives usually follow nouns.

For observational learning to happen, however, students must relate or feel some degree of similarity to the model and must perceive that they are capable of performing the behaviors. For example, misbehavior of a well-liked classmate that goes unchallenged in the classroom may result in similar incidents of misbehavior by others in the class. Likewise, rewards for desired behavior to one classmate may result in an increase in the same kind of behavior by other students. However, a person must feel capable of performing the behavior. A short person might relate to Hakeem Olajuwan and observe the accolades that he receives for his slam dunk of the basketball. Nevertheless, the person who is 5'3" with no hope of growing taller, might not perceive that he or she is capable of ever performing a slam dunk and therefore probably would not play basketball.

Several processes determine the success of modeling as a classroom strategy. Observers first must attend to the desired behavior and retain it in memory so they can subsequently perform it. Then they must reproduce the behavior. Finally they must be motivated to performance of the behavior. Motivation, in this case, refers to the reinforcement received by the model for performance. If the observer does not view the reinforcement as desirable, motivation to perform will be low. For example, middle school students may not view a teacher's public praise of a fellow student's assistance with chores in the classroom as desirable. For this reason, they would not assist the teacher for fear of receiving similar praise. Look at the following example and try to identify the processes involved in observational learning.

A ninth-grade English teacher passes out graded essay exams. She then places one of the answers copied onto a transparency on the overhead projector. She says: "Look at the answer one of your classmates wrote [no name appears on the example]. I gave this an A grade. Let's look at it together and see why. First notice the thesis sentence . . ."

What does the teacher do to enable her students to learn from the example? How does she focus attention? What reinforcement does she provide? Would students likely be motivated to reproduce this behavior? Why or why not?

Educators often fear that sports or music heroes who behave in an immoral or unethical manner but retain their standing and wealth in society may reinforce undesirable behaviors by our youth. Since identification with the model is an important aspect of vicarious conditioning, the shortage of females and minorities in certain professions also becomes a source of concern to educators who want to raise the aspirations of underrepresented groups.

Applying Behavioral Theory in the Classroom

Behavioral learning theory has had considerable impact on the strategies teachers use in classrooms because it provides tools for planning for instruction, teaching skills and knowledge, managing student behavior, and assessing the impact of teachers' classroom behaviors. Planning tools include guidelines for formulating behavioral objectives that explicitly describe the observable, measurable behavior targeted, the conditions under which this behavior will be performed, and the criteria by which success will be judged. In addition, behavioral theory contributes procedures for task analysis to aid teachers in breaking down tasks into sequential, component skills that they can teach by using shaping and chaining processes. The creation of token economies, use of the Premack principle, and adherence to appropriate reinforcement schedules, all described previously, enable teachers to strengthen desired behaviors.

Rosenshine's Direct Instruction Model

The teaching model presented in Figure 5.1 has been used extensively in the classroom and as a basis for evaluation of teachers. The model's teaching functions are consistent with behavioral learning theory. Look at each of the functions. What principles that you have read about in this section are embedded in these functions? What kinds of outcomes would use of this model be likely to facilitate in students?

Figure 5.1
Teaching Functions

1. *Daily Review and Checking Homework*

   Check homework (routines for students to check each other's papers).
   Reteach when necessary.
   Review relevant past learning (may include questioning).
   Reveiw prerequisite skills (if applicable).

2. *Presentation*

   Provide short statement of objectives.
   Provide overview and structuring.
   Proceed in small steps but at a rapid pace.
   Intersperse questions within the demonstration to check for understanding.
   Highlight main points.
   Provide sufficient illustrations and concrete examples.
   Provide demonstrations and models.
   When necessary, give detailed and redundant instructions and examples.

3. *Guided Practice*

   Initial student practice takes place with teacher guidance.
   High frequency of questions and overt student practice (from teacher
   and/or materials).
   Questions are directly relevant to the new content or skill.
   Teacher checks for understanding (CFU) by evaluating student responses.
   During CFU, teacher gives additional explanation or process feedback, or
     repeats explanation—where necessary.
   All students have a chance to respond and receive feedback; teacher ensures
     that all students participate.
   Prompts are provided during guided practice (where appropriate).
   Initial student practice is sufficient so that students can work independently.
   Guided practice continues until students are firm.
   Guided practice is continued (usually) until a success rate of 80 percent is
     achieved.

4. *Correctives and Feedback*

   Quick, firm, and correct responses can be followed by another question or a
     short acknowledgment of correctness (i.e., "That's right").
   Hesitant correct answers might be followed by process feedback (i.e., "Yes,
     Linda, that's right because . . .").
   Student errors indicate a need for more practice.
   Monitor students for systematic errors.
   Try to obtain a substantive response to each question.
   Corrections can include sustaining feedback (i.e., simplifying the question,
     giving clues), explaining or reviewing steps, giving process feedback, or
     reteaching the last steps.
   Try to elicit an improved response when the first one is incorrect.

Becoming a Teacher in a Field-Based Setting

Guided practice and corrections continue until the teacher feels that the group can meet the objectives of the lesson.

Praise should be used in moderation, and specific praise is more effective than general praise.

5. *Independent Practice (Seatwork)*

Sufficient practice.

Practice is directly relevant to skills/content taught.

Practice to overlearning.

Practice until responses are firm, quick, and automatic.

Ninety-five percent correct rate during independent practice.

Students alerted that seatwork will be checked.

Student held accountable for seatwork.

Actively supervise students, when possible.

6. *Weekly and Monthly Reviews*

Systematic review of previously learned material.

Include review in homework.

Frequent tests.

Reteaching of material missed in tests.

Source: Rosenshine, B., & Stevens, R. (1986). Teaching functions. In M. C. Wittrock (Ed.), *Handbook of Research on Teaching* (3rd Edition, pp. 376–391). New York: Macmillan.

World Wide Web Site: You may learn more about Direct Instruction at: http://jan.ucc.nau.edu/~dlk/direct.html

Use of behavioral theory for assessment of the effects of instruction provides teachers with a means of improving their own teaching and assisting others in improvement. The focus on observation and measurement of observable behaviors has resulted in a number of behavior checklists or observation instruments that can be used by teachers in their own classrooms or in the classrooms of their peers (see e.g., Good & Brophy, 1997). The use of instruments that simply record behavior, without providing an inference or judgment, provide objective data about students as well as nonthreatening data about teacher behaviors. Teachers can use the data in reflection about their own practice, in teacher research, in peer coaching, or to identify and resolve instructional and managerial problems in the classroom. The Interaction Seating Chart Inventory (Stallings, 1997) in Figure 5.2 is one example of an instrument designed to provide teachers with information about teacher and student behavior.

Figure 5.2
Interactive Seating Chart

This chart provides a means for recording student and teacher interactions in the classroom. To use it, first familiarize yourself with the codes for certain behaviors listed at the top of the chart. Then make a seating chart for students in a class you plan to observe. Using the codes provided, record next to the names of students on the chart the type of interaction each has with the teacher as it occurs.

? Asks a direct question	+ Praises or supports responses	✓ Social comment
? Asks an open-ended question	C Corrects a response	* Student-initiated comment
✓ Checks for understanding	G Corrects & guides response	– Reprimands behavior

Teacher's Desk	T1–T10	Supplies

?+ ?G+ * ?+ * **Sarah**	✓?+ ?+ ?G **Jill**	✓ ?C ?+ * **Kay**	✓ * ?+ **Tim**	?+ **Olga**
✓ + ? + *+ **John**	?C ?C + * **George**	✓ ?+ ?+ **Francis**	?+ **Bob**	**Shirley**
?C ?+ ?+ **David**	**Hazel**	* ?+ **Robin**	?+ **Elaine**	– – **Ken**
?C – * **Evan**	* – ?C **Tony**	– ? **Bill**	?C **Ellen**	– – **Tom**
?C – – **Charles**	* – ?C **Lucy**	– ?C **Betty**	– – **Harry**	– **Dick**

Bookshelf · Bookshelf · Pencil Sharpener · Trash Can · Door

Source: Stallings, J. A. (1997). *Learning to teach in inner city schools training manual.* College Station: Texas A&M University, College of Education.

Experienced teachers learn how to use numerous teaching and learning strategies and will select activities that motivate their students and meet individual needs.

Learning as Cognition

Mr. Garcia is teaching the concept of density to his elementary science students. He provides groups of students with a number of different types of clear liquids (e.g., water, alcohol) and a bucket of ice cubes. He asks students to drop ice cubes in each of the liquids, record what happens, and discuss their findings in groups. Many students are surprised to find that the ice cubes float in some liquids but sink to the bottom in others. The next day he engages the entire class in a discussion of their findings and elicits their theories concerning the experiment.

Ms. Lee teaches secondary economics. Prior to beginning a series of lectures on international trade, she describes the different kinds of bartering for playthings that might take place among children at a playground and relates this to some of the concepts they will encounter in her lectures.

Mr. James is teaching his fifth-grade students about the Civil War. He puts a chart on the overhead projector that has Political Beliefs, Social Beliefs, and Economic Beliefs as column headings, and Northern Leaders and Southern

Leaders as row headings. He assigns groups of students to gather information about each of the cells in the charts and to fill them in. During the discussion following the group work, they look for similarities and differences in the two groups and predict how that might impact the struggle. Mr. James also encourages the class to change the chart to better capture the information they have gathered.

What do all these examples have in common? Each vignette provides an example of a different type of cognitive theory about how people learn. As was true for behavioral theory, cognitive theory consists of many different approaches. However, they all share certain underlying principles that make them look somewhat alike when they are applied to classroom instruction. In addition, they all differ from behavioral theory in ways that are evident in classroom applications as well. As was true for behavioral learning theories, this section will review only a few of the many cognitive learning theories that might help you make decisions about instruction. In addition, we will discuss how these theories are similar and different from one another and how they are different from behavioral learning theories in their application, and then we will provide a rationale for using both in the classroom, depending on the kinds of student outcomes you want.

Comparing Behavioral and Cognitive Approaches

Earlier, we discussed common features of behavioral learning theory. All shared an emphasis on observable, measurable behavior and the importance of reinforcement in the strengthening of desired behaviors. From this perspective, teachers need to break tasks, skills, and knowledge into smaller components in order to teach and reinforce performance of component behaviors. Repetition or practice of these component skills is a key feature of most of the models drawing on behavioral theory. In many ways, the learner emerges as rather passive, reacting to the environment in ways that respond to the reinforcement received.

FIELD-BASED ACTIVITY 5.5

As you observe in classrooms, find examples of teachers using the two different approaches to learning. Do some classrooms seem more "behavioral" in their approach? Are others more "cognitive"? What makes you think so? Do some mix the two approaches? How do they do this?

Behaviorists see knowledge as learned patterns of associations and define learning as acquiring new associations. Applications derived from this theory will be particularly helpful in determining basic classroom management procedures, teaching basic skills and knowledge, and teaching psychomotor skills. The teacher's role consists of arranging the environment so that students make the desired associations. Since motivation depends on external reinforcement for behavior, extrinsic rewards such as food, money, and grades are important.

Cognitive learning theories view the learning process from a very different perspective (see e.g., Phye & Andre, 1986). They focus on covert activities of the mind rather than on overt behaviors. The learner actively tries to understand what's going on in the environment rather than passively responding to associations between stimuli and responses. Cognitivists define knowledge as organized sets of mental structures and procedures and learning as the change in these mental structures brought about through mental reasoning. Students do not merely receive information—they construct knowledge by incorporating new information into existing knowledge. This may require them merely to add on to existing knowledge or to change either the existing or the new knowledge in some way. (This may sound familiar to those of you who have studied child development. Piaget's conceptions of assimilation and accommodation describe these processes.) When students alter incoming information so that it will fit with what they already know, misconceptions often occur. Applications from this theory emphasize the active role of the learner in exploring the environment and tend to focus on learning of complex skills and knowledge. The role of the teacher consists of providing students with opportunities to explore their environment and facilitating this discovery. Since motivation is related to the need for learners to make sense of their world, intrinsic rewards connected with successful problem solving, accounting for phenomena that are contrary to expectations, and accomplishment of tasks are important in this theory. The experiment with the ice cubes and the liquids described in the vignette about Mr. Garcia's science class should be intrinsically motivating to students since they observe a puzzling situation that they cannot initially explain.

Traditional Cognitive Theory

While traditional cognitive learning theory has often been associated with discovery learning, discovery is not a requisite element of applications of this approach. The issue is how to make learning meaningful. Two cognitivists who have had considerable influence on elementary and secondary classrooms disagree about how meaningful learning occurs, but they concur that the emphasis should be on meaningful understanding of the substance of material rather than verbatim recall. They both accentuate the importance of seeing relationships among ideas, learning generalizable concepts and principles, and organizing information both in written and oral text as well as in the mind of the learner. However, Jerome Bruner advocates student discovery of concepts and principles through experiences in which the student observes specific instances of the concept or principle (Bruner, 1966). In other words, he suggests that students engage in more meaningful learning when it is accomplished inductively. The vignette describing the way that Mr. Garcia "teaches" density to his science students is an example of discovery learning in which students inductively discover scientific principles through exploration of specific instances.

David Ausubel, on the other hand, advocates presentation of information to students in a deductive manner often referred to as reception learning (Ausubel, 1968). In other words, students should be able to infer specific instances from a general principle or rule presented by a teacher during lectures or text. The key to making learning meaningful lies in enabling students to connect new information with what they already know, rather than merely memorizing information. He counters Bruner's assertion about discovery learning by claiming that both discovery learning as well as reception learning can be either rote or meaningful depending on students' ability to connect the new learning to something they already know. From this perspective, rote discovery learning is just as likely to occur as rote reception learning without specific attention to meaning. For example, have you ever participated in a science lab experiment in which you were able to fill in the blanks of the lab sheet but had absolutely no idea what you were supposed to have "discovered"? Since discovery learning can require a great deal of time and effort and can often result in mere rote learning or the discovery of incorrect principles, Ausubel suggests the incorporation of advance organizers in lectures or texts to enable students to make connections during the more efficient reception learning.

Advance organizers present information at a higher level of abstraction than will be utilized later, so that subsequent subordinate concepts can be incorporated into the more general concepts presented in the organizer. The organizer

FIELD-BASED ACTIVITY 5.6

Can you think of examples from your own experience or from classroom observations that could be considered rote discovery learning or rote reception learning? Now think of examples of meaningful discovery learning and meaningful reception learning. How were the meaningful experiences different from the rote ones?

Becoming a Teacher in a Field-Based Setting

uses language that is easy for learners to understand. In the work of Ausubel, advance organizers generally took the form of shorter, more abstract readings or oral summaries prior to a lecture or reading, but other research has supported the use of concrete models, analogies, examples, organizing principles or rules, and discussion of primary themes (Mayer, 1983). Ms. Lee, in the vignette presented at the beginning of the section, provided the playground analogy as an advance organizer for the less familiar concepts and principles to be introduced in her international trade lecture. Graphic organizers, such as Venn diagrams or webbing, may achieve the same objectives.

Cognitive Information Processing Theory

One of the most useful approaches to learning is also one of the most recent. Based on cognitive theory but with several elements compatible with behavioral theory (including an attempt to make covert processes overt so they can be observed and measured), cognitive information processing (CIP) theory uses the computer as its model for how humans process information. Theorists from this perspective (there are actually various theories, but for the sake of simplicity, they will be treated in this section as one) are interested in how humans acquire, store, and retrieve information. Examination of mental structures and processes have implications for the design of effective instruction and may help us better understand instructional failures as well.

Early theory characterized the human mind as a multistore model that was selective in the type of information acquired and stored (Klatzky, 1980). Although this theory has been replaced with other, more current theories, the implications for instruction remain similar. Data from our environment enters our sensory register (SR) through our various senses. However, due to the sheer volume of environmental data, we understandably must screen and reduce these data. Teachers can help ensure that students attend to desired information by providing visual and verbal cues that some information is more important than other. Cues such as "Listen carefully to the following because . . ." or underlining or highlighting important information on overheads or on the board help focus attention. Discrepant events also attract our attention since we tend to try to make sense of our world. Mr. Garcia's ice cube experiment presented at the beginning of this section would tend to direct student attention to the behavior of the ice cube in liquids since the ice behaves in a manner inconsistent with our typical experience with ice in water.

Despite their utility, external cues are not sufficient to focus attention. What we attend to in the environment is influenced by our previous experiences as well as by the context of the situation. The tendency for humans to try to make new information meaningful may result in different perceptions of the same environmental stimuli by different people or revisions of what they hear or see in order to make the information more compatible with what they already know. For example, I observed a group of kindergarten students learning the national "Pledge of Allegiance to the Flag" in a Houston, Texas, classroom. The teacher recited the pledge slowly, phrase by phrase, emphasizing key words. The young students immediately repeated what she said. When they came to the part that says "with liberty and justice for all," one young girl loudly repeated "with liberty and Joske's for all." At that time, Joske's was a large department store in Houston near the elementary school that the students attended. While justice was not a familiar term, the idea that everyone should have a Joske's seemed perfectly reasonable to this little girl and that is what she thought she heard!

The implication of this tendency to perceive information in a personally meaningful way is that we cannot assume that each student perceives messages, information, or experiences in the same way. Knowing our students' backgrounds and previous experiences in an area, consciously creating a context that will elicit related experiences or information, and continually checking student perceptions will help students learn and perhaps prevent development of misconceptions. However, directing students' attention to important information and determining whether their perceptions of information are consistent with the teacher's intent reflect implications for only a part of the process.

FIELD BASED ACTIVITY 5.7

Teachers call attention to important information and focus student attention in many ways. The following categories provide a framework for thinking about strategies that focus attention. As you visit classrooms, look for examples of the ways teachers focus attention, and list as many of these as you can under the category headings. Which ones seem to be most effective?

Verbal statements

Visual displays

Demonstrations

Unusual or puzzling events

Thought-provoking questions

Emphasis—verbal or visual

Use of student names

Becoming a Teacher in a Field-Based Setting

Data selected for attention in the SR are transferred to short-term memory (STM), also referred to as working memory or consciousness. This structure is the site of conscious thought and processing of data. STM has a limited capacity of seven plus or minus two "chunks" of information (Miller, 1956) that will be lost within thirty seconds unless they are rehearsed (repeated over and over as we might do when we have looked up a telephone number and need to remember it long enough to get to a phone and dial it) or transferred into long-term memory (LTM) for later retrieval. Long-term memory, on the other hand, has, for all practical purposes, an unlimited storage capacity. One of the teachers' goals, then, is to enable students to retain important information in STM long enough to be able to process and transfer it to LTM. To do this, the teacher must facilitate student attention so they focus on appropriate information in their environment, provide information in a way that does not overload the capacity of STM, and facilitate student acquisition of strategies that aid in processing information for storage.

Understanding how to help students overcome some of the limitations of STM related to the amount of information that can be processed is important for teachers. A chunk of information refers to a meaningful piece of information. For example, the numbers 1, 4, 9, and 2, considered separately, would constitute four chunks of information. However, considering them together as a date that has meaning to us, such as 1492, would constitute only one chunk of information. Therefore, we can improve the capacity of our working memory by organizing smaller pieces of information into meaningful chunks.

Students who do not possess strategies for organizing information in meaningful ways or for making connections between new and existing information can be taught to do so with a resulting increase in memory capacity and problem solving (Pressley et al., 1989). Teachers can model strategy use for students as well as teach strategies explicitly to students. Knowledge about students' existing strategies and the strategies most successful for a given task enable teachers to integrate strategy instruction into specific content areas. Figure 5.3 provides a list of the kinds of strategies students may use to facilitate learning and problem solving (Knight & Boudah, 1997).

While lack of strategies may negatively impact student learning, another reason we may not achieve the learning results we intend in the classroom relates to the way we present information. Due to the limitations of STM, students may not be able to handle the amount of information we present at one time. For example, consider the following dilemma and try to explain it in terms of information processing theory.

A math teacher complains: "I stood there for fifteen minutes and explained the procedure for dividing fractions until my throat hurt from talking! I know fractions are hard for fifth-graders—and it took a long time for me to describe the process—but this morning they came in and it was if they hadn't even been there—or had only been there for part of the time! They just have no initiative! I just don't get it—what do I have to do to get them to pay attention?"

This math teacher was frustrated because she thought the students were not listening. In reality, she may have overloaded their working memory and caused a STM bottleneck that prevented them from being able to retain the information long enough to transfer it to LTM. The students also may not have had strategies to organize this incoming information, and there is no clue that the teacher helped them by providing the material in an organized fashion or in a way consistent with STM capacity.

Another way of overcoming limitations of STM can be achieved by making some of the operations that are typically carried out in STM automatic or externally supported so they do not take up limited processing space. For example, students working on math word problems may not have enough processing capability for understanding the problem and for determining and implementing appropriate algorithms or strategies to solve the problem if they also must perform certain computations (e.g., addition, subtraction, multiplication) simultaneously. If computation is automatic, as in retrieval of products of the multiplication of two numbers, space becomes available for other processes. For students who have not yet mastered these basic skills, external supports such as calculators or computers may free up processing capability so that higher-order tasks like solving word problems can be accomplished concurrent with acquisition of basic skills.

FIELD-BASED ACTIVITY 5.8

Practice or drill to facilitate memorization or automatization of certain skills is important in both behavioral theory and CIP theory. However, the reasons for memorization and the emphasis on memorizing are quite different and may make a marked difference in the overall curriculum and instruction in classes based on behavioral approaches, and those based on cognitive approaches, despite the presence of drill and practice in both. What reason would behaviorists give for drill and practice? What reason would CIP advocates give? How would these be different when implemented in classrooms? Ask a classroom teacher who uses drill and practice why she uses it. Does her explanation sound more behavioral or cognitive?

Figure 5.3
Sample Learning Strategies

Reading Comprehension

>Looking up unknown words in the dictionary/glossary
>Guessing at the meaning of unknown words by examining the context of the sentence
>Stopping and rereading when a passage is difficult to understand
>Asking yourself questions about the passage
>Predicting what will come next in a passage
>Summarizing passages/portions of text when reading for extended periods of time

Main Idea

>Searching for and identifying the main idea of a lecture or passage
>Determining what is the main idea of a passage or assignment

Mathematical/Science Problem Solving

>Defining the problem (clear idea of the concepts involved)
>Selecting important information in the problem
>Mentally representing the problem (draw a diagram)
>Applying appropriate heuristics
>>Work backwards
>>Work forwards
>>Means-ends analysis
>>Solving a simpler problem within the problem
>>Relating to a similar problem
>>Trial and error
>Applying appropriate algorithms

Knowledge Acquisition

>Mentally linking new material to previously learned material
>Using visualization techniques to help remember new material
>Using mnemonic devices
>Summarizing information mentally to self
>Teaching information to someone else
>Keeping up with reading and assignments so that new information is gained gradually
>Asking questions during class

Attention/Concentration

>Studying in an area that is free of external distractions
>Clearing the desk of unneeded items while working or studying
>Refocusing when your mind "drifts" during a lecture or while studying/reading
>Maintaining your focus while completing a task

continued on following page

continued from previous page

Motivation

> Reminding yourself of the importance of completing a task
> Looking for something interesting in assignments/tasks
> Rewarding yourself when successfully completing a task

Study Skills

> Having a designated place in which to study
> Taking notes during a lecture
> Reviewing notes as soon as possible after a lecture
> Using underlining, note-taking, highlighting, outlining, concept mapping
>   during studying/reading
> Skimming over material or readings before a lecture is given

Time Management

> Beginning an assignment soon after it is assigned
> Keeping a systematic record of tasks that need to be completed
> Being aware of which tasks need to be completed first
> Being aware of how long tasks will take to complete

Test-Taking

> Brainstorming possible questions that might appear on a test
> Underlining key words in a test question
> Crossing out possible incorrect answers to a multiple choice question
> Marking difficult items and returning to them after attempting other
>   items

Source: Knight, S., & Boudah, D. (1998). *Teacher research training manual.* College Station, Texas A&M University.

The manner in which information is transferred, or encoded, into LTM is important since it will impact how we retrieve it. The more connections that exist among pieces of information, the more likely we will be successful in retrieving what we need. Encoding is the process of forming internal mental representations, or schema, by making connections in LTM between new information and existing information. As described earlier, meaningfulness is one of the characteristics of learning considered desirable by cognitive learning theorists. Meaningfulness, from an information processing perspective, refers to the number of connections between ideas in LTM. Therefore, increasing connections among ideas or pieces of information serves two purposes—we have a more complex, or meaningful, representation of information, and we are more likely to be able to retrieve relevant information when we need it because we have increased the number of means of access.

The information and arrangement of information within a schema may be differently arranged depending on the learners' prior experiences. Culture and language histories, unique environmental contexts and experiences, interactions with various adults, and individual abilities are some of the many influences on schema. Humans construct knowledge in ways that are uniquely theirs. Although students in classrooms may be taught the same basic concepts, all children will not learn exactly the same thing, in the same sequence, or in the same way.

A very simple interaction can illustrate how a young child becomes an active participant in learning and predicts, confirms, or integrates new information. A young child looks out the window and sees something flying through the sky. Using prior knowledge already available in established schema, the child points to the airplane and predicts by saying "bird, bird!" The mother standing close by provides a reaction to the prediction by saying, "It looks like a bird doesn't it, but hear the noise, that is an airplane." The child is unable to confirm the original prediction but has modified his or her schema to include flying objects that are not birds but that are noisy and called airplanes. The existing schema is modified and a new category of flying objects is added.

Applying Cognitive Theory in the Classroom

Given the manner in which we process information, the teacher's goal in the classroom is to facilitate the construction of meaningful representations by arranging instruction so that students make appropriate connections and increase the number of connections between old and new information. To do this, we need to ensure that students actively process information rather than merely memorize material. The notion of active student involvement in processing information differentiates behavioral from cognitive approaches. While few behaviorists would deny the need for active engagement in academic tasks (see e.g., Brophy & Good, 1986), the nature of that engagement is different from a CIP perspective and may not always be visible to external observers. To actively engage students mentally, the teacher can employ strategies that prevent mere

FIELD-BASED ACTIVITY 5.9

Listed in this section are several ways that teachers can facilitate active student involvement in creating meaningful connections rather than rote memorization (i.e., questions, paraphrasing, problem solving, writing, hands-on activities). Choose one of the categories and ask a teacher for some specific examples of this category used in the classroom. Ask about advantages and disadvantages of using the particular examples.

rote association or memorization of information: Asking questions or having students ask questions that cue students to think about connections or to analyze examples or applications, asking students to paraphrase content, giving them opportunities for problem solving, having students write about what they're learning, and engaging them in hands-on activities as often as possible are ways to initiate active involvement and discourage rote memorization.

In addition to providing opportunities for active mental processing of content, teachers can also use and teach students to use strategies for organizing information in ways that expose possible connections between existing pieces of information and between prior and new knowledge. Strategies for organizing information into patterns or categories can be used by teachers to present information in a way that makes connections clear and by students to make sense of material from lectures or text. For example, providing graphic organizers that show relationships among concepts, such as concept maps, flow charts, graphs, diagrams, and tables, may help students see connections that might otherwise not be seen. Having them use graphic organizers helps them discover patterns and relationships.

The vignette depicting Mr. James's class at the beginning of the section on cognitive theory provides a concrete example of several teaching strategies compatible with cognitive approaches. First, the teacher actively involves students in using a chart to discover patterns and relationships. While he provides some initial structure, students are responsible for seeking information, rather than passively receiving it. Since Mr. James gives students the initial structure for the categories, he reduces the difficulty of the organizing task that their age and prior knowledge might have made too difficult. The partial assistance he provides, which will be gradually removed or reduced as students gain competency in the use of graphic organizers, is referred to as scaffolding. Just as scaffolds are used to support the erection of a building and then removed as sections of the building are completed, assistance provided to students can be reduced when no longer needed. In addition to providing scaffolding, the teacher systematically addresses both the content of the activity and the process used to organize information in the following discussion. Engaging students in a discussion about how the categories of the chart might be revised to better fit the information they collected will encourage them to explore and develop their own organizational strategies.

While actively engaging students in processing information and using and teaching organizational strategies may facilitate meaningful connections, other teaching strategies may also be necessary to consciously increase the number of connections within existing knowledge frameworks and between new and old knowledge. Teachers may need to help students make connections by explicitly pointing out differences and similarities. For example, a second-grade teacher may need to show a series of examples of problems that require subtraction without regrouping and a series of problems that show subtraction with regrouping and make the differences explicit. Teachers can also use and have students use analogies that show the similarities in dissimilar objects or ideas. Strategies to create meaning where none exists initially for the student may also be necessary at times. The use of verbal mnemonics (using an acronym such as HOMES to remember the Great Lakes) or imagery (using a method that associates words or ideas with familiar places that are easily recalled) can aid both encoding and later retrieval of information that students want to remember.

Perhaps one of the most important tasks of the teacher from an information processing perspective is to provide students with the means to improve their own learning. Metacognition is the term used to refer to conscious awareness of the way in which we process information, our effectiveness in doing so, and the-means for improving effectiveness when needed. As with strategy use, teachers can directly impact students' metacognitive abilities. "Thinking out loud" for students while demonstrating procedures or solving problems, including modeling of difficulties encountered while doing so, provides students with a model for strategy use as well as diagnosis and repair of errors in thinking. Having students "think out loud" while they are performing tasks or solving problems, either with you or with a peer, makes thinking processes public and available for discussion. Often you or the students themselves will become aware of the effectiveness of specific strategies as they are engaged in thinking aloud. Asking students to explain how they arrived at an answer or if they can provide an alternate way of arriving at a similar or different conclusion or answer emphasizes the importance of the process used to arrive at answers and provides additional models of thinking. Metacognitive awareness provides a valuable first step in enabling students to become independent learners in an era in which the sheer volume of information available makes efficient and effective information processing a priority for our schools.

In summary, cognitive theory has replaced behavioral approaches in the past decade as the dominant theory underlying the development and implementation of new instructional models and strategies. Educators have found both traditional and information processing cognitive approaches particularly useful in providing students with opportunities to acquire meaningful knowledge and to develop higher-order skills such as problem solving and reading comprehension. In addition, information processing theory has focused attention on the importance of understanding students' prior knowledge, the strategies they use to process information, and the way they approach and solve complex problems. Information processing theory has also emphasized the importance of "thinking about our own thinking" and provided the tools to make our own as well as our students' intellectual processes more visible and more effective.

Learning as Constructivism

A third approach to learning theory that holds promise for classroom instruction, but that does not yet have the strong research base that the other two theories offer, focuses on the role of social interaction in learning. Compatible with cognitive approaches that emphasize the active, constructive nature of learning and development of meaningful connections, social constructionist approaches focus on the role of peers and adults in construction of knowledge. This theory suggests that cognitive abilities are acquired through interactions with others, particularly through assistance provided by others that enable us to accomplish tasks that we may not be able to do on our own. As the learner actively transacts, interprets, and interacts with the environment and with other people (Strickland, 1995), understandings and knowledge that reflect the learner's background begin to guide the learning process. A great deal of learning occurs in social contexts, and the learners' relationships with others serve a vital function in communication. How people interact, what comments they provide, and how they view the world become part of learning. The following vignette provides a preservice teacher's view of one classroom that takes a constructive approach to learning and instruction.

The work of Vygotsky (1962, 1978) has been particularly influential in the development of this theory. From this perspective, students learn best when provided with tasks that are within their zone of proximal development. This zone encompasses behaviors that the student cannot yet perform alone but can accomplish given assistance. Peers, teachers, or other adults who are more competent provide prompts and assistance as needed in the course of interacting toward accomplishment of a meaningful task. This concept is similar to the notion of scaffolding discussed earlier in relation to cognitive information processing theory.

Apprenticeship models best reflect the type of instruction consistent with a Vygotskian approach to learning. Apprenticeships have long been common means of learning and acquiring skills in medical schools, doctoral institutions preparing future professors, and trades such as carpentry or tailoring. Students learn by interacting and working with those skilled in the profession or trade, and they learn in an authentic context, such as a hospital or factory, as opposed

VOICE OF A PRESERVICE TEACHER

The classroom looked as though some catastrophe had occurred and everyone had made a mad dash for the exit—collecting and dropping valuable and invaluable items along the way. The desks were in disarray. I couldn't quite determine whether they were arranged or disarranged that way. No desktop was visible. Books stacked on books, stacked on paper, game pieces and other indescribable objects covered each desk as well as much of the floor. Five birds filled the air with song and the splats of birdseed dropping to the floor. A ship's sail, made from a bedsheet hung from the ceiling, a wooden plank stretched from one desk to another, and a wicker basket lid resting on a desk looked as though it might be used for a helm. What a mess, I thought to myself. How could children possibly learn among all of this?

And then the children came in, filling the room with third-grade talk. Mostly, I heard, "Mr. Landmann, Mr. Landmann" as they asked question after question. The class began with the activity of rewriting the script of The Tempest. Each child had been assigned a character who they were going to portray in a video filming of the play at a later date. Children simply began calling out their invented script lines and asking questions, such as, "Will the audience know what a sprite is?" Then someone said, "Ariel should say, 'Father, don't get so overheated.'" I was surprised at their maturity, cooperation, and wonderful ideas. They conducted themselves much like a team of writers might behave working on a movie script or Broadway play. Mr. Landmann's position was that of coordinator and editor, reminding the students of time restraints and prop limitations. Again, I was dumbfounded and very impressed.

Two words best describe the reasons for successful learning—autonomy and interaction. The children were involved. They—not the teacher—were the creators of almost every activity that took place. Mr. Landmann had only to initiate and then the students took over the responsibility to make it work.

I wonder if I'll be a teacher like Mr. Landmann. One who is open to all kinds of possibilities for teaching and learning. One who raises expectations and limits for teaching and learning and who provides opportunities for children to excel beyond what the curriculum expects of them. I hope to teach lessons that require students to discuss and interact with each other so that talking and listening is not considered disruptive chatter, but reflective thinking.

to a simulation of the context. While this may not be possible to a great extent in elementary or secondary schools, the challenge becomes to create an environment as similar to the real-world as possible so that tasks are tied to real-world situations.

World Wide Web Site: You may learn more about Vygotsky and metacognition at: http://www.massey.ac.nz/~i75202/lect18/lect18.htm
http://www.oise.utoronto.ca/~ggay/metacogn.htm

The work of several theorists who have studied the elements of successful apprenticeships (Collins, Brown, & Newman, 1989; Rogoff, 1990) may facilitate transfer of the apprenticeship model to school settings. Students need to have opportunities to observe skilled peers and adults as they are modeling the skill—in other words, as they are engaged in the skill or learning to be acquired. Students need to perceive that the mentor's engagement in the task is actually connected to real-world settings rather than to artificial tasks performed only in schools and classrooms. Beyond mere observation, more skilled adults or peers need to provide coaching in the form of direct instruction and feedback in the skill or learning. In conjunction with coaching, they need opportunities to practice and to receive assistance as they practice commensurate with their skill level at the time. Earlier, we labeled this activity as scaffolding, but Rogoff refers to it as *guided participation* and stresses the importance of the role of the skilled mentor in assessing the demands of the task in relation to the skills of the apprentice and in structuring tasks so that apprentices are constantly increasing their skill level. Mentors encourage apprentices to reflect on their performance in comparison with experts and peers and may require apprentices to articulate what they are doing as a means of testing their knowledge. However, this practice should not be limited to mere imitation, but should provide opportunities for apprentices to explore new ways of approaching and accomplishing tasks.

Putting It All Together: Using Behavioral, Cognitive, and Constructivist Theories

The three theories discussed in this section define learning from three very different perspectives, and the skilled classroom teacher will find value in the use of all three, depending on the needs of the students in the classroom and the kind of learning outcomes desired. Behavioral theory provides ways to manage classroom behaviors and to teach basic intellectual and motor skills. Instructional strategies based on this theory have been particularly helpful with younger students, students with learning or behavioral disorders, and students of low ability. Cognitive theory suggests ways of promoting student acquisition of dispositions and skills associated with complex tasks or tasks that have multiple solution paths or right answers. In addition, information processing theory enables us to understand and assess students' cognitive processing so that we can encourage more effective processes and ultimately transfer control of the learning process to the student. Finally, constructivist theory suggests ways we can take advantage of the social nature of the classroom and provide meaningful experiences for students that may be more likely to transfer to the world outside of the classroom.

PORTFOLIO REFLECTIONS AND EXHIBITS

Throughout this chapter, you completed a series of field-based activities. The activities may serve as the basis for a portfolio representation, you may develop your own exhibit, or you may complete one of the suggested portfolio activities listed below.

Suggested Exhibit 5

1. Use the Interaction Seating Chart Inventory in Figure 5.2 while observing in a classroom. Analyze your findings using the questions provided below. Show the teacher your data and ask him or her to comment on it. How were your analyses similar and different? Would you revise your interpretation in any way after talking with the teacher? If this were your class, what would you do based on the data obtained? Include your data and a summary of your analysis with the teacher's comments in your portfolio.

2. Discuss problems of classroom management or motivation with one of the teachers in your school. Together, select a target behavior of a student (or students) that needs changing. Define the behaviors clearly. Choose a period of time during which the behavior is likely to occur and keep a baseline record of the behavior. In other words, make a note each time the behavior occurs during that time period. Share your data with the teacher and discuss possible cues or reinforcements that contribute to the behavior. Include your data, a summary of your interpretation of it, and possible ways to extinguish the behavior and/or strengthen more positive student behaviors in your portfolio.

3. Conduct a think-aloud interview with a student to determine what strategies the student is using to approach and solve complex tasks. Choose a task requiring higher-level thinking typical of the content area and age group of the student you plan to interview (i.e., math word problem, science experiment, summary of a reading). Using the protocol suggested in Figure 5.4, interview the student, transcribe the tape of the interview, and analyze the kinds of strategies the student uses in relation to his or her success on the task provided. Figure 5.4 may help you identify some of the strategies used.

Figure 5.4
Think-Aloud Protocol

Phase I. General Instructions

I'm going to ask you to solve some problems about (social studies, science, reading, math). You can solve these problems any way you like. In fact, I'm really not even interested in whether you get the right answers. But I am interested in what you do when you read passages, answer questions, or solve the problems—the strategies you use. For this reason, I'm going to ask you to talk aloud as much as you can while you work. I'm going to turn on the tape recorder when you begin in order to help me remember what you are saying (optional). OK?

You won't have to do anything special. Just work like you normally would. Some students tell me that they "mumble to themselves" when they're reading or solving problems. If that's what *you* do, then all you'll have to do today is mumble a little louder. In any case, try to talk constantly when you're not reading silently. Say what you're thinking and doing even if it doesn't make sense.

Phase II. Problem Solution and Student "Think-Aloud"

Read the instructions to the student and ask him/her to begin. Turn on tape recorder (optional). Say as little as possible, being careful to use only neutral, nondirective phrases. Use *only* the following prompts:

Can you say what you're thinking?
That's very clear.
Please tell me what you are writing.
Mmm.
OK.
I see.

Continue this until the student has answered the questions following the passage.

Phase III. Debriefing

Even if the student talked continually, there may be many unclear points in the protocol. Ask the following clarifying questions after the student has finished:

Could you summarize for me how you got your answer?
Can you say some more about it?
Can you explain to me what you were thinking when you (asked yourself that question, got that picture in your mind, made those notes, etc.)?
Is there anything else you can think of?

Source: Knight, S. & Boudah, D. (1998). *Teacher research training manual*. College Station, Texas A&M University.

Related Readings

Aaronsohn, E. (1996). *Going against the grain: Supporting the student-centered teacher.* Thousand Oaks, CA: Sage.

   This book tells the story of a new teacher who tries to use new theories in her classroom. It describes her efforts to overcome the resistance from other teachers in her new school and she learns how to handle her own uncertainties about her nontraditional curriculum.

Brooks, J. G. (1993). *The case for constructivist classrooms.* Alexandria, VA: American Association of Curriculum Development.

   This book describes activities and teaching principles in which a constructivist theory is applied to classroom contexts. Some of this book focuses on research and inquiry, but there are some good examples of how the constructivist learning theory will translate to teacher practice.

References

Alexander, P. A., & Knight, S. L. (1993). Dimensions of the interplay between teaching and learning. *The Educational Forum, 57*(3), 232–245.

Ausubel, D. P. (1968). *Educational psychology: A cognitive view.* New York: Holt, Rinehart & Winston.

Bandura, A. (1982). Self-efficacy mechanism in human agency. *American Psychologists, 37,* 122–148.

Brophy, J. E., & Good, T. L. (1986). Teacher behavior and student achievement. In M. C. Wittrock (Ed.), *Handbook of research on teaching* (3rd ed., pp. 328–375). New York: Macmillan.

Bruner, J. (1966). *Toward a theory of instruction.* Cambridge, MA: Harvard University Press.

Collins, A., Brown, J., & Newman, S. (1989). Cognitive apprenticeship: Teaching the craft of reading, writing, and mathematics. In L. Resnick (Ed.), *Knowing, learning, and instruction: Essays in honor of Robert Glaser* (pp. 453–494). Hillsdale, NJ: Erlbaum.

Gage, N. (1984). *Hard gains in the soft sciences: The case of pedagogy.* Bloomington, IN: Phi Delta Kappa.

Good, T., & Brophy, J. (1997). *Looking in classrooms* (7th ed.). New York: Longman.

Klatzky, R. L. (1980). *Human memory: Structures and processes* (2nd ed.). San Francisco: W. H. Freeman.

Knight S. (1990). The effort of cognitive strategy instruction on elementary students' reading outcomes. In S. McCormick & J. Zuttell (Eds.), *National reading conference yearbook* (vol. 38, pp. 241–251). Chicago: National Reading Conference.

Knight, S., & Boudah, D. (1997). *Participatory research and development for the improvement of teaching and learning.* Paper presented at the annual meeting of the Southwest Educational Research Association, Austin, TX.

Knight, S., & Boudah, D. (1998). *Teacher research training manual.* College Station, Texas A&M University.

Knight, S., Waxman, H. C., & Pedrone, R. N. (1989). Examining the relationship between classroom instruction and elementary students' cognitive strategies in social studies. *Journal of Educational Research, 82*(5), 270–276.

Mayer, R. E. (1983). *Thinking, problem solving, and cognition.* San Francisco: W. H. Freeman.

Miller, G. A. (1956). The magical number seven, plus or minus two: Some limits on our capacity for processing information. *Psychological Review, 63,* 81–97.

Palincsar, A. S., & Brown, A. L. (1984). Reciprocal teaching of comprehension-fostering and monitoring activities. *Cognition and Instruction, 1,* 117–175.

Phye, G. D., & Andre, T. (1986). *Cognitive classroom learning: Understanding, thinking and problem solving.* San Diego: Academic Press.

Premack, D. (1965). Reinforcement theory. In D. Levine (Ed.), *Nebraska symposium on motivation* (Vol. 13). Lincoln: University of Nebraska Press.

Pressley, M., Johnson, C., Symons, S., McGoldrick, J., & Kurita, J. (1989). Strategies that improve children's memory and comprehension of text. *Elementary School Journal, 90*(1), 3–32.

Rogoff, B. (1990). *Apprenticeship in thinking: Cognitive development in social context.* New York: Oxford University Press.

Skinner, B. F. (1954). Science of learning art of teaching. *Harvard Educational Review, 24,* 86–97.

Skinner, B. F. (1958). Teaching machine. *Science, 128,* 969–977.

Skinner, B. F. (1963). *Science and human behavior.* New York: Macmillan.

Skinner. B. F. (1968). *Technology of teaching.* New York: Appleton Century Cross.

Skinner, B. F. (1969). *Contingencies of reinforcement: A theoretical analysis.* New York: Appleton Century Cross.

Stallings, J. A. (1997). *Learning to teach in inner city schools training manual.* College Station: Texas A&M University, College of Education.

Strickland, K. (1995). *Literacy not labels: Celebrating students' strengths through whole language.* Portsmouth, NH: Boyton/Cook.

Thorndike, E. L. (1913). *Educational psychology: The original nature of man* (Vol. 1). New York: Teachers College Press.

Vygotsky, L. (1962). *Thought and language.* Cambridge, MA: MIT.

Vygotsky, L. (1978). *Mind and society.* Cambridge, MA: Harvard University.

Wang, M., Haertel, G., & Walberg, H. (1993). Toward a knowledge base for school learning. *Review of Educational Research, 63*(3), 249–294.

6
Establishing a Successful Classroom Environment

In this chapter

- Establishing a Personal Management Style
- Factors Influencing Classroom Procedures
- Developing Effective Classrooms
- Organizing Students, Time, and Materials
- Discipline

I took Steven aside during a calm interval and told him I was very unhappy about all the hitting he was doing. I thought he would stop it because there are so many things he does well. Now, however, when he hurts someone, he will have to sit alone, away from the class, in a "time-out" chair, and do nothing for ten minutes. I showed him the chair, and he nodded.

He wandered around the room, looking at the chair. I became involved in writing down a story Jan was dictating. Suddenly Steven pushed Jimmy down and began kicking him. I jumped up, grabbed Steven, and dragged him to the chair. He would not come by himself and he would not remain seated. He screamed furiously. I said nothing, but held on to both his arms and sat next to him. He struggled and tried to kick me. I said, "Steven, don't even think of kicking me. I can't ever let *you do that. I have to make you sit here because you won't do it by yourself. Every time you hurt someone you must sit here."*

I told the children, over his screaming, that Steven needed me to sit here with him. They must have understood that I was upset and Steven was upset, and we were trying to work something out. They stayed away from us and their play was subdued. They were upset too.

This was a Monday. We did this twice on Monday, and twice on Tuesday. On Wednesday, Steven sat on the time-out chair by himself with no complaint. After that, he stopped hitting children. I had won because of superior strength and size. I was not sure what was won and what was lost.

—Vivian Gussin Paley, *White Teacher*

Establishing effective learning environments is a demanding task. The most successful teachers are recognized for their ability to fashion environments where all learners have the potential to succeed. To have everyone benefit from educational opportunities, competent teachers must orchestrate many factors and make multiple decisions. In addition to dealing with twenty or thirty students for only one teacher, instruction involves such factors as managing materials, scheduling activities, moving from activity to activity, and managing behavior. Management approaches and decisions reflect beliefs about learning, student development, and the roles of teachers and students. Managing classrooms is an extremely complex task that requires a great deal of effort, thought, and reflection on the part of the teacher.

Organizing and managing classrooms is a major concern of both beginning and experienced teachers. Many strategies have proven successful with classroom organization and management, and the knowledge in this area is expanding. Nevertheless, classroom management also involves a personal approach that reflects the personality of the teacher and the students who are in the classroom. While some techniques will emerge from experience, you can learn a great deal by observing veteran teachers who maintain effective and well-ordered classrooms, acknowledging your own beliefs about power and control, participating in field experiences that provide you opportunities to plan and manage instruction, and reflecting about your perceptions and experiences.

Becoming a Teacher in a Field-Based Setting

Effective teachers coordinate and balance a complex set of learning processes, interpersonal relationships, individual differences, and instructional strategies to establish a successful learning environment for their students.

This chapter discusses several aspects of classroom environment, organization, and instructional planning and specifically answers the following questions:

- What factors must be considered when establishing effective learning environments?

- What factors contribute to a teacher's personal view of effective learning environments?

- How does a teacher encourage student involvement and positive behavior?

- What are ways that students can be grouped for maximum instructional effectiveness?

- What instructional arrangements, approaches, and strategies can contribute to effective learning environments?

Careful planning encourages and motivates students and helps avoid behavior and discipline problems. Planning and organization should result in predictable classroom procedures, a comfortable environment, and realistic teacher expectations. Teachers who plan and organize daily routines and schedules based on the needs of their students, the nature of the learning process, and the desire to provide motivating instructional strategies and materials are more likely to have successful classrooms.

Establishing a Personal Management Style

A teacher can select from a wide range of management styles. When you think about your own education, you may be able to remember teachers who were extremely strict and enforced rules and regulations, and teachers who were very warm, interactive, and flexible. One teacher might have encouraged a great deal of drill and memory work, whereas another teacher focused on exploration, multiple responses, and active participation in interpreting and solving problems. Some teachers avoided controversial issues, choosing to focus their students on teacher-selected topics. Other teachers included a wide range of issues, encouraged debates and ambiguity, included current topics, and capitalized on the curiosity of students. Almost all of these approaches can be successful with most students and in some situations.

Although there are many ways to describe effective classrooms, establishing healthy learning environments means that students will learn designated content, misconduct is diminished, and worthwhile academic activities occur (Brophy, 1988). Effective classrooms do not emerge by chance. Classroom environments that work require personal reflection about teachers' roles, an understanding of what works in classroom organizations, a view of the relationship between management and instructional decisions, and the ability to use multiple methods while organizing classroom components of classroom organization.

FIELD-BASED ACTIVITY 6.1

Describe the learning environments in the school setting where you are currently working. Are they structured, highly defined classrooms where teachers deliver traditional lectures and make assignments that are graded and returned? Or are they more relaxed environments in which there are discussions, small group activities, and student directed lessons? Which of these provides a more comfortable learning environment for you? Develop a list of descriptors that make you the most comfortable, keep you interested, and help you learn most effectively.

Becoming a Teacher in a Field-Based Setting

The manner in which a teacher goes about establishing a positive classroom climate is a central issue in learning to be a teacher. Although a wide variety of processes and techniques are used to set up learning situations, teachers' authority is most effective when based on respect and caring for students. Classrooms require structure and rules designed to produce situations in which all students feel safe and look forward to academic success. Care and control in the classroom can be blended. The combination of the two important elements empowers students and clarifies their roles. In addition, classroom interactions can demonstrate and teach caring, communication skills, and democratic principles (Ames, 1992). A balanced approach to classroom management includes respectful treatment and avoids producing situations in which students feel alienated and disenfranchised.

Factors Influencing Classroom Procedures

There are many factors to be considered when a teacher is setting up the classroom for instruction. Some factors are implemented by teachers and other factors exist independent of teachers' actions. Outside influences impact the establishment of a positive learning environment in numerous ways. Recognizing the various influences upon classroom environments is important, even though teachers are not always able to control or change the life situations involving their students. While Chapter 2 provides a more in-depth review of societal conditions that affect classrooms today, the following sections provide a context for considering classroom learning environments.

Home and Social Contexts

Some student behavior and attitudes can be traced to factors outside the school environment. Violence, gangs, drugs, poverty, and homelessness impact some students directly and others in more subtle ways. These factors have traditionally been associated with inner-city schools, but they are now more and more evident in small cities, rural communities, and suburbs. Students are exposed to some tough situations at younger and younger ages. Reports of gang activity at fourth grade, alcohol abuse among eleven- and twelve-year-olds, and pregnancy among young teenagers are not uncommon. There is some evidence that young peoples' attitudes and beliefs are influenced by the representation of society on television, in movies, on e-mail, and on the Internet.

Family life can impact students' school behaviors and responses. Families have changed a great deal, and students may live in situations that are different than traditional ideas of family life. Aunts, uncles, grandparents, or older brothers and sisters may be the heads of some households. Homes where children live are headed by single, divorced parents or by two parents who both work, so parents are not always present to oversee their children. Some schoolchildren leave school and let themselves into an empty, unsupervised home. Almost all families care and want the best for their children, but changing family structures have impacted the educational system. Schools are assuming more and more responsibilities for teaching lessons once taught by parents and for providing after-school care and other support systems.

Probably no other circumstance affects children and their learning as much as poverty and the resulting conditions. Nearly one-third of the nations' children are living in poverty. Not all poor children live in inner-cities or are members of minority cultures, but there are large pockets of poverty in large cities and an overrepresentation of family poverty in minority groups. Poverty inevitably affects the health and well-being of children. Children from poor families may not receive the nutrition or health care necessary to maintain good health. They come to school hungry or sick. Poverty can affect the experiences and resources that a family can provide for its members. Experiences taken for granted by middle-class parents—vacations, visiting zoos and museums, attending cultural events—may be beyond the reach of poor families. Even more dramatic is that schools located in poverty areas may not have the same access to resources as schools in the affluent areas. Poor schools won't have the textbooks, computers, or wide variety of class offerings found in schools with more adequate resources. So, in one way or another, poverty makes a great impression on the school experiences of some children.

Many students and their families overcome great odds to succeed. Stories of success usually occur with a strong community and family support system and role models that encourage students to value their school experiences. There are many students from all economic groups who do not receive the support to help them deal with many hard societal issues, and teachers are usually well aware of their plight. Students make decisions each day about their response to society, and schools can play a role in the way they respond to some issues.

Despite the difficulty educators may have in impacting societal conditions, schools do make a difference in the lives of students. For example, positive, well-managed classrooms and school environments have been connected to prevention of delinquency, teen pregnancy, and drug abuse (Dryfoos, 1990). Effective processes can enhance student self-understanding, self-evaluation, and self-control (McCaslin & Good, 1992). An effective learning environment provides

Becoming a Teacher in a Field-Based Setting

students with a sense of community and with opportunities to develop interpersonal communication and conflict management skills and to take the risks necessary for learning.

Students' Characteristics and Needs

Students' characteristics are extremely varied. They may differ in developmental levels, culture, experience, gender, language, and intellectual and physical abilities. The differences represented in the classroom offer both the joys and frustrations of teaching.

A key element in classroom management is attention to developmental issues of students. One of the first considerations in implementing classroom instructional procedures is that of age and maturity of students. Older students, for example, might be much more sensitive to issues of power and control (Glasser, 1988) and need more experiences with choice and negotiation. Younger children will need more opportunities to learn how to make good decisions. The nature and complexity of the content presentation changes as children gain more academic experiences. Most teachers focus on a particular age, primary or high school for example, study the behavior, and become experts of learning abilities of children at that age. Consideration of age differences appears to be one of the most natural factors in instructional processes.

Students' cultural and experiential backgrounds also need to be considered when developing instructional and management methods (Kuykendall, 1992). The diversity of today's classrooms requires teachers to consider multiple ways of interacting. Teachers who are aware of the diverse characteristics in their classrooms will take responsibility for how teacher behavior is interpreted and internalized by students who come from different backgrounds and have different experiences than their teachers (Dana, 1992). (See Chapter 2 for a complete discussion of student differences.)

As the year 2000 approaches, teachers will have more chances than ever before to hear many different languages in their classrooms. All children who come to school speaking languages other than English are not the same and will possess different levels of fluency and literacy. Bilingual and bicultural education is designed to meet the needs of students who do not speak English. Programs run the gamut of teaching skills needed for transition to English, maintaining support for continued growth in the native language, and providing intense study in English language. Bicultural, bilingual programs help build pride in native culture while preparing for success in the English schools and society.

There are also gender differences in the way that students respond to classroom procedures. In the 1992 report *How Schools Shortchange Girls* (AAUW),

VOICE OF A TEACHER

There has been so much written about how teachers treat girls and boys differently, and I worry that I am not conscious enough of what I do in the classroom. I try to call on everyone equally. I use girls and women as examples during my teaching. I also try to select literature that shows women in strong roles. But it's hard to do this all the time. Textbooks aren't always helpful. Media, television, and newspapers don't always provide female role models. When I make an explicit attempt to be gender conscious, I find it takes additional time to add examples, watch my own behavior, and rethink my actions. I am not sure that I am gender conscious in everything I do. It's easy to forget this concern when things are moving quickly in the classroom.

a case was made for the different learning styles and requirements of boys and girls. Some differences in classroom experiences between the sexes is caused by how teachers respond to girls and boys. Classroom contributions, the feedback the two sexes receive, the representation of sexes in content areas, and the interactions between teachers and the two genders establish and support lifelong beliefs about the capabilities of men and women (Orenstein, 1994). All of this has a great deal to do with how teachers set up and manage the classrooms where boys and girls are learning.

World Wide Web Site: You may learn more about the American Association of University Women at: http://www.aauw.org/

Specific management skills are required for students with special intellectual and physical needs, including gifted and talented students, special education students, and students with behavior disorders. With the passage of Public Law 94-142, special education students were given the right to receive public education in the least restrictive environment. Originally, the law was interpreted to

---

FIELD-BASED ACTIVITY 6.2

Go into a classroom. Look at the students. Make a list of the ways that students differ from one another in this class. Be sure to include individual (i.e., ability, motivation, physical attributes) and group differences (i.e., culture, gender). Compare this list to the previous text discussion. What are some of the ways that these differences may impact teaching and learning processes in the classroom?

Becoming a Teacher in a Field-Based Setting

provide special teachers, classrooms, and conditions for students who might have special needs. This practice isolated students from their peers, and the labeling of being "special" often reduced expectations of their performance. A more recent approach, often referred to as "inclusion," is to include special students in regular classrooms, mainstreaming them with all children, and providing additional support such as modified inclusion or special teachers to help them succeed in the classrooms with their peers. Students participate in specialized and limited environments only when their needs cannot be met in regular classrooms. This approach can put a great deal of pressure on regular classroom teachers who will need to plan and implement many types of instruction for a diversity of student characteristics, including those with handicaps or gifts.

World Wide Web Site: You may learn more about Public Law 94–142 at:
 http://www.ridgewater.mnscu.edu/EA/Special/sld001.htm

Expectations of Teachers and Learners

Researchers have recently demonstrated that the expectations related to what it means to be a teacher and a student in a particular classroom are established within the first few days of school (Fernie, Kantor, & Klein, 1990). However, classroom expectations and perceptions reflect more than the immediate interactions between students and teachers. Teachers enter the classroom with preconceived expectations, beliefs, and attitudes about classroom life (Chandler, 1992). Students, like teachers, come to the learning context with certain expectations, beliefs, and attitudes developed through messages from society and family that enhance or detract from their cognitive, physical, linguistic, and problem-solving abilities. They gain ideas of what should happen in a classroom from their brothers and sisters and from television and other media. Parents' attitudes toward education impact students' views of what should happen in classrooms. As students proceed through school, their own life experiences have taught them what they should expect from school and what teachers expectations of their own behavior and academic achievement might be. Both student and teacher expectations can influence the curriculum, the organization, and the everyday events of a classroom.

Teachers' expectations of students' achievement is an important influence on classroom behavior. Expectations affect what is taught, how it is taught, and the attitudes of both the teacher and the learners. General expectations may emerge from personal beliefs about gender, race, and other equity considerations or they can be personally directed toward one learner. What and who learns particular content can be greatly affected by socialization processes. Expectations can override teacher effectiveness as well as student abilities. When teachers hold low expectations for the learning achievement of some students, the most advanced teaching strategies are sure to be ineffective (Bartolome, 1994).

The problem of low teacher expectations for various socioeconomic, ethnic, and language minority students is pervasive. Some teacher behaviors and school practices reflect a belief that students who represent a minority group or are poor will not have the experiences, language, or support to succeed in school. Often this results in lower expectations for poor minority students. For many years there has been a discrepancy between the achievements of some minority students and white students. This can be seen in the high minority representation in low ability and remedial groups versus the white middle-class membership in gifted programs. Some prejudices, perceptions, and misunderstandings can be overcome in classrooms where activities are well planned and highly organized. Teachers can counter the problem of low expectations by providing learning environments that facilitate successful teaching of students who typically do not succeed in schools.

The most effective contexts leading to optimum student achievement are classrooms where all students feel valued, respected, and capable of succeeding despite their differences (Olsen & Mullen, 1990). Effective classroom organization is built on the understanding that children have different interests, learning styles, and abilities and will require different considerations during instructional planning. Understanding the potential differences and using that knowledge to organize instruction can improve the learning environment for all students.

The School Context

School contexts have substantial impact on classroom processes. The climate, organizational structures, decision-making procedures, and the types of professional support available will play a role in teachers' personal approaches to classroom management. Schools in which teachers work collaboratively and have developed a common vision of success will be able to offer support and establish healthy classroom contexts. An overall positive environment is established when a sense of belonging exists for all students. Some secondary schools are establishing different types of schedules to provide extended periods of time with one adult and one group of peers to help their students have time to develop healthy relationships. The quality of life within a school is an essential consideration for ongoing efforts to create healthy learning environments.

Instructional Tasks

Management procedures are most effective when tailored to instructional methods. What is being taught and how it is being taught is important when making decisions about classroom management and organization. Some information might be best delivered through direct instruction by the teachers, while other information may be learned effectively through discussion or independent reading. Using a variety of instructional tasks will assure that differences in learning preferences will be taken into account, but changes in tasks can also require differences in management techniques. When teachers move away from lecture and presentation methods and reliance on more interactive, small group discussion practices, then managing the classroom becomes more complex (McCaslin & Good, 1992). As a beginning teacher, you will need to consider various types of management methods in order to facilitate varied instructional methods such as whole language approaches or cooperative learning techniques. The use of various instructional methods will require teachers to help students be successful when working with groups, sharing ideas, debating issues, and providing peer assistance. The following chapters contain much more about designing instructional processes.

Developing Effective Classrooms

The previous sections demonstrate an overwhelming number of factors influencing classroom environment that cannot be changed or altered by schools and teachers. On the other hand, some fundamental factors related to classroom management can be fostered by teachers and can positively impact classroom environment.

Recognizing Effective Teaching Behaviors

What does a good teacher do? What behaviors do they display? There are many ways to answer that question. Classic educational research has described the behaviors of teachers who are most successful during traditional teacher-centered whole class instruction (Brophy & Evertson, 1976; Emmer, Evertson, & Anderson, 1980). Although these teacher behaviors have not been researched in more interactive, student-centered classrooms, the series of proactive behaviors associated with early research seem to make sense in most settings and can serve as general principles to guide teacher behavior (Jones, 1996). The teacher actions most associated with effective teaching include an explicit awareness of what is going on in the classroom or "withitness" (Kounim, 1970). Most good teachers know their students, understand interactions, and can usually predict behavior and responses from their students. Teachers who are "with it" know when students are not attending to instruction or when they are upset or happy, and can redirect classroom activities to take advantage of or defuse classroom attitudes. A change of pace or activity can result when a teacher maintains close contact with what is going on in the classroom.

Good teachers also plan smooth transitions between activities. They understand that procedures for moving from one activity to another should be clearly understood by students. Routines are introduced to change activities and to move from small-group to large-group instruction. Rules for transitions are clearly articulated. Students don't lose valuable time in making instructional transitions and disruptive behavior is avoided when classes are in transition.

Good teachers also find ways to hold students accountable for assignments and classroom activities. They expect assignments and activities to be completed in thoughtful and productive ways and to provide feedback when students respond or provide a product. The feedback is appropriate, and students understand how and when feedback will occur.

Each of these characteristics makes very good sense in any type of instructional setting. They have become the mainstay of expected teacher behaviors, although some educators encourage more consideration of instructional objectives and methods in defining good teacher behaviors (Jones, 1996). For example, the concept of "withitness" might change if a teacher uses a great deal of small-group work and independent work where students may find ways to deal with problem solving that is not as controlled as in traditional classrooms. Teachers may not control each aspect of problem solving and learning, and the smoothness of transitions may be interrupted when students are developing their own learning processes. A more modern approach to identifying effective teacher behaviors is to see how instructional goals guide the classroom management techniques as opposed to imposing specific teacher behaviors before the instructional outcomes are identified.

Creating Positive Interpersonal Relationships

The extent to which students will have their needs met in an educational setting will be dependent upon the relationships between teachers and students. Understanding that classroom organization and effectiveness are impacted by the beliefs and perceptions of the teachers and the learner suggests that roles and relationships of learners and teachers must be considered when planning for instruction (Green, Kantor, & Rogers, 1990). The relationships between teachers and students are dynamic and change with each new class or when a new learning strategy is introduced (Zaharlick & Green, 1991).

Teacher Student Relationships Interacting with young people is one of the major reasons individuals become teachers. The same interactions can also be the greatest source of frustration and stress to teachers. Teachers report that much of the stress associated with their work comes from managing student behavior (Jones, 1996). Experienced teachers explain that students and their behavior have changed dramatically since the 1980s, making it more difficult to plan and manage instruction. Teachers are being asked to deal with a wide range of students in their classrooms, including students with special needs—academic, social, personal, and emotional characteristics that require a great deal of attention and can cause unpredictable results during class interactions.

The quality of interactions between teachers and students impacts students as well as teachers. Since the 1960s, educators have known that positive relationships between teachers and students can improve academic behavior. Students do care about what their teachers think about them. When students believe that their teachers care and respect them, they are more positive and have higher academic achievement (Phelan, Davidson, & Cao, 1992).

Students who are more at risk of failure in school environments need more support from teachers than students who are more successful need (Wehlage et al., 1989). Those students at risk need to feel that they belong in the classroom and that their teachers care about them. Several educators have made this point regarding the relationships between teachers and minority students. Comer (1988) wrote that "no matter how good the administration, teachers, curriculum, or equipment; no matter how long the school day or year, and no matter how much homework is assigned, if students do not attach and bond to the people and program of the school, less adequate learning will take place." Most important, teachers should realize the importance of expressing a sense of optimism that all students can learn (Wehledge et al., 1989, p. 135).

In addition to teacher expectations discussed previously, the feedback of teachers to students about their work plays an important role in positive learning environments. Clear and specific feedback that is immediate, focuses on students' performance and effort, and avoids comparisons with others is most effective. This is when grades and test scores establish environments where comparisons are made and success and failure is numerically calculated. Providing feedback related to school achievement and promoting a cooperative as opposed to a competitive environment may be difficult for teachers in standardized test-driven settings.

Peer Relationships An important aspect not often discussed, but related to positive learning environments, is peer relationships. More effective classrooms are established when the students within the classroom get along and can work together. A classroom personality develops from the combination of students in the classroom. Classrooms offer an opportunity for prolonged contact with peers, and interactions serve more than an educational role in students' development. Interactions between peers in classrooms contribute to social roles, adult personality patterns, and future peer associations. Instructional strategies requiring students to accomplish tasks cooperatively and in small-group settings make positive peer relationships even more important in today's classrooms.

Some research has shown that students' achievement increases when they are accepted by their classmates, and students work together to establish norms related to how they perform and respond in the classroom (Jones, 1996). Teaching students to interact and collaborate more with each other may ultimately enhance classroom behavior, increase school achievement, contribute to positive learning environments, and develop important life skills (Jones, 1996). Attention to student relationships and developing a culture of cooperation encourages behavior skills that are valued in society and the workplace.

Enhancing On-Task Behavior

The amount of time that a student is actively engaged in learning tasks, known as on-task behavior, is related to successful learning. Consideration of the amount of time involved in learning is a classic way of looking at classroom management as well as instruction. To plan instruction that achieves the most on-task behavior, teachers must establish goals, design instruction to reach the goals, and provide immediate feedback to students during learning attempts.

FIELD-BASED ACTIVITY 6.3

Observe in the classroom setting and determine what types of behavior students display when off-task. What are they doing when not paying attention to their teacher or when they quit working on the classroom assignment? Are they reading, talking to each other, or distracted in other ways? Complete the chart in Table 6.1. Compare your findings in a class discussion and define task-oriented behavior. Are you tolerant or intolerant when students do not do what the teacher expects? What does this tell you about your view of teaching and authority?

Table 6.1

Off-Task Behaviors

Behaviors	Descriptors	Observation Notes
Chatting	Student is talking with others.	
Disruptive Behavior	Students are making noices, teasing others, roaming around the classroom.	
Personal Needs	Students are sharpening pencils, being excused to go to the bathroom, getting a drink of water.	
Uninvolved	Students obviously are not listening or taking part in classroom activities, and are daydreaming, staring.	
Waiting	Students are standing in line, raising their hands, waiting on teacher.	
Sleeping	Students have their heads on their desks, eyes closed.	
Other Behaviors		

Motivate   The ability to motivate, to engage students in learning, is a most crucial element of establishing a positive learning environment. Children are born with the motivation to learn (Wlodkowski & Jaynes, 1990). The curiosity of infants, toddlers, and preschool children who ask questions, experiment, and acquire new information on what seems like an hourly basis is a joy to watch. Too often the child's entry into formal educational practices results in a loss of the spontaneous joy of learning evident with younger children. Competition for a child's motivation, formalized approaches to learning, constant evaluation, and grading are a few of the factors that may change motivational factors related to school learning.

The motivation to learn must become a habit, a routine, and a priority in young people's lives that contributes favorably to learning in school (Wlodkowski & Jaynes, 1990). Many factors impact motivation. Culture, family, school, organizational structures, and individual personality all come to bear on the learners' motivational levels. Despite a large number of outside influences, motivation to learn can be taught and encouraged. A good teacher increases the potential for academic motivation to learn in several ways.

Provide Support for Success Students will work to accomplish learning tasks if a support system exists to help avoid frustration and confusion. Teachers support student efforts by making tasks manageable, providing models for accomplishing tasks, and being sure that students understand explanations and processes (Blumenfeld, Puro, & Mergendoller, 1992). Additional support can be provided for learning demanding material through small group collaboration and opportunities to share learning. Scaffolding, initially giving a great deal of help and facilitative encouragement and gradually requiring students to do more and more on their own, is also an important way to provide support during learning activities.

Successful teachers make sure that their students can take part in the learning activities. When introducing a particular routine or strategy, everyone should know how to participate and what is required for successful involvement. Students must often be taught some of the instructional procedures that will help them succeed in the classroom. They may not automatically know how to do what is required for academic achievement. For example, if the teacher is using a particular cooperative learning technique and students are taking on roles such as leader, timer, and question poser, then the students should be taught what is expected of each role.

Communicate High Expectations Teachers' expectations and student motivation are linked. Teachers and students must believe that success is possible, that tasks are reasonable, and that all students can do the work. Students are willing to attempt difficult tasks if it is clear that those around them believe that they can succeed. All students should be expected to do their best, and no exceptions should be made because of gender and/or culture. Developing the perspective that all students can and will achieve, no matter what their gender, ethnic, or linguistic background, is a belief fostered throughout teacher careers.

Provide for Flexibility and Variation An important factor related to motivation is having available a multitude of tasks at appropriate levels of difficulty. Students who are able to select their mode and method of learning in various situations will be more motivated to focus on their learning tasks. Nevertheless, there may be some tasks that all students must complete, and there will be times when the teacher will select the focus, but when it is appropriate for students to learn different information or in different ways, they can be given choices. If they are allowed to select from a range of tasks, then they will come closer to selecting the activities that are most motivating to them. The tasks should be challenging but at the same time realistic and should provide choices for learning in varied and different ways.

Ability grouping and other comparative and competitive approaches can have a negative impact on motivation in some circumstances. Whenever possible, teachers should minimize processes that compare students or require them to compete against each other. The practices associated with comparison and competition can send the message that not everyone is expected to succeed in the same way. On the other hand, teachers who use flexible grouping techniques based on achievement of specific skills or knowledge as opposed to grouping by ability, for example, treat their students as if they all can learn. Several types of flexible grouping arrangements are described later in this chapter.

Plan Relevant and Meaningful Activities A most important contribution to the motivation of student learning is how much they value and are interested in the material. Learning activities that allow opportunities for students to relate their ordinary life experiences to the content presented in schools and encourage them to use their real-life experiences to understand new information are meaningful to students. Learning does not occur in a vacuum. Connections to students' lives and opportunities to transfer their knowledge and strategies to new learning situations will motivate their learning.

Relevant learning activities produce the active and personal engagement that demonstrates motivation. Individual contributions, discussions, and sharing of life experiences are simple ways to make learning relevant. Focusing on topics that students find interesting, such as current events, popular culture, and media will also increase the relevancy of learning activities. Sometimes the teacher must help make connections to develop interest and relevancy. Presenting Shakespeare

---

FIELD-BASED ACTIVITY 6.4

Look back at Field-Based Activity 6.3. Rethink your responses and consider the impact of motivational factors. Does that change your attitude about on-task behavior? Or do you still think the same way? Reframe your response to Activity 6.3 and include your ideas on motivation.

---

as an analogy for a contemporary problem is an example of connecting topics to relevant issues.

Stress Cognitive Engagement Students must be encouraged to answer questions, complete assignments, and, as a result of their work, receive feedback (Blumenfeld, Puro, & Mergendoller, 1992). Cognitive engagement is encouraged when students synthesize, represent, demonstrate, and apply their knowledge in a variety of ways. Feedback requirements should be more than coming up with one right answer; they should involve manipulating the information, considering multiple answers, and sharing predictions and hypotheses.

Provide Feedback In order to motivate continued learning, students need to know when a learning component ends and be able to make some judgment about their impact of the activity on their own personal learning (Brophy, 1988; Lepper, 1983). The more learner goal-setting and self-monitoring that can be implemented, the more motivated the students will be. Students should be held accountable for learning and understanding material, not just for getting the answers correct or making good grades. The frequency and form of teacher feedback play an important part in the classroom motivational process.

The teacher is key in motivating students. In addition to using all the techniques described, teachers can do a great deal to motivate students by being an enthusiastic learner themselves. Providing a good example for motivated learning is one of the most successful techniques that teachers can use to encourage attention to learning. Students want to know what activities and abilities interest adults. Reading, for example, is very easy to model. Sharing information and personal reading can be a powerful lesson in motivation to read and learn. When teachers share their excitement about learning new information, students are intrigued and interested. When teachers believe that learning is important, motivating, and relevant, students will become increasingly self-motivated to be active learners. One way for teachers to demonstrate their enthusiasm for learning is to involve students in collaborative learning. Working and learning together is an excellent way to involve students in the learning process.

Organizing Students, Time, and Materials

Schools provide some students with a structure not present elsewhere in their lives. Other students will find that the regular routines of home life are consistent with school schedules and routines. This adherence to a certain structure does not mean that the plans and organizations of the classroom can't be responsive to children's needs. On the contrary, effective teachers are willing to accept their students desires, interests, and concerns into the daily routine. Teachers who demonstrate flexibility with daily plans and routines will better meet the needs of their students. Personal events, such as neighborhood or family emergencies or crises within their peer groups, affect student interests and attentions. Worldwide events such as wars, national disasters, and presidential elections impact the classroom. Sometimes teachers may abandon regular routines and refocus instruction to recognize relevant and current student interests. Generally, however, students should know what to expect from classroom instructional routines.

Organizing Students

There are several ways to organize a classroom full of students. When planning for instruction the teacher must consider the goals of instruction, the desired nature of interaction, and the responses required during lessons to make decisions about organizing students for instruction. Small groups, large groups, or individual student arrangements are all viable grouping procedures depending on the instructional objectives.

Grouping Learners Students can be arranged and grouped in many different ways during instruction. Different activities and goals, of course, will require various groupings. Distinctive classroom mixtures will require a variety of arrangements since the way individuals work together commands various organization patterns. The key to arranging and managing the classroom is to be flexible and to experiment with different groupings to find the best one for the students, activities, and materials involved.

Students can benefit from varied grouping arrangements since different reactions and responses are produced when students interact with small groups of peers, peer pairings, or large groups. Small-group arrangements may ensure that all students will have an opportunity to take part in discussions. Not all children will volunteer in large-group settings, and small groups can encourage a great deal of interaction. Large-group work can provide a good opportunity to hear many ideas or to summarize learnings and new knowledge. Large groups can present a wider range of ideas and solutions than small-group processes. Small groups may be more manageable than whole classes and can be assigned special projects.

There are many ways to arrange students during the school day. While a teacher can use most any method for making group assignments, he or she should avoid any organization that labels the learner. It is much more beneficial and positive to organize the class based on student and instructional needs.

• *Ability Grouping.* Grouping by ability or special talents is a controversial issue in schools and classrooms. Educational arrangements have placed students into groups according to some measure of their abilities. Usually, ability levels are measured by some form of standardized testing, and students are placed together according to common performance. Ability grouping is designed to reduce the wide range of differences among students so that more effective instruction can be provided.

Recently, however, ability grouping has come under intense scrutiny and is no longer viewed as the optimum method of organizing students for instruction. There are several detrimental practices associated with ability grouping:

1. Ability grouping labels students. Often the placement of students in groups will affect their perception of their learning abilities for years to come. The results of grouping have been shown to be long lasting; most adults can remember which group they were in during their school experiences.

2. The groups remain constant through several years of schooling. It is seldom that students move from one group to another.

3. Instruction varies among groups. Instruction directed at students identified with less ability is usually more focused on simple tasks, less reading and problem solving, and more rote learning. Many of these differences in instruction only maintain the differences in school performance.

4. For years, members of minority groups and poor children have been overrepresented in low groups. Students whose language, experiences, and culture are different seem to be at risk on achievement tests. Ability groups reflect this discrepancy.

Teachers may have reason to establish ability groups to help students learn a particular skill or strategy, but once the strategy has been learned, the group could be disbanded.

• *Flexible Grouping.* One way to arrange the class in small, manageable groups is to establish flexible grouping practices. Membership in flexible grouping terminates when the reason for establishing the group is accomplished. Small groups can be established for long periods of time or may be set up for short-term projects or objectives.

The goals and objectives of the small groups should be explicitly delineated and understood by the teacher and the students. The types of follow-up activities should be carefully described and monitored. There are several types of small flexible groups that can contribute to successful learning environments:

1. Special project groups can work on activities that accompany instruction. A teacher may arrange students to conduct lab experiences, read similar content, or interview other students in the school about a particular topic. Small flexible groups can be assembled to complete problems or other skills related to content areas.

2. Interest groups can be established to allow groups of students to read, discuss, and complete activities based on common interests. Interest groups provide students more opportunity to make decisions about classroom activities. For example, a group of students may group together because they are all interested in science fiction. However, they may read different books and share their stories or identify common elements of the genre they are reading. Another interest group could be formed to study poetry and songs. They might all share poetry orally or write their own poetry as a result of their common interest.

3. Research groups are established to locate, organize, and report information. Research groups are particularly appropriate for instruction in the content areas. Before research groups set out to work on their own, they should be taught research skills needed in the small group. Many of the skills can be demonstrated in whole class settings before children are placed in small groups.

4. Instructional groups are formed when more than one student could benefit from teacher-led instruction. For example, a group of children who are having difficulty with long division processes involving remainders would meet together to receive extra instruction. These groups are disbanded when all group members understand the strategy, skill, or concept.

5. Brainstorming and categorizing groups are usually short-lived and are established to begin reading, discussing, or writing. Students are placed in small groups to list everything they know about a concept or a topic or to design questions they would like to answer during study.

6. Expert groups may be formed and assigned a topic on which they are supposed to become "experts." After studying and researching, they become resources for the rest of the class. Expert groups may be required to do the research, be familiar with a particular portion of the text, or perfect some skill that can be taught to others in the class.

- *Cooperative Grouping.* Cooperative learning describes a certain type of student-grouping arrangement that may or may not be used in conjunction with the flexible grouping options previously described. Activities from any content area are planned and common goals are established to be met by assigning responsibilities for learning within the group. In most cases, four or five students form cooperative groups that work together to solve a problem or complete a task. Individual evaluation may be included as in Slavin's (1987) cooperative grouping approaches. However, individual competition is downplayed, and the work of the entire group is recognized for evaluation. The entire team is responsible for motivating all in the group to complete their tasks.

Although cooperative learning has been set up in many different ways, there are basic guidelines for introducing the instructional strategy:

1. Clarify rules and procedures before implementing the procedures. After a teacher decides what is to be accomplished cooperatively, then demonstration and instruction should accompany the task so that students are assured of success. Students should be explicitly aware of the goals and intentions of cooperative groups. Sample rules for the procedure might include the following:

   Know your responsibilities.
   Understand one another's roles.
   Help others who need help.
   Do your part and contribute to group activities.
   Use rules for disagreements and discussions
   Ask the teacher for help only as a last resort.

2. Organize the groups. Most cooperative learning activities arrange the class in groups of three to six students. Each student is assigned a specific role. The individual is responsible for that role, and his or her contribution is necessary to complete the tasks successfully. Some of the tasks that might be assigned include:

   Encourager
   Observer
   Materials monitor—makes sure that all students have materials
   Recorder—writes responses from group members during group activities
   Reporter—reports responses from group members during large-group
      discussions

3. Clarify purpose. Describe the goals for the activity and describe the task that is to be completed. Cooperative learning groups can accomplish reading activities, discussion and/or problem-solving activities, research activities, or any other work that is logical for more than one person to do.

Table 6.2

Sample Cooperative Learning Lesson

Task: Each group will compare two reading selections. The teacher will have discussed methods of comparison in advance.

Group Responsibilities

1. Be sure that all group members have a copy of the two reading selections.
2. Involve each group member.
3. Assign roles and responsibilities.
4. Use the format provided by the teacher.
5. Share group work with the rest of the class.
6. Evaluate group performance after completion.

Individual Responsiblities

1. Read the selections to be compared.
2. Contribute to the summaries of the two texts.
3. Contribute at least two ways the stories are alike.
4. Help the entire group complete the format provided by the teachers.
5. Help the group contribute information to the whole class activity.

Evaluation (by the teacher)

1. Review the small-group summaries.
2. Evaluate group skills in making decisions, achieving goals, and helping each other.
3. Evaluate small group's contribution to class summary.

4. Explain and demonstrate procedures. Students must be clear about procedures and logistics of the group work. It may take time to teach students what will happen in small groups. The small-group activity can be introduced through whole class discussion, role-playing, or demonstration. Some of the skills students may need to learn to work in cooperative groups include making space for people, communication skills, elimination of put-downs, taking turns, and active listening (Hill & Hill, 1991). Students may need time to practice these skills before working together in cooperative groups.

5. Observe student interactions. Cooperative learning teaches students how to be independent and interact with others, but it will require careful monitoring from the teacher. During activities, the teacher moves from group to group, noting problems, suggesting solutions to any potential

conflicts, and generally guiding activities. Even though students are held responsible for their own learning, the teacher still is involved actively in the students' work.

World Wide Web Site: You may learn more about cooperative learning at:
http://www.memphis-schools.K12.tn.us/schools/douglass.htm/

Whole Class Instruction Working with the entire class may not be the best arrangement for all types of instruction, but there are activities that can be very successful if the whole class is involved. Discussions, enrichment activities, concept introduction, reading aloud, and direct instructional procedures can be accomplished with the whole class. It is a useful arrangement for presenting information for several reasons:

1. Whole class instruction is efficient. Presenting the information to the entire class at one time can free the teacher to provide more attention to individuals and smaller groups who may need more intense and repetitive instruction. Whole class instruction can be more economical when presenting some strategies and information. It is an excellent way to present routines, discuss new approaches, and respond to information. Small-group work can follow whole class instruction and focus on different aspects of the main theme of instruction.

2. Whole class instruction provides students with time to interact with those of differing abilities and opinions. Whole class approaches avoid labeling or focusing on special abilities and offer an opportunity for a wide range of interests and abilities to be recognized. Students at all levels of ability can participate easily in whole class sharing and instruction, thus feeling that they are a part of the class. Even if all students do not participate in discussions, they can learn a great deal by listening.

3. Whole class activities contribute to establishing a classroom community. Students who share and interact together build common experiences, languages, stories, and procedures. This is a time when all students in the class can share their ideas and understand others' perspectives. It is a time to get to know each other.

   Almost any type of activity that can be accomplished in small groups can be done in whole classes and vice versa. The activities for the entire class should offer something for everyone. In-depth discussions or strategy instruction that applies only to a few students should be saved for small groups.

Becoming a Teacher in a Field-Based Setting

While others in the class work independently, a teacher provides one-on-one attention to this student. Student-teacher conferences provide opportunities for teachers to evaluate student learning and help them with the specific learning needs.

Teacher-Student Conferences Conferences are an instructional strategy that can be used to encourage, monitor, evaluate, and guide students. Conferences can be conducted for individual students, small groups, or whole classes. The teacher is responsible for planning and organizing the structure normally used in each situation.

Conferences are individual or small-group meetings that provide teachers and students an opportunity to discuss a wide array of academic issues. The teacher has a different role during conferences than might be expected in other grouping arrangements. While the structure for what happens during the conference is provided by the teacher, the activities are guided by students who are responsible for establishing the topic or focusing on strategies. A teacher must remember that students should do most of the talking during a conference. Conferences are a time for teachers to listen and support students during the learning process. The discussions provide teachers with information that can help and guide student learning.

Conferences may be regularly scheduled with students or can be initiated by the teacher or student if there is a need. The main objective is to provide students an opportunity to discuss their individual learning with the teacher. While conferences have been used extensively in teaching reading and writing (Wiseman, 1992), they could be adapted for use across the curriculum. Conferences have four parts (Pappas, Kiefer, & Levstik, 1990): sharing, questioning, interacting, and guiding.

1. Sharing: Conferences can begin by allowing children to share what they have been learning or accomplishing in class. If they have been keeping journals or other written records of class work, they can be encouraged to share some examples of their work with the teacher.

2. Questioning: The teacher listens to the student and asks questions about what the student is sharing. If the teacher is meeting with more than one student, then other students are invited to ask questions about each other's work.

3. Interacting: The conference includes opportunities to share new information, read orally, provide examples of learning, or share favorite or interesting issues. During the conference, the teacher notes and records discussion topics and examples for later reference.

4. Guiding: The teacher and the student(s) discuss future plans for learning. Students can identify what else they need to learn, and the teacher can guide them to the next steps. At the conclusion of a conference, students know their next step in relation to the learning activity.

A conference can be used at any grade level to encourage independent learning and respond individually to students. Once students learn the logistics of a conference, they can conduct conferences with each other.

Peer conferences give students an opportunity to share their learning and may be effective at the secondary as well as elementary levels. Conferences may

---

FIELD-BASED ACTIVITY 6.5

Use the text to produce a list of different ways of grouping students. Invite some of the teachers or student teachers from your school into your classroom to talk about how they organize their students for instruction. Share the list with them, and ask them what grouping arrangements they have used. What classroom management concerns do these different kinds of grouping arrangements present? What do they see as the pros and cons of different grouping procedures?

Highly capable students can work on their own. A student's ability to engage in independent study is often dependent upon a teacher's skill in organizing lessons and motivating students.

be arranged and encouraged by the teacher or may occur spontaneously when a collegial atmosphere is established in the classroom. In a classroom that values the learning of individuals, it is not unusual to have student-initiated conferences. Often, informal conferences between students are reflections of teacher-led conferences (Graves, 1994).

Student Pairs Students can be paired in numerous ways to support instructional organization. Pairs can be used to accomplish a goal, clarify an instructional objective, or tutor each other in a particular strategy. Students will need to experience responses to their own work to develop ways to respond to each other. They need to have guidance in how to respond to the work and ideas of classmates and this requires teaching and demonstration opportunities.

Students can be paired to accomplish a specific goal. Teachers can pair students to provide each with practice in a particular strategy. Sometimes students can explain a new idea more clearly to their peers than a teacher can. Paring students can provide opportunities for each to share his or her understanding of a topic.

One adaptation of student pairs is cross-age tutoring. Arranging for situations in which older students tutor younger students can provide teachers with some help and allow younger students to receive some individual attention.

Individual, Independent Activity There are many times when students work independently. Daily plans will include projects and assignments for students to complete on their own without direct teacher supervision. While students are working independently, the teacher can meet with small groups and individuals. Individual activity must be planned carefully because of the potential for off-task behavior.

Organizing Time

Scheduling requires consideration of many activities and school structures. The elementary teacher may schedule four or five subject areas for 20–25 children. Students leave the classroom for physical education, music, art, library, and special classes. The high school teacher may schedule one or two content courses for 125–150 students. There are countless other interruptions throughout the day. Class pictures must be taken, assemblies must be attended, and guest speakers heard. In both extremes, the school day is full of many activities. The main thing is for administrators and teachers to experiment and learn about a variety of ways to organize their days.

The modular scheduling concept has existed in elementary and secondary schools for many years and establishes specific amounts of time for instructional blocks. Usually it is set up around thirty-minute blocks in elementary schools and forty-to-sixty minute blocks in high schools. For example, we are all familiar with science period, math period, and band period. These time blocks remain constant regardless of learning requirements or learning demands. A more recent trend has been to consider more flexibility in school days and take into account learning needs when developing effective schedules. Some subjects can be best taught in short time blocks where other learning might be most effective in longer in-depth sessions. Likewise, some content might be best taught in small classes and other content can be addressed in larger classes. When the modular and flexible concepts of scheduling are combined, there are endless possibilities for arranging time schedules. This flexibility leads to a more student centered approach to scheduling and can make fairly dramatic changes in the nature of schools (Johnson et al., 1991).

An important element in scheduling the day for elementary students or the weekly class schedule for secondary students is that they learn a predictable schedule. Students want to know what to expect in their classes. At times they can be flexible, but overall predictability helps them feel in control and allows for some understanding about expectations during the school day. Most elementary school day schedules and secondary schedules viewed in the context of an entire week will include time for the following daily activities.

1. Whole class activities or focus time. The teacher should plan for time and activities when the entire class works together. This is the time when the teacher focuses the activities and organizes the day, class period, or week. Whole class instruction is a time to teach new strategies, discuss new information, or talk about the behavior that is expected of each student. The teacher might use this time to lecture, read aloud, have students read, or have discussions of general or topical interest. This time is very flexible depending on the teaching objectives and the developmental level of the students.

2. Independent work time. There are scheduled times in a daily or weekly class schedule when students will work on their own, making independent selections of reading material, working lab problems, or writing responses to assignments. Even very young students will have some daily independent work time. Some independent work time can be assigned in response to assignments or discussions introduced during whole class activities. Independent work time may occur with the entire class working at the same time or with part of the class working independently while the teacher works with small groups. The rules for independent work should be established early, and everyone should be aware explicitly of how this time is conducted.

3. Discussion or sharing time. Discussion or sharing sessions culminate the time allotted for planned instruction. Discussion provides opportunities to verbalize and talk about what the students have read and written in their independent work. Sharing time provides opportunities to discuss books, share personal writing, check lab problems, reteach, and evaluate the effectiveness of instruction. Sharing time may be different from class focus time, when teachers may have specific plans and objectives since it may be guided by what the students wish to discuss or share.

Organizing Materials

Materials used in the classroom are diverse. Schools usually provide basic textbooks, some selected lab materials, and access to multimedia. Teachers may contribute some of their own books, references, and media equipment to the classroom. Students may provide materials they have written and designed to classroom instructional processes.

Basals and Textbooks Instructional organization traditionally relies upon textbooks, which are provided in most classrooms. There are textbooks for almost all content areas. Although lessons designed to accompany textbooks may vary somewhat from subject to subject, most lesson structure includes before-reading, during-reading, and after-reading activities and discussions. The before-reading activities provide background information, develop vocabulary, and establish purpose and learning objectives. Skills instruction can be part of the introductory activities or part of the conclusion of a lesson. The skills emphasized in the introductory phase are subject-related. For example, social studies might focus on globe and map skills, and science might focus on laboratory skills. Teachers are given guidance in directing the activities through lesson plans suggesting discussions and activities that reinforce, reteach, or enrich the concepts and allow the teacher to establish what their students have learned.

Textbook publishers provide teachers' editions that have many suggestions for instruction as well as specific lesson plans for particular units and concepts. They include supplemental materials. For example, a social studies series might include maps, globes, and atlases. A science series might include lab manuals, microscopes, and charts.

Almost all states have approved textbooks and basal readers that school districts can select for use. These approved texts usually reflect the statewide curriculum and make sure that objectives and goals identified by the state are covered. The school districts select their texts from the list of textbooks on the state-adopted list.

Textbooks can play an important role in the instructional process as one source of material for teachers. The suggested plans accompanying the textbooks can be used as a framework or plan for instruction. Suggestions can give teachers ideas about where to start their instruction, introduce and augment discussions of topics, serve as surveys to begin the study of a concept, and establish initial concepts about a topic before students begin a self-directed study. It is not unusual, however, to see a single textbook adopted and used in classrooms as the sole source of information on a subject. When there is total reliance on basal readers and textbooks, they control what is taught, how it is taught, and in what order instruction is presented to students. There are several reasons why this total dependence may not be desirable. One of the first problems that arises is that learners come to classes with differences in prior knowledge and interest about the topic. Sometimes children need different levels of motivation to encourage their interest in a topic, and textbooks do not always present material in an interesting way. The concerns associated with the misuse of textbooks are enough to demonstrate that textbooks alone are not adequate for teaching most subjects.

Students have more potential to read and learn concepts and information if a large variety of printed and other media is available. Effective use of texts suggests that teachers should make decisions, use their knowledge of the content, the student, and instructional methods, and select a variety of materials to support the instructional approaches used in the classroom.

Children and Young Adult Literature Teachers of elementary, middle, and high schools can take advantage of the wide range of children's and young adult literature available to teach almost any subject. Literature, both fiction and nonfiction, provides an excellent resource in planning instruction. Students can learn concepts, facts, and ideas from both expository and narrative literature. Literature can be incorporated into almost any subject taught in schools. The range of topics of children and young adult literature can be used to build knowledge, motivation, and interest. Supplementing textbooks with literature increases opportunities to read about, write about, and discuss many different subjects.

Newspapers, Magazines, and Other Current Periodicals Today's world is changing so rapidly that current publications will sometimes have the most up-to-date information about topics being presented in the classroom. Options for classroom reading material include materials that are regularly read in the home and workplace. Popular periodicals can serve an important role during instruction. Current periodicals can be written for school students or directed toward adult readership. *Weekly Reader* and *Scholastic Magazine*, written for young people, are two periodicals found in many classrooms. Other available magazines and periodicals reflect a wide range of interest and concerns—for example, outdoor life, science, sports, and cultural activities. Use of magazines and periodicals enrich the classroom and assure that a wide range of interests, cultures, and perspectives are represented during instruction.

Computers and Multimedia More and more teachers now have the opportunity to utilize computers and other multimedia technology in their classrooms. With modern methods of communication, such as CD-ROMS, e-mail and the Internet, the resources available in the classroom are greatly expanded. Teachers can use the technology to find new instructional approaches, access teaching units, and identify resources from all over the world. Students can use the technology to complete research projects, communicate with others, and identify sources for further contact. Only the teachers' and students' imaginations will limit the ways that new technology can contribute to classroom planning.

Much information can be provided in print, film, and recordings, and there are many effective ways to use tapes, CDs, television, movies, and VCRs in instruction. These common technological tools can add a great deal to classroom instruction through enrichment activities to units of study or reading assignments.

Physical Arrangement

The physical arrangement of classrooms should support routines, grouping, and instructional activities. Arrangements will vary according to the amount of space, equipment, and furniture available. The room's size, space, and shape are relatively constant, but teachers can arrange the furniture and equipment to suggest an emphasis on group work, individual work, or whole class discussions. Classrooms should invite movement from small groups to individual work to whole class sharing. Materials should be easily available to students. If possible, quiet spaces for individuals as well as small-group work space should be provided during learning opportunities. The classroom becomes a space that reflects a teacher's philosophy and the students' work.

Some teachers will need a classroom with movable desks, chairs, and tables so that the room arrangements can be changed for certain activities. In general, a room should provide a large space for whole class instruction and sharing, a smaller area for small-group work, display and book shelves, and individual work spaces.

The physical arrangement of the classroom, materials, and equipment can make a statement about the philosophy of instruction. Classrooms can be

FIELD-BASED ACTIVITY 6.6

Have everyone in your class sketch the design of the classroom to which they are assigned. During classroom observations, watch carefully to see what student behavior is encouraged by the physical arrangement of the room. Watch what students do as they walk into the classroom and prepare for the day's activities. Watch how the arrangement of the room contributes to the ongoing instructional processes in the room. Share your observations in class and associate particular types of classroom learning and interactions with various classroom physical arrangements. Can you identify a link?

arranged to say "Let's read, talk, and write about what interests us." Classroom arrangements may also suggest a student-centered focus and a challenge to try things. Circular arrangements or round tables stimulate interactions. The arrangement of the classroom can reflect different instructional approaches and different student needs. Teachers will recognize what arrangements are most advantageous to their teaching style over time and with some trial and error.

Discipline

Teachers who attend to many of the aspects of classroom management identified as crucial to positive learning events will avoid a great many conflicts and have significantly fewer classroom disruptions. Even so, there will be times when students bring problems to the classroom, and even teachers who are very effective classroom organizers will be confronted with unproductive student behavior that requires intervention. Disciplining students for disruptive behavior should be part of a continuous plan that is explicit to the teacher and students. Skills necessary for teachers during disciplining procedures are the ability to listen, the knowledge of conflict-resolution techniques, the ability to work with teams of professionals who can focus on the disruptive behavior of a particular student, and the knowledge to develop and carry out management and discipline plans.

The most important aspect of attending to disruptive behavior is to return the classroom to a constructive atmosphere. Regaining control of the classroom quickly and avoiding involvement of more students than necessary is a goal following any type of disruptive behavior or confrontation. There are several strategies that teachers should remember when responding to disruptive student behavior.

1. Try not to make unreasonable requirements or overreact to disruptive incidents. There are times when teachers contribute to the crisis at hand by exerting too much control or power, responding in a prejudicial or grudging manner, or not attending to students' behaviors (Seeman, 1988). Teachers should examine their own contributions to disruptive situations.

2. Be honest about your feelings. If you are upset, disappointed, or angry, then explain that to students. They will be the first to know if you are trying to mask your feelings. They will respect you for your honesty and realize that you have emotions and reactions that are similar to theirs.

VOICE OF A TEACHER

Keeping a classroom on-task and involved is complicated. It's hard to explain to someone else about your own classroom discipline since it is such a personal thing. I have developed a discipline system that reflects my personality, experience, and philosophy. Students contribute to the organization in a classroom, too. The makeup of the class makes a big difference about how I manage instruction and keep order and discipline. Some years my discipline is much easier to establish than others.

I believe that management and discipline are closely related. I have found that good organization helps reduce the discipline problems in my classrooms. When my students understand what is expected of them, know what work they need to finish, and how I will respond to them . . . most of them will work in class. They really want to be actively engaged—they like to interact with each other while engaged in interesting, meaningful activities.

Don't get me wrong. There are times my students don't go along with my planning. They may not be motivated to learn what I am trying to teach. Or they may need a great deal of structure to get them into the learning mode. Kids do need limits. I have to establish limits, rules, and follow through—do what I say I will do.

Another important aspect of classroom management and discipline is to figure out how you can show respect for your students. I try and listen to what they say and listen carefully to what they are telling me. I try to see the movies they see and read what they are reading. I can't always understand or enjoy their music—but I try. When I show that I know about some of these things, my students are really impressed. They know that I am interested in what they are doing.

I worried more about classroom management and discipline when I started teaching than I did any other thing. It didn't matter how much anyone talked to me about it—it's hard to know how to juggle all the aspects of classroom discipline and management—it is mostly learned while you are in front of a classroom. And each teacher will have their own individual way of approaching classroom organization. If I were to give a new teacher advice, I would suggest that they read as much as they can and then approach their first classroom with the idea that they will be organized, well planned, and respectful. And then I would tell new teachers to remember that classroom management and discipline will get easier with experience.

3. Be consistent and follow through with what you have said you will do. When rules of discipline are established, then it is crucial that the teacher follow through with what processes have been established. Threats should be avoided—they will only encourage student challenges.

4. Above all, be fair with your students. If you have made a mistake, applied rules indiscriminately, or have implemented actions that are not working or were not fair in the first place, apologize to your students. Again, they will respect you for your honesty and openness.

Becoming a Teacher in a Field-Based Setting

Punishment

Often when students' misbehavior is serious and teachers' efforts fail to result in appropriate behavior, more severe strategies are needed. Usually, this occurs with collaborative consultation between classroom teachers and other educational resource staff. Consequences may involve corporal punishment in states where it is allowed and/or suspension from school.

Corporal punishment (spanking) is the punishment dreaded by all schoolchildren. Most educators believe that the use of force does little to encourage compliance with rules or promote good behavior since punishment may have unintended consequences that make it a desirable option. Suspension from school is another severe response for violation of school rules. Except in cases in which students are dangerous to themselves or others, school suspension should be discouraged (Pinnell, 1985). In cases of corporal punishment and suspension, student behavior is controlled by outside forces and the student is not developing and internalizing self-controls. In some schools, educators provide in-school suspension centers, which serve to remove students from the classroom but enable them to continue their studies.

Classroom management is a series of teacher decisions that happen in a fast-paced, complex environment. Teachers are facilitating appropriate behavior and reacting to student misbehavior, and their responses often reflect their own views of power and authority. For these reasons, classroom management might come more from intuition than from thoughtful, reflective plans. Sometimes, a teacher's own experiences play the biggest role in how classroom management proceeds. How you have been disciplined and punished in your home and at school will impact the way you feel that your students should be disciplined. Given the complexities of classrooms, the many needs of students, and the greater knowledge of good classroom management techniques and understandings, it seems obvious that classroom management skills will continue to grow and expand as a teacher gains experience and confidence.

PORTFOLIO REFLECTIONS AND EXHIBITS

Choose one of the field-based activities suggested in the text, develop an exhibit that represents what you have learned during the readings and discussions accompanying this chapter, or complete the suggested portfolio exhibit below. Your response to the activities or your exhibit may become part of your teaching portfolio.

Suggested Exhibit 6: My Emerging View of Classroom Management
1. Review your responses to each of the field-based activities in this chapter. Compile your personal list of the descriptors that emerged after each of the activities. Summarize in writing what your responses to each of the activities had in common. Identify the descriptors that were mentioned with each of the activities.

2. Represent your responses to classroom management and organization in some explicit and descriptive way. Use a graphic, such as a continuum, a computer program, a drawing, an essay, or a collage, to describe how you see yourself as a classroom manager. Will you be flexible, traditional, creative, structured, eclectic? How can you describe your thoughts about classroom environments? Be prepared to share your representation with your classmates.

Related Readings

Collins, M., & Tamarkin, C. (1990). *Marva Collins' way: Returning to excellence in education.* New York: Putnam.
>   *Marva Collins, a successful Chicago teacher, presents some inspiring ideas about establishing a successful classroom environment. She talks about how she motivates children who might normally be unsuccessful in our schools to achieve.*

Paley, V. G. (1990). *The boy who would be a helicopter: The uses of storytelling in the classroom.* Cambridge, MA: Harvard University Press.
>   *This book tells the story of a troubled child who continually disrupts the classroom. The teacher uses storytelling to help him become an effective classroom participant. This story will help you understand how flexible teachers must be to meet their students' unique needs.*

References

AAUW report: How schools shortchange girls. (1992). Washington, DC: National Education Association.

Ames, C. (1992). Classrooms: Goals, structures and student motivation. *Journal of Educational Psychology, 83*(3), 261–271.

Bartolome, L. (1994). Beyond the methods fetish, toward a humanizing pedagogy. *Harvard Educational Review, 64*(2), 173–194.

Blumenfeld, P. C., Puro, P., & Mergendoller, J. R. (1992). Translating motivation into thoughtfulness. In H. H. Marshall (Ed.), *Redefining student learning* (pp. 112–125). Norwood, NJ: Ablex.

Brophy, J. (1988). Educating teachers about managing classrooms and students. *Teaching and Teacher Education, 4*(1), 1–18.

Brophy, J., & Evertson, C. (1976). *Learning from teaching: A developmental perspective.* Boston: Allyn & Bacon.

Chandler, S. (1992). Learning for what purpose? Questions when viewing classroom learning from a sociocultural curriculum perspective. In H. H. Marshall (Ed.), *Redefining student learning* (pp. 86–99). Norwood, NJ: Ablex.

Comer, J. (1988). Educating poor minority children. *Scientific American, 359*(5), 42–48.

Dana, N. (1992). *Towards preparing the monocultural teacher for the multicultural classroom.* Paper presented at the 72nd annual meeting of the Association of Teacher Educators, Orlando. (ERIC Document Reproduction Service No. ED 350 272.)

Dryfoos, J. (1990). *Adolescents at risk: Prevalence and prevention.* New York: Oxford University Press.

Emmer, E., Evertson, C., & Anderson, L. (1980). Effective classroom management at the beginning of the school year. *Elementary School Journal, 80*(5), 219–231.

Fernie, D., Kantor, R., & Klein, E., (1990). *School culture and peer culture influences on adult and child roles in a preschool classroom.* Unpublished paper presented at AERA, Boston.

Glasser, W. (1988). On students' needs and team learning: A conversation with William Glasser. *Educational Leadership, 45*(6), 38–45.

Graves, D. (1994). *A fresh look at writing.* Portsmouth, NH: Heinemann.

Green, J. L., Kantor, R. M., & Rogers, T. (1990). Exploring the complexity of language and learning in classroom contexts. In B. Jones & L. Idol (Eds.), *Educational values and cognitive instruction: Implications for reform* (Vol. II, pp. 400–422). Hillsdale, NJ: Erlbaum.

Hill, S., & Hill, T. (1991). *The collaborative classroom: A guide to cooperative learning.* Portsmouth, NH: Heinemann.

Johnson, J. A., Collins, H. W., Dupuis, V. L., & Johansen, J. H. (1991). *Introduction to the foundations of American education,* (8th ed.). Boston: Allyn & Bacon.

Jones, V. (1996). Classroom management. In J. Sikula (Ed.), *Handbook of research on teacher education* (pp. 503–524). New York: Macmillan.

Kounim, J. S. (1970). *Discipline and group management in classrooms.* New York: Holt, Rinehart & Winston.

Kuykendall, C. (1992). *From rage to hope: Strategies for reclaiming Black and Hispanic students.* Bloomington, IN: National Educational Service.

Lepper, M. R. (1983). Extrinsic reward and intrinsic motivation. In J. Levine & M. Wang (Eds.), *Teacher and student perceptions: Implications for learning* (pp. 212–232). Hillsdale, N. J.: Lawrence Erlbaum.

McCaslin, M., & Good, T. (1992). Compliant cognition: The misalliance of management and instructional goals in current school reform. *Educational Researcher, 21*(3), 4–17.

Olsen, L., & Mullen, N. (1990). *Embracing diversity: Teachers' voices from California's classrooms.* San Francisco: California Tomorrow Project.

Orenstein, P. (1994). *School girls.* New York: Doubleday.

Pappas, C. C., Kiefer, B. K., & Levstik, L. S. (1990). *An integrated language perspective in the elementary school: Theory into action.* New York: Longman.

Phelan, P., Davidson, A., & Cao, H. (1992). Speaking up: Students' perspectives on school. *Phi Delta Kappan, 73*(9), 795–704.

Pinnell, G. S. (1985). The "catch-22" of school discipline policy making. *Theory Into Practice, 24,* 289.

Seeman, H. (1988). *Preventing classroom discipline problems.* Lancaster, PA: Technomic.

Slavin, R. E. (1987). Ability grouping and student achievement in elementary schools: A best evidence synthesis. *Review of Educational Research, 57*(3), 293–336.

Wehlage, G., Rutter, R., Smith, G., Lesko, N., & Fernandez, R. (1989). *Reducing the risk: Schools as communities of support.* London: Falmer Press.

Wiseman, D. L. (1992). *Learning to read with literature.* Boston: Allyn & Bacon.

Wlodkowski, R. J., & Jaynes, J. H. (1990). *Eager to learn: Helping children become motivated and love learning.* San Francisco: Jossey-Bass.

Zaharlick, A., & Green, J. L. (1991). Ethnographic research. In J. Flood, J. Jensen, D. Lapp, & J. Squire (Eds.), *Handbook of research on teaching the English language* (pp. 205–225). New York: Macmillan.

Becoming a Teacher in a Field-Based Setting

7

Teaching Lessons in Today's Classrooms

In this chapter

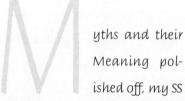

Myths and their Meaning polished off, my SS class was given a collection of simple contemporary short stories; fortunately, there was a surplus in the Book Room. The first one dealt with a child who was allergic to sweets, his mother, who had admonished him never to eat them, and a good-hearted but misguided neighbor who believed the child's stories about his cruel mother and his deprivations, and who fed him sweets until he became violently ill. The mother threatened to sue the neighbor. End of story.

The discussion I started in class—about good intentions and responsibility—proved so lively, that I decided to follow it up with a dramatization. I asked them to come prepared the next day to transform the classroom into a courtroom; and we would plead the case, as a sequel to the story . . . I assigned the roles: mother, father, neighbor, child, prosecuting attorney, defense attorney, witnesses for the defense and the prosecution, even the doctor. I realized we had left out the judge. Through one of those swift moments of inspiration, I turned to Jose Rodriguez and asked him to be prepared to act the judge. A few in class snickered; Jose nodded; and I myself had no idea what to expect.

The following day he appeared in class in a cap and gown—a black graduation gown and mortar-board, borrowed or rented at what trouble or expense I could only guess, and a large hammer for a gavel. He bore a look of such solemn dignity that no one dared to laugh.

He sat at my desk and said: "The court clerk is supposed to say they gotta rise."

There was such authority in his voice that slowly, one by one, the class rose. It was a moment I don't think I will ever forget.

The class was directed to sit down, and the wheels of justice proceeded to turn . . . When anyone spoke out of turn, Jose would pound on the desk with his hammer: "This here court will get quiet, or you will be charged with contempt."

He overruled every objection . . . And when Harry Kagan challenged him on court procedure, he said, with quiet assurance: "I ought to know. I been."

The court ruled for the defense.

When the bell rang, Jose slowly removed his cap and gown, folded them neatly over his notebook, and went on to his next class; but he walked as if he were still vested in judicial robes.

I don't think he will ever be quite the same.

And that's it; that's why I want to teach; that's the one and only compensation: to make a permanent difference in the life of a child . . .

—Bel Kaufman, *Up the Down Staircase*

Becoming a Teacher in a Field-Based Setting

eachers are involved in making decisions every day. Decisions about what they should teach. Decisions about what materials they should use. Decisions about how to encourage learning in the classroom. Clarke and Peterson (1986) report that teachers make a decision on how to best affect student learning about every two minutes in the classroom.

Many factors are considered when a teacher begins the planning process. This chapter will answer the following questions:

- How do teachers decide what to teach?

- What resources are available to teachers?

- How can teachers use technology in the classroom?

- How is integrated instruction different than discipline-based instruction?

- How do teachers plan for individual lessons?

- How can teachers evaluate the success of their teaching?

Setting Up Instruction

Throughout this chapter you will see entries from a reflective journal in which a preservice teacher corresponded in writing with a mentoring classroom teacher about her experiences and thoughts as she began the process of planning, teaching, and reflecting on learning in the classroom. You will also be able to hear the voices of teachers and preservice teachers throughout the chapter as they talk about planning for instruction.

The activities in this chapter are designed to guide you through planning and teaching a lesson with your students in your field placement.

FIELD-BASED ACTIVITY 7.1

Write a letter to a classmate as you begin the planning and teaching cycle. What are your concerns about planning a lesson and writing a lesson plan? What concerns do you have about teaching a lesson in your classroom? Respond to your classmate's concerns.

Interdisciplinary planning can be effective at any age level. When teachers plan instruction together, content areas such as English, social studies, and science are integrated with drama, art, and music.

Approaches to Classroom Instruction

It would take several books to explain and describe all the different concepts, definitions, models, and approaches used to describe how teachers plan, organize, and implement their instruction. A description of two general categories, teacher-centered approaches and student-centered approaches, provides a good overview of the choices available to teachers.

Teacher-Centered Approaches

Teacher-centered approaches hold the teacher responsible for all classroom activity. The teacher identifies topics of study, conceptualizes the goals, establishes the sequence of learning activities, presents the materials, and develops assessment procedures. The teacher explicitly identifies outcomes and controls and determines instruction. A common type of a teacher-centered approach is direct instruction, during which the teacher relies on a structured process to

REFLECTIVE JOURNAL ENTRY

VOICE OF A TEACHER

I was thinking last night that my struggle to learn to teach is similar to the struggle the students are having learning descriptive writing. It's so easy for me to sit here and watch you teach and recognize those things that make you a good teacher. However, it's very difficult for me to actually get up and do those things. These children can pick out the things that make description good, but getting them to be successful at doing those things is a different story. We all need PRACTICE at what we're trying to learn. We also need to be reflective. These are the keys to learning. How do we get the children to recognize this and truly care about what they are learning? I guess part of it is choice. I am choosing to be a teacher, so I have a passion for learning this. The students, however, don't always get to choose what they learn about, so it's harder to instill in them this attitude toward obtaining knowledge.

VOICE OF A CLASSROOM TEACHER

You are so right about practicing what we are learning. Expect to get better at time management this semester, but it will take years to be really good at it. I still haven't mastered it! We also need to focus on students' practicing. Let's do some good practice with small groups on descriptive writing next week.

direct the students' thinking and participation. Instructional activities include whole group review, instructional input, guided and independent practice. The teacher constantly checks for understanding and relies on drill and practice activities.

Direct instruction presents learning in small structured steps requiring practice and structured feedback to make sure the student is learning. The teacher plays a major role and presents material, guides the student, and provides the students with extensive practice routines. This approach is especially useful when students are required to learn and master well-defined concepts and skills such as mathematics computations. Direct instruction illustrates many of the characteristics common to behavioral learning theory discussed in Chapter 5.

Student-Centered Approaches

Student-centered approaches to instruction require a great deal of student participation and interaction between teachers and students and among students. Although the teacher facilitates and structures learning, students have a lot of responsibility and are delegated with a portion of the authority during learning activities. The focus of instructional strategies is on cooperation and class cohesiveness.

Student-centered approaches are also known as indirect methods because the teacher is involved less directly. Teachers are encouraged to shift from their traditional roles as information providers and toward a more facilitative, supportive role. The emphasis is on teaching students how to learn through peer and teacher interactions. Students are involved in goal-setting, and as a result of participation, they develop and share multiple opinions, question ideas and positions, and refer to multiple sources. Students may be asked to contribute personal experiences that offer information and clarify issues. Learning strategies are focused on the scientific or discovery method of gathering facts, hypothesizing, testing solutions, and revising solutions.

Student-centered approaches appear to improve students' attitudes toward learning, increase motivation, and develop social skills. There is some indication that student-centered approaches encourage higher-level thinking skills, but critics of student-centered approaches maintain that basic skills learning is less emphasized in a total student-centered approach.

Establishing Goals for the Classroom

Goals and objectives are used by teachers to select the topics and activities for the day. Goals are what teachers expect students to learn if their teaching is successful. Ideally, all the materials, methods, and climate of the classroom are manipulated to successfully attain these goals. Effective teachers not only understand these goals and how they fit into the larger framework of the total curriculum, but also make sure students understand as well.

District, state, and national educational guidelines can begin to define a teacher's academic goals. According to Tyler (1974), goals establish priorities for what students learn and should be based on subject mastery, student needs and interests, societal concerns, community priorities, instructional theory, and research. Essential content for each grade level and learning objectives for each subject are often outlined by standards set outside the classroom. Standardized testing requirements can also influence the curriculum content of the classroom, as teachers are often accountable for student achievement or mastery of test objectives.

State and National Goals

In recent years, several national teacher organizations, such as the National Council of Teachers of Mathematics, the National Council for the Social Studies, the National Council for Improving Science Education, and the National Council of Teachers of English, adopted curriculum frameworks designed to develop learners who can think independently in real-world situations. These frameworks shifted the focus from curriculum based on isolated skills and memorization of basic facts to more complex thinking and problem solving (Borich, 1996). In 1990 the president and the governors met to adopt six educational goals for the United States (see Figure 3.1, page 53). Goals 2000, as they are known, and the national curriculum focused on developing students who can think for themselves in a rapidly changing world and on maintaining high expectations for all students.

World Wide Web Sites: You can learn more about the National Goals at
http://hp877.odedodea.edu:8001/dnatlgls.htm
http://www.ed.gov/legislation/ESEA/Guidance/app-c.html

Address: Department of Defense Education Activity (DoDEA)
4040 North Fairfax Street
Arlington, VA 22203-1635

State educational guidelines also effect the goal-setting process of the individual teacher in the classroom. State-mandated tests are often required at specific grade levels and media pressure to perform well can be intense. Figure 7.1 is a sample of instructional targets for mathematics for the Texas Assessment of Academic Skills test. Fourth-grade teachers in Texas, who know that they and their schools will be held accountable for their students' achievement in these areas, study these state guidelines and incorporate them into their curriculum in order to ensure student coverage of the material to be tested. Check the web site

---

FIELD-BASED ACTIVITY 7.2

Reflect on your experiences in the school setting and identify activities that relate directly to Goals 2000. Can you find teaching and learning activities that reflect each of the goals? If not, why?

Figure 7.1

Example of Objectives and Instructional Targets for the Texas Assessment of Academic Skills Test

Mathematics, Grade 4

DOMAIN: Concepts

Objective 1: The student will demonstrate an understanding of number concepts.
- Translate whole numbers (name to numeral/numeral to name).
- Compare and order whole numbers.
- Use whole numbers place value.
- Round whole numbers (to nearest ten or hundred).
- Recognize decimal place value (tenths and hundredths; using models).
- Use odds, evens, and skip counting.
- Recognize and compare fractions using patterns and pictorial models.

Objective 2: The student will demonstrate an understanding of mathematical relations, functions, and other algebraic concepts.
- Use whole number properties and inverse operations.
- Determine missing elements in patterns.
- Use number line representations for whole numbers and decimals.

DOMAIN: Operations

Objective 6: The student will use the operation of addition to solve problems.
- Add whole numbers and decimals (tenths and hundredths; using models).

Objective 7: The student will use the operation of subtraction to solve problems.
- Subtract whole numbers and decimals (tenths and hundredths; using models).

of your state educational agency or other state educational resources to determine if you have guidelines or standards that will need to be incorporated into your lessons.

School districts also develop curriculum guides for teachers to use in their planning. These guides often incorporate national and state standards and may be organized into subject matter units of study or around specific disciplines. School districts may also adopt special units of study, such as dental care or AIDS awareness, that teachers are required to teach at certain grade levels.

Becoming a Teacher in a Field-Based Setting

Planning for instruction requires a teacher to understand small- and large-group interactions. Group work or class discussions may result in a chart or overhead summary that students use for reference as they work on their assignments.

Assessing Curriculum Needs

Successful teachers serve as translators between the written curriculum and the needs of the students, constantly striving to define the written curriculum in a comprehensible, meaningful way for students. Bringing a written curriculum and preset curriculum goals to life in a real classroom, with a wide range of students operating at various levels of achievement, requires constant problem solving and critical thinking skills related to assessment of the important need for curriculum and instruction.

At the beginning of any curriculum unit is the assessment of need. Need can be defined at several different levels. There are subject matter and grade level needs defined by the state and district curriculum guidelines, and there are also interest and ability needs of the students.

Long-range planning decisions often occur before the semester or year begins. Teachers decide on broad topic areas or upcoming units of study based on what they want students to be able to do at the completion of the unit. They estimate the time needed to accomplish their learning goals and plan a calendar

I also agree with you on the necessity of us being actively engaged with the students at every opportunity in the classroom. It is very easy to get so caught up in planning that we forget about what is important every day at every moment—the students! After all, that's why we're teaching. We're not teaching so we can plan.

for the year, knowing it will change constantly as students' interest and academic needs demand.

One technique for assessing what Pre K-12 students already understand and what they want to learn about a topic is K-W-L (Carr & Ogle, 1987). The K column represents what students already know about a topic and reflects the need to link prior knowledge with new information, as discussed in Chapter 5. Students can work individually, in small groups, or with a whole class to discuss and record information they already know about the topic. The students then record or dictate the information to the teacher to complete the K column. The W column is for what students want to know about a topic. Questions are generated individually and in small groups and then reported to the class for recording and categorization. This information can help teachers increase student motivation by making class topics interesting and relevant to students as they assist in the goal-setting for their own learning. The last column on the K-W-L chart is for recording new learnings—for what students learned about the topic. The K-W-L chart serves as a guide throughout the unit or lesson. Questions

---

FIELD-BASED ACTIVITY 7.3

Fill in the following K-W-L chart for your own learning. Complete the first two columns now, before you have taught your lesson. Use the correspondence from Field-Based Activity 7.1 to help you generate ideas for your first two columns. Discuss your charts in small groups and then compile lists with the whole class. Fill in the last column after you have taught the lesson. Ask yourself these questions: What do I already know about planning and teaching a lesson? What do I want to know? What have I learned?

Topic: Planning and Teaching a Lesson

K	W	L
What I know . . .	What I want to know . . .	What I learned . . .

REFLECTIVE JOURNAL ENTRY

VOICE OF A PRESERVICE TEACHER

I felt a little nervous during the quotation lesson. I think part of the problem was I had not made a formal lesson plan for it—I had only thought about it. Next time I will write at least some sort of lesson plan on paper, even if it is not something that will have to be turned in. I am not at the point where I can do lessons automatically, without forcing myself to think about the various parts. Thank you for going over those parts with me. I've written lesson plans before and I know what it entails, but I just needed to be reminded of them, so that I could make sure I was doing everything. I need to be reminded, too!

I tried to do all the parts of the lesson cycle today and I definitely think I made progress since last time. I really wrote out the lesson last night, so the key word to today's progress was PLANNING!

VOICE OF A CLASSROOM TEACHER

Great job of getting the students interested in the quotation lesson! They always want to find our mistakes. Your original story was also a great attention getter. I missed some of the lesson because the volunteer came, but it seemed to go really well. I will talk to you more about it later.

asked before the lesson are answered and crossed off the list as new learning occurs. New questions are added to the list, which may lead to extensions of a unit or topic.

After looking at goals set outside the classroom and at the learning needs of the students, teachers continue the individual planning process by reflecting on past experience. Based on previous experience with a grade or subject, they begin to establish short- and long-range goals. Retaining successful practices and

---

FIELD-BASED ACTIVITY 7.4

Schedule a teacher planning conference. Discuss the following questions with your teacher before beginning to plan your lesson. Record the answers.

- What subject will I be teaching?
- Are there district and state guidelines for this subject?
- How will my lesson fit into a larger unit of study?
- What time constraints will I have? How long should my lesson last?
- What resources are available?
- What should the student be able to do on completion of the lesson?

---

redefining activities or processes that were unsuccessful, they learn to adopt high expectations, yet are able to recognize unrealistic expectations.

Short-range planning occurs every day in a variety of ways as teachers assess learning needs on a weekly or even an hour-by-hour basis. Short-range plans are constantly changing. A math concept is more difficult than expected and tomorrow's lesson must be adjusted for reteaching. A writing activity needs more time than planned, so the activity is extended into several more upcoming class periods. Students became very interested in a current event in the news, and the social studies unit is modified to include this new topic of interest.

Creating, Selecting, and Adapting Resources

When students actively participate in acquiring new knowledge and are allowed to take some responsibility for their own learning, teachers must seek out many materials and resources to support the variety of classroom activities. Textbooks are supplemented with children's literature, reference materials, current periodicals, audiovisual aids, and computer software related to the topic. Needed materials can, however, be just as individual as the learning taking place in each classroom. Mr. Landmann, the third-grade teacher we met in Chapter 5, is constantly seeking out costumes and props suitable to portray the major characters in history so that when the third-graders present their research in a living history museum at the end of each six weeks, they are properly attired. As a part of her unit on insects, one first-grade teacher worked to find live silkworms so that her students could observe them growing, spinning a cocoon, and eventually hatching into moths.

Using Technology

Computer learning has traditionally been seen as rote learning, where students are presented several screens of information and then asked to answer questions about the material presented (Grabe & Grabe, 1996). In some classrooms, however, technology is becoming an extension of the teacher's lesson plan, not a replacement. "Student motivation, attention and enthusiasm increases with technology in the classroom. Through technology, students become active participants, who are encouraged to creatively problem solve, explore and expand their horizons beyond the classroom" (Franzee & Rudnitski, 1996, p. 310). The following technological tools provide a variety of modes for students to actively participate in their own learning and construct new meaning.

- *Multimedia Presentations.* Multimedia presentations are computer-based presentations that can include text, pictures, sound, and even video. Such presentations can help students make learning meaningful and personal (Wilson, 1991), and students need to make these personal connections for learning to occur (Hawkins & Collins, 1992). Commercially or teacher-prepared multimedia presentations can be used in interactive ways, with students selecting the path of their own learning and moving through the material in ways that are individually meaningful to each student. Jonassen (1986) suggests that this non-linear presentation of material is similar to the way the brain stores information naturally and is a way of encouraging students to find relationships among the pieces of information presented. Students can also create their own presentations on the computer, manipulating new learnings into a creative presentation that reaches all the senses. These presentations produce a sense of ownership in producing a physical product as evidence of their understanding (Bruder, 1991).

- *Telecommunications.* With a computer, modem, and a phone line, classrooms are able to interact with the world. With Internet access, learners can communicate with other classrooms in different locations, contact experts in a field of study, and access resources in various libraries around the world.

- *Instructional Games and Simulations.* Games and simulations can provide practice, remediation, and enrichment for students in the classroom. Lessons introduced in a whole class setting can be expanded into individual or small-group practice in an instructional game provided by computer software. Some simulations are appropriate for use in a discovery lesson, allowing students to discover concepts and information first through their interaction with the computer, leading to later discussion and further instruction by the teacher.

- *Computer-Assisted Instruction (CAI).* One of the first ways computers entered the classroom was through computer-assisted instruction. CAI provides tutoring and practice with instant assessment and feedback capabilities. Students are presented new material, student responses are assessed by the computer, and the computer can provide immediate reteaching based on student responses. The level of difficulty is adjusted automatically by the computer so instruction is individualized to meet each learner's needs (Borich, 1996).

New technological innovations continue to emerge at a rapid pace, requiring continuous learning on the part of the teacher and the students. Many students have access to computers at home and come to school with a wide range of technological expertise.

Creating Relevant Curriculum

Today's curriculum for students is often a sequential, skill-oriented continuum, involving direct teacher instruction, with many educators believing a fundamental set of basic skills must be mastered before moving on to more complicated higher-level thinking activities. Mathematical concepts are taught as discreet skills, such as how to multiply a two-digit number or how to add three numbers together. Individual language arts skills might include how to decode a word with a consonant blend, divide words into syllables, or how to use capital letters correctly in a sentence. Skills are isolated and practiced until students are able to demonstrate understanding. There are benefits to this kind of instructional approach based on behavioral theory described in Chapter 5. A list of sequential skills helps teachers diagnose specific learning weaknesses, so individual student deficiencies can be identified and a specific plan of remediation designed to address student needs. This diagnosis and remediation cycle allows for frequent feedback, rapid pacing, and repeated opportunities for practice. Teachers are able to assess students' achievement easily and make adjustments as needed.

Even though test results can improve with such a planned approach to remediating student deficiencies, studies have found the skills approach, especially for disadvantaged students, more repetitive and less challenging, with students receiving fewer opportunities to learn higher-order skills (Allington & McGill-Franzen, 1989). A skills-based curriculum can keep traditionally low achieving children from progressing to more challenging, meaningful activities until they demonstrate mastery of a set of identified fundamental skills. This philosophy often results in a curriculum that fails to encourage problem solving, reading comprehension, and meaningful writing activities (Knapp & Shields, 1990). Children in such an environment often have difficulty making the connection between skills practiced in isolation and integrated, more meaningful tasks. Those students who already find school alien to their personal experience see little reason for completing isolated skill activities and end up falling further and further behind since they must master basic steps before they can move on to more challenging, and interesting, activities. By underestimating what students are capable of accomplishing, teachers may postpone more interesting work and keep students from having the chance to apply the skills they have been taught (Knapp & Shields, 1990).

In contrast, some schools are looking at the strengths students bring with them to school rather than at the deficiencies. Children from poor and affluent backgrounds alike come to school with important skills and knowledge about the world around them—including sophisticated language abilities and numerical concepts. Instruction in advanced skills allows students to integrate prior learning in the process of knowledge and building on existing basic academic skills. Instead of looking at what children do not know, a curriculum based on integrated skills acknowledges what children already know (Means & Knapp, 1991).

In mathematics, schools can offer a more challenging curriculum by emphasizing mathematical concepts along with computational skills. Students at all levels need frequent opportunities to apply mathematical concepts to real-life problems so that connections can be formed that help students draw on past experiences. Students are involved in solving complex, meaningful problems about issues they consider important. Computational skills are embedded into the more global task of problem solving, allowing students to see the big concepts rather than spending the majority of their school time on the memorization of isolated and unconnected facts. Students learn basic mathematical skills as they are needed and are able to understand the connection between the skill and a meaningful purpose for learning the skill.

REFLECTIVE JOURNAL ENTRY

VOICE OF A CLASSROOM TEACHER

Great job of leading the Venn diagram lesson! It is hard to lead a discussion that is so open-ended. As long as the students can give proof for their answers, accept them. Reason with them if they are on the wrong track. This kind of discussion is so good for them.

Before the lesson, make sure you have the attention of all the students. Ask them to put their pencils down and look at you. Don't start until they do this! Steve has a tendency to keep doing his own thing otherwise.

VOICE OF A PRESERVICE TEACHER

You are right about getting their attention. I mumble too much. I have a tendency to do this when I'm nervous. Instead, I need to speak up and command attention.

At the elementary level, a challenging reading curriculum is focused on comprehension, not just decoding skills. All skills instruction is focused on gaining meaning, giving students a purpose for using skills within the context of a story. Children's literature and reading material reflecting a diversity of backgrounds and cultures is integral to the reading program. Within such a reading curriculum, students are often allowed to select their own reading material, increasing interest and building on prior experience. Teachers, and sometimes whole schools, implement a time of sustained silent reading, where students are allowed to choose their own books and read silently for a set amount of time each day. At the secondary level, teachers can incorporate approaches to reading for knowledge in specific content areas that continue to build comprehension skills.

A strong curriculum for writing draws on the experiences and knowledge of students, with less emphasis placed on the mechanics of writing such as spelling, punctuation, and grammar, and more emphasis placed on the process of writing. Students are encouraged to brainstorm for writing ideas using past experiences, write several drafts with input from teachers and peers, apply mechanical skills to revisions, and then produce a final piece of writing to share with others. Stories of experience, community, and family are shared in the classroom, and all students have the opportunity to bring their out-of-school experiences and culture into the classroom through shared writing. Students are consistently involved in reflecting on their own lives through autobiography and story. Written biographies of community elders or other influential adults in the community can also bridge the gap between home and school. Writing skills, formerly taught in isolation, are taught as a necessary part of the process, when the

Becoming a Teacher in a Field-Based Setting

need for understanding arises. Students are able to see the purpose of learning the skill when it is embedded in the writing process.

A strong curriculum for all students also emphasizes verbal communication, with constant dialogue as the central form of communicating knowledge. Teachers are no longer responsible for transmitting knowledge to a passive student. Students must be engaged in the learning process as a two-way communication between the teacher and the student or among students.

Just as skills are no longer viewed as isolated pieces within subject areas, individual subjects are also viewed as pieces of a larger integrated curriculum. Reading, writing, and mathematics are all combined across the curriculum. Readers comment on literature with written responses. Writers seek examples of style and tone through reading a variety of authors. Mathematicians write out answers to complicated problems in narrative form. Verbal communication is also important, as students are encouraged to talk about their solutions with teachers and other students in a variety of formats.

World Wide Web Site: If you wish to learn more about how teachers are connecting through the web, you may do so at: http://www.teachnet.com

Integrated Instruction

Integrated instruction includes several important concepts. First, it can refer to how teachers approach skills instruction. Integrated curriculum embeds basic skills instruction into processes that demonstrate real uses of the skill. Students learn the skills by using phonics and addition facts during reading and mathematic computations that resemble actual reading and mathematics calculations. The skills may be the focus of instruction when initially presented to the students, but their relevance to learning and understanding how to comprehend reading material or how the addition facts relate to mathematic computations is a formal overall goal of instruction. While drill and practice of basic facts is used in integrated curriculum, the skills learned are repeated and linked into the total process. Learning skills related to specific subject areas is more meaningful and relevant when integrated into real uses.

Second, integrated instruction has to do with overlapping the learning of different subject areas. There are times when different subjects are easily integrated together for more meaningful instruction. For example, when studying a particular country in social studies, students can read literature presenting characters from the country's culture, use mathematic skills required for graphing population or determining distances on a map, look at art and listen to music of a specific culture, and review the types of animal and plant life associated with the country's geographic area, thus bringing many subjects together in one unit of study. Elementary teachers do this quite easily since they are usually responsible for one subject. Integrated instruction is somewhat more difficult for middle school and secondary teachers, since this means that they must work together with teachers across the content areas. However, participating in cross-content planning teams can help bridge traditional barriers between content areas. Secondary teachers may make a special effort to seek out colleagues who will collaboratively plan and participate in integrated thematic units across the content areas. For example, English, history, art, and music teachers may collaborate on a Shakespearian unit focusing on appropriate literature, history, art, and music associated with a specific play.

Linking Disciplines

An integrated curriculum that links the disciplines throughout the day may be a preferred way of teaching for many teachers. As students get older and move into the more discipline-structured environment of the secondary schools, integrated instruction becomes more difficult. Teachers who want to integrate subjects across disciplines often have to locate a willing partner in another discipline, and even then they face the further difficulty, when schedules cannot be coordinated, of not sharing the same students. Some secondary schools arrange their schedules to encourage cross-disciplinary teaching. They schedule classes such as math and science together in two- or three-hour blocks. The shared blocks of time for two different subject areas provide opportunities for students and teachers to work together across the disciplines. Some universities have integrated mathematics and science methods courses to set examples for future teachers.

Learners must continually search for connections between new learning and familiar concepts in order to make sense of the new information. An integrated curriculum can help in that process by making it easier for students to see patterns and connections between disciplines. By providing the brain with a way to connect and organize new information, students are able to understand the content more deeply and are then able to transfer this new information to other areas (Franzee & Rudnitski, 1996). "Because the learner is constantly searching for connections on many levels, educators need to orchestrate the experience from which learners extract understanding. They must do more than simply provide information or force the memorization of isolated facts and skills" (Caine & Caine, 1994, p. 5).

Some research has shown that the majority of teachers in the United States, especially in secondary education, are still following the prescribed written

REFLECTIVE JOURNAL ENTRY

VOICE OF A PRESERVICE TEACHER

I need to make sure that I realize discovery learning does NOT mean random or chaotic learning. It requires as much or even more planning as other types of instruction. I fell into this trap today, and I don't plan on doing it again. A good reflection of whether or not I make progress on this will be on my sound lesson Friday. This lesson uses the same type of instructional strategy. We'll see how it goes.

VOICE OF A CLASSROOM TEACHER

It is a good idea to lay out everything the afternoon before you do the lesson. Think hard about materials, worksheets, groups, etc. I know we will have a great week.

recipe of the textbooks with little deviation—students read the chapters and answer the questions at the end of the book (Goodlad, 1984; Sizer, 1984). However, some teachers are breaking new ground in developing curriculum that is student-centered and organized to help students make connections between subjects. Recent research has shown that such integrated techniques involving students in problem solving and critical thinking can lead to greater achievement and more meaningful learning (Aschlbacher, 1991).

Teachers who use an integrated approach often build classroom activities around problem solving and projects that incorporate higher levels of thinking (Jacobs, 1989). As students work to apply and demonstrate their knowledge, effective teachers begin to allow students to have a greater voice in the curriculum, and the roles of the teacher and student begin to change (Franzee & Rudnitski, 1996). Teachers who use a thematic or integrated approach to curriculum believe not only that subjects should be interrelated but also that children should be a part of the goal-setting process. No longer is the teacher seen as the source of all knowledge in the classroom, directing all classroom activities and learning. Today's teacher is seen as a guide and a resource for students as they need assistance in getting meaning from the curriculum.

Thematic Teaching

Thematic teaching is an effective strategy for helping students make connections between the disciplines. Units of study may last only a week, usually in the lower grades when students stay in the same classroom the whole day, or six weeks or longer in upper grades. These units integrate learning objectives from many different subject areas under one thematic umbrella and are often selected from children's interests, a piece of children's literature, seasonal topics, or other material. Classroom space is designed with collaboration in mind. Children are expected to be active participants, and classroom areas are provided to encourage reading, writing, listening, and speaking.

Including Cultural Diversity

Attention to equity and diversity should be included in every curriculum area, not just for special units of study. A two-week unit on African American leaders or on women's issues, while still better than no mention at all, leads students to believe these issues are outside the mainstream of the normal curriculum. Every unit taught can have a story of a different culture in it. Examples that reflect the history of *all* groups should be integrated throughout the curriculum, not set apart as a special event to be studied in isolation at a special time of the year.

The materials a teacher selects for the classroom can impact the success of all students. Diversity in the classroom should be reflected in the diversity of curriculum materials. Texts and other materials should reflect a variety of cultural backgrounds and be free of stereotypical language and characters.

Textbooks are often criticized for presenting history from a single majority viewpoint. For example, the stories of Thanksgiving and Christopher Columbus have long represented the European perspective, but as classrooms become diverse, so must the perspectives of historical events. Textbooks also often use stereotypical images and language that can be nonrepresentative of student background and culture.

Classroom libraries need to have a variety of multicultural books. No one book can represent one subject or one culture perfectly. Within each multicultural group are many different experiences and personalities. While books may show some similarities among people of all colors, they should not make all characters talk and act the same regardless of color. Culture brings individual, distinct differences to characters and stories.

Books also need to reflect changing times. Folktales from a particular culture can provide information on values and traditions of a group of people, but current stories from a variety of cultural backgrounds are also needed to tell the full story of how a culture has evolved.

Effective teachers are familiar with the cultural background of students in the classroom. Such knowledge helps teachers learn to accept and respect students for their differences, realizing differences are strengths rather than deficiencies. Teachers learn to appreciate the variety of backgrounds and experiences that students bring with them into the classroom. Each person in the classroom, including the teacher, brings a unique perspective into the room. Each person has something to offer to the learning community. Good teachers encourage positive self-esteem when they recognize, validate, and respect each individual student's unique cultural background, making connections constantly with the students' out-of-school experiences and cultures.

Instructional Guidelines

The content of the curriculum and the materials used to convey concepts are critical to the success of all students, but individual teachers bring their own personalities into the classroom again as they seek out the best strategies for teaching the content. The selection of equitable instructional strategies is an important teaching responsibility. Several guidelines exist to help in this selection process.

- *Maximize time on task.* Students are engaged in learning activities for the majority of the academic time. In order to accomplish this, teachers have to spend time planning and preparing for the learning activities before the instructional time. All necessary materials must be ready and organized for easy distribution so that students can begin work quickly with all the materials they need. Routines are established to make transition times move quickly and efficiently. The focus of the classroom and the majority of the time is spent on meaningful learning activities.

- *Model thinking strategies aloud.* Effective teachers constantly model powerful thinking strategies—talking through their thought process as they explain solutions and responses. Every step of the learning task is modeled carefully to ensure success for all students. Students are routinely expected to follow the teacher's example and are often asked to "think aloud" so that others can learn the process they went through to solve problems.

- *Encourage multiple ways of solving problems.* Effective teachers encourage multiple approaches to academic tasks. Students are encouraged to come up with creative ways of approaching problems. The process of how students reach a solution is just as important, if not more so, than the correct answer. Teachers encourage students to use their own background and knowledge of the world to reach a solution that is unique to them. Problems must, therefore, be centered in the real world and applicable to the age group and interest of the student.

- *Make dialogue an integral part of the teaching process.* Effective teachers make dialogue the central means for teaching and learning. Students are engaged in discussion about their learning, not only with the teacher but with each other, and are constantly called upon to explain or justify their responses to others. Throughout the process, student language is not devalued.

- *Use cooperative learning activities in the classroom.* Cooperative learning is a way of promoting respect, understanding, and positive relations in a diverse classroom by encouraging students to work together in small groups to maximize their own learning and that of their peers (Johnson, Johnson, & Holubec, 1984). Cooperative tasks can encourage teamwork, intercultural understanding, and positive interactions when group members realize that they must combine their talents and abilities to complete the required task. Leadership responsibilities are shared, and students learn to help each other succeed.

Lesson Planning

An experienced teacher's lesson plans are usually little more than a written outline to follow. The lesson plan may describe the instructional goal, the behavioral objective, the activity, and the materials needed, but these plans usually serve as a means for teachers to organize their thoughts. Much more planning occurs in the teacher's mind than is ever written on the lesson plan.

For preservice teachers observing in an experienced teacher's classroom, this internalized decision making can be deceiving. Because extensive lesson plans are not specifically written down, some may think little planning was done prior to the lesson.

When teachers are beginning to learn how to plan, clearly written lesson plans provide a necessary reminder of the thought processes that experienced teachers may have internalized through many years of practice.

There are many different formats for lesson plans and teachers often experiment with several until they find one that works well with their particular style of instruction. Most lesson plans have some basic components in common as they guide a teacher through planning and teaching the important components of a lesson.

- *Objectives.* The learning outcome described in an objective is what students should be able to do upon completion of the lesson. The language of the objective must be specific enough so that the learning can be measured and the stu-

REFLECTIVE JOURNAL ENTRY

VOICE OF A PRESERVICE TEACHER

I really love watching you teach. You are so sure about what you're talking about. It makes them pay attention. I also think it's neat that you read about something and then you try it—for example, the writing in math. You're also to the point when you're teaching of knowing when you can go on. I think sometimes I do too much practice and it drags out too much and becomes boring.

VOICE OF A CLASSROOM TEACHER

Knowing when to move on in a lesson is really something that comes with experience. (I know you just love to hear that!) Remember that I taught this similar lesson the three previous years. I think part of it also involves really observing the students and scanning the room throughout the lesson.

dent outcome observable. Were students able to achieve the objective? How did they demonstrate their understanding?

• *Motivation/Introduction.* Starting a lesson and gaining the attention of the learner is a critical, and often overlooked, part of teaching a lesson. Each lesson should begin with an instructional focus that prepares the learner for active engagement in the lesson and should be designed to arouse curiosity and interest. Depending on the readiness of the learners and on the learning environment, this activity can be as simple as leading the class in a review of a previous lesson on insects or as complicated as a dramatic retelling in costume of the Gettysburg Address. Student motivation must be taken into account when planning a successful opening, and all students must be actively engaged in the lesson from the very beginning. In classrooms with young learners, this may mean physically moving students to a location in the room where they can focus on instruction. The introduction is also the time to inform students, in vocabulary suitable to the age group, about the objective of the lesson and what they will be required to do at the completion of the lesson to demonstrate understanding.

• *Teaching Activities.* The direct instruction segment of the lesson is the time to help students recall past learning. Previously learned information can be recalled from past experiences outside of school or from the lesson the previous day, but the connection to past learning is critical. The actual teaching portion of the lesson can take many forms. A teacher can guide a whole class in a discussion of new concepts, or students can work together in small groups to discover new learnings. Whatever the format, careful planning is necessary to ensure maximum time on task.

• *Student Activities*. Students need the opportunity to interact with new concepts and learning materials independent of the teacher. Student activities provide necessary practice for students to achieve the objective. Activities can involve everything from independent seat work, lab activities, or creative writing and art demonstrations. Teachers monitor and provide feedback to students as they practice and interact with the materials.

• *Closure/Evaluation*. At the close of the lesson, a teacher restates the learning objectives, summarizes the activities, and provides opportunities for students to demonstrate mastery of the objective. The closure of the lesson should have a direct relationship to the objective and the desired outcome.

• *Classroom Management Concerns*. Teachers must provide a positive learning environment in the classroom where students feel safe from physical and emotional abuse—a classroom climate free of intimidation, insult, and criticism. Talking about respecting others is not enough. The environment of the classroom must encourage students to display responsible behavior and discourage abusive and disrespectful behavior. Effective teachers don't assume students come to school with strong interpersonal and social skills. They teach these important life skills along with the academic subjects. Planning for classroom management concerns should also be a part of the lesson planning process. How should students move from one activity to another to ensure little wasted time? Who might have difficulty working together? Where in the lesson might potential problems develop?

Evaluation and Assessment

Structured evaluations, anecdotal records, interviews and interest inventories, and student self-evaluations are all examples of ways that teachers can be informed about their students' learning. A most recent trend in assessment and evaluation is the use of a portfolio system. Portfolios traditionally are used by artists, actors, and models to demonstrate their work and potential, but students can demonstrate their work and potential by collecting samples, examples, and responses to chronicle their learning, growth, and development. A portfolio is a collection of materials indicating an individual's thinking, problem-solving abilities, attitudes, beliefs, and knowledge acquisition. Portfolios are more than collections of responses to class assignments; they include self-reflections, summaries of work, and descriptions of students' work.

The lesson plan in Figure 7.2 was completed by a preservice teacher as a part of a thematic unit on ecology and habitats for first-graders. Notice how carefully she planned out each part of her lesson—estimating the time needed for each part of the lesson, writing notes to herself on questions and content information, and anticipating possible classroom management concerns before they occurred.

World Wide Web Site: You may learn more about creating lesson plans at:
   http://www.ericsp.org/lesson.html

FIELD-BASED ACTIVITY 7.5

Using the following sample lesson plan, or one provided to you by your instructor, plan for a lesson that you will be able to teach in your field-based placement.

LESSON PLAN OUTLINE

  I. Objective

 II. Materials needed

III. What I want to accomplish

IV. Focus Area

 V. Procedure

     Motivation/Introduction

     Teaching Procedures and Student Activities

     Closure/Evaluation

VI. Evaluation and Assessment

VII. Classroom Management Concerns

Figure 7.2

Sample Lesson Plan

Week One, Day One
General Introduction
First Grade

OBJECTIVE (what students should be able to do after completing the lesson):

- The students will be able to define the terms *ecology* and *habitat* in their own words.

MATERIALS NEEDED (all the resources needed to teach the lesson):

- word cards (ecology and habitat)
- *Professor Noah's Spaceship* by Brian Wildsmith

WHAT I WANT TO ACCOMPLISH (personal teaching goal for this lesson):

- I want the students to have a basic understanding of the terms *ecology* and *habitat* because the rest of the unit will build on these terms.

FOCUS AREA (If someone were observing this lesson, I would want them to help me by concentrating on the following . . .):

- Are the students on task? Have I organized the discussion to ensure everyone the opportunity to participate?

Brief Outline of Lesson and Times (step-by-step description):

MOTIVATION/INTRODUCTION: **2–3 min.

- Show printed vocabulary word cards and ask students to predict their pronunciation and meaning. Record predictions.

TEACHING PROCEDURES AND STUDENT ACTIVITY: **5–8 min.

1. Show and pronounce the first word (*ecology*) and have students tell what they may already know about the word.

   Once prior knowledge is activated, then add to definitions to provide a clear understanding. Ecology is the relationship between an organism and its environment. Different animals live in all different parts of the world and do different things to survive in their environments. The way humans treat these different places affects the health of the animals who live there. What are some things that people may do to prevent animals from being able to live in a certain place any more? (pollute, litter, cut down trees, destroy environment)

2. Repeat step one with the word *habitat.* **5–8 min.
   Explain that the different parts of the world where animals live and grow are called habitats. As humans we need a special kind of habitat. What are some of the different things humans need to live and grow? Name them

Becoming a Teacher in a Field-Based Setting

(food, shelter, clothing). What kind of habitat do we need? Could we live in the forest or desert? Because all animals are different and need different things to live and grow, all habitats are different. Think about all the different kinds of animals and where they live. Can anyone name some habitats? (desert, forest, swamp, rain forest)

3. Share book with students. **10–12 min.

    Today I am going to share a book with you about animals that live in a forest as their habitat. They live there happily until something happens to their habitat. Listen while I read the book aloud and then we will talk about it.

4. Ask higher-level thinking questions. **5–8 min.
    • What part of the story could really happen? Could not really happen?
    • Are the animals in our world in danger? Why or why not? Share pictures of panda bears and black rhinos.
    • How can we help solve this problem?

5. Share information on chart tablet with students. **8–10 min.

    Have one student read a part of this summary information and then discuss what the student has read. Have the class read this part chorally. Continue this process until all the information is shared.

CLOSURE/EVALUATION (How do students demonstrate new learning?): **5–8 min.

Return to the predictions of the meaning for habitat and ecology and have students decide what predictions were correct. Each student will then write or dictate a simple definition of each new vocabulary word in their own words.

CLASSROOM MANAGEMENT CONCERNS (Where can problems be anticipated and planned for?):
• Have all materials ready to share.
• Have brainstorming chart paper available.
• Watch the transition to and from floor—plan for orderly transition.
• Enforce good listening skills—raising hands.

Becoming a Reflective Teacher

Teachers who are effective in classes with a wide range of student differences are self-reflective about their own attitudes, beliefs, and actions. They constantly work to recognize and eliminate teacher expectations based on race, class, and/or sex and are continually asking questions at the completion of each lesson, looking for the strengths and weaknesses that will impact future improvements. Here are some questions you can ask yourself after teaching your lesson:

- What was the most effective part of the lesson? the least effective?
- What were students most enthusiastic about and why?
- If you had the opportunity to teach this lesson again, what would you do the same? What would you do differently?
- Were there any surprises, and how did you handle them?

Reflecting on Learning

As discussed in Chapter 6, successful teachers maintain high expectations for all students. The influence of teacher expectations on student achievement is strong (Brophy & Good, 1974). Teachers' attitudes, and resulting actions, about students in the classroom can help or hurt their performance. Teachers can perpetuate a self-fulfilling prophecy, where a teacher's beliefs about a student's abilities are continually reinforced until the student conforms to the expectation and the teacher's beliefs become reality. Teachers can also influence student achievement by sustaining effects, where a teacher expects a certain academic performance from a student because of past experience and fails to see any change in that pattern. Teachers translate their expectations in a variety of ways. Low achieving students are often located further away from the teacher in the classroom. Low achieving students receive less time to respond to a teacher's questions, less

---

FIELD-BASED ACTIVITY 7.6

Teach the lesson you have planned. Reflect on your teaching based on the questions above. Reflect on your concerns outlined in Activity 7.1. Have these concerns or questions changed? If so, how?

---

attention, fewer opportunities to answer questions, and less feedback on responses. Self-reflection and careful monitoring of classroom response patterns can help teachers see when lowered expectations are keeping students from higher academic achievement.

Teachers must become "kid-watchers" (Goodman, 1977) and continually work to get to know each individual learner in a crowded classroom of diverse students. Anecdotal records are notes teachers keep as they observe students' learning. They can be brief notes kept in a notebook or on index cards. Teachers might also record reflections in their lesson plan books about the success of a particular lesson and suggestions for future improvements. One teacher spaces out a classroom set of notes on a clipboard, and as she walks around the room observing students, she records the information she observes on the note for that particular child. Later the notes are placed inside the child's portfolio.

Anecdotal records readjust teachers' vision of who and where the student is and sharpen teachers' insight into how students travel along the paths to learning. Only when we look as if with a magnifying glass can we see and hear individual and idiosyncratic child-based standards of growth, accomplishment, and failure (Mathews, 1992).

Peer coaching is defined as "the assistance that one teacher provides another in the development of teaching skills, strategies, or techniques" (Strother, 1989, p. 824). Teachers in peer coaching situations can observe in each other's classrooms, work together on classroom research, study current practices as a part of a study team, or just work together to solve common problems; with the idea that peers—not supervisors or evaluators—are working together to learn more about teaching and learning (Strother, 1989). Peer coaching is a form of direct assistance that helps teachers improve instruction; however, the observer is not an evaluator or a supervisor. "The process is intended to examine the efficacy of the teacher's practices, not the teacher's competence" (Nolan, Hawkes, & Francis, 1993, p. 53). Peer coaching is a supportive, not evaluative, process that encourages professional, not social, interactions in a school (Robbins, 1991) and has a teacher-specified focus.

The process requires training and time for teachers to observe in each other's classrooms in a supportive, nonthreatening environment. After the structure has been defined and teams of teachers identified, the inviting teacher schedules a preconference with an observing teacher to identify concerns and a focus for the upcoming observation. A teacher may want an observer to watch for off-task behavior in the classroom during the lesson or to listen for the types of questions being asked most often.

REFLECTIVE JOURNAL ENTRY

VOICE OF A PRESERVICE TEACHER

Well, I'm lying here in bed about to go to sleep and get ready for another week. Looking at my schedule this weekend, I began to get a little nervous about my math unit. It's difficult to get everything ready for the present week, and it seems almost impossible to look ahead, but I know it will get done.

Looking over the entries for last week helps me conclude that it was a good one. I seem to be learning a lot in a short period of time, but that's probably just because I'm writing it down and my learning is actually being recorded. It would be great if we could get students to record their learning in this manner without it being artificial. How is that possible? I have heard of learning logs, but I don't know how you get children to keep them without it being just another task they complete.

I could probably go on forever, but I should probably end this and get some sleep. This week my goal is not really an intellectual one. For right now, my goal will be to get as much done on my math unit as I possibly can before I get too busy to work on it. As far as other goals are concerned, let's see what tomorrow calls to my attention.

VOICE OF A CLASSROOM TEACHER

I liked your idea of learning logs for the kids. We should try to come up with something. It doesn't have to be anything tedious, just a sentence or two. We could possibly pick a subject a day and have the kids write about it and what they learned. Think about it anyway.

I thought the reference lesson went well today and it was fun. We were organized, the lesson flowed, and the students understood. Yahoo! I'm always excited when the kids get excited.

One inviting teacher asked a peer coach to "map" her movements around the room when she taught to see if she was unintentionally ignoring any students. The observing teacher watched the lesson and drew lines on a seating chart to show the movement of the teacher around the room. Each time the teacher stopped, the observer marked an X on the chart. The observation chart was left with the inviting teacher so she could reach her own conclusions. The resulting observation report was clear—a table of students in the front was not receiving the same teacher attention as the rest of the class. In a postconference, the inviting teacher and the observing teacher discussed possible ways to alleviate the problem and then discussed further areas for focused observation.

Related Readings

Ladson-Bilings, G. (1994). *The dreamkeepers: Successful teachers of African American children*. San Francisco: Jossey-Bass.

> *This book talks about successful teaching and learning strategies used by African American teachers. The author allows the teachers in the book to tell their own story, and as a result, we are able to envision intellectually rigorous and culturally relevant classrooms. This book will teach you important lessons about teaching all children.*

Schaafsma, D. (1993). *Eating on the street: Teaching literacy in a multicultural society*. Pittsburgh: University of Pittsburgh Press.

> *This is an interesting example of the different ways that culture affects instruction. Not only will the reader learn about cultural differences, but he or she will read an account of seven teachers who guided fifth-, sixth-, and seventh-graders to explore, interpret, and write about their community.*

References

Allington, R., & McGill-Franzen, A. (1989). School response to reading failure: Chapter 1 and special education students in grades 2, 4, and 8. *Elementary School Journal, 89*, 529–542.

Aschlbacher, P. R. (1991). Humanitas: A thematic curriculum. *Educational Leadership, 49*(2), 9–16.

Borich, G. (1996). *Effective teaching methods*. Englewood Cliffs, NJ: Prentice Hall.

Brophy, J., & Good, T. (1974). *Teacher-student relationships: Causes and consequences*. New York: Holt, Rinehart, & Winston.

Bruder, I. (1991). Guide to multimedia: How it changes the way we teach and learn. *Electronic Learning, 11*(1), 22–26.

Caine, R. M., & Caine, G. (1994). *Making connections: Teaching and the human brain*. Palo Alto, CA: Addison-Wesley.

Carr, E., & Ogle, D. (1987). K-W-L plus: A strategy for comprehension and summarization. *Journal of Reading, 30*(7), 626–631.

Clarke, C., & Peterson, P. (1986). Teachers' thought processes. In M. R. Whitrock (Ed.), *Handbook of research on teaching* (3rd ed., pp. 255–296). New York: Macmillan.

Darling-Hammond, L., & Ascher, C. (1991). *Creating accountability in big city school systems.* ERIC Clearinghouse on Urban Education and the National Center for Restructuring Education, Schools, and Teaching. New York: Teachers College, Columbia University.

Franzee, B., & Rudnitski, R. (1996). *Integrated teaching methods: Theory, classroom applications, and field-based connections.* Albany, NY: Delmar Publishers.

Goodlad, J. I. (1984). *A place called school.* New York: McGraw-Hill.

Goodman, Y. (1977). Kid watching: An alternative to testing. *Elementary Principal, 57,* 41–45.

Grabe, M., & Grabe, C. (1996). *Integrating technology for meaningful learning.* Boston: Houghton Mifflin.

Hawkins, J., & Collins, A. (1992). Design-experiments for infusing technology into learning. *Educational Technology, 33*(6), 26–31.

Jacobs, H. H. (1989). *Interdisciplinary curriculum: Design, development, and implementation.* Alexandria, VA: Association for Supervision and Curriculum Development..

Johnson, D. W., Johnson, R. T., & Holubec, R. (1984). *Circles of learning: Cooperation in the classroom.* Alexandria, VA: Association for Supervision and Curriculum Development.

Jonassen, D. (1986). Hypertext principals for text and courseware design. *Educational Psychologist, 21,* 269–292.

Knapp, M., & Shields, P. (1990) Reconceiving academic instruction for the children of poverty. *Phi Delta Kappan, 71*(10), 753–758.

Mathews, C. (1992). An alternative portfolio: Gathering one child's literacies. In D. Graves & B. Sunstein (Eds.), *Portfolio portraits* (pp. 158–170). Portsmouth, NH: Heinemann.

Means, B., & Knapp, M. (1991). Cognitive approaches to teaching advanced skills to educationally disadvantaged students. *Phi Delta Kappan, 72*(4), 282–289.

Nolan, J., Hawkes, B., & Francis, P. (1993). Case studies: Windows onto clinical supervision. *Educational Leadership, 51*(2), 52–56.

Robbins, P. (1991). *How to plan and implement a peer coaching program.* Alexandria, VA: Association for Supervision and Curriculum Development.

Sizer, T. (1984). *Horace's compromise: The dilemma of the American high school.* Boston: Houghton Mifflin

Strother, D. (1989). Peer coaching for teachers: Opening classroom doors. *Phi Delta Kappan, 70*(10), 824–827.

Tyler, R. W. (1974). Considerations in selecting objectives. In D. A. Payne (Ed.), *Curriculum evaluation: Commentaries on purpose, process, product.* Lexington, MA: D. C. Heath.

Wilson, K. (1991). New tools for new learning opportunities. *Technology and Learning, 11*(7), 12–13.

8

Outlining School Organization and Leadership

In this chapter
- Contexts of Today's Schools
- Organizational Contexts
- Leadership in Today's Schools
- Perspectives of School Leadership

Alphonse Laudato, the principal, arrived first in the morning and did not leave until long after most teachers went home. During the day, Al roamed the hallways, a short man in an oxford shirt with a clip-on necktie and, though in his forties, very trim. He had gone to college to play baseball and football he said, and had drifted into education. He looked like an athlete. He rarely stayed still.

Al belonged to Kelly School, and Kelly School belonged to Al. He once said, "I'm responsible for every teacher who walks in this door. Not that I'm in charge of everybody, the only one in charge, but I'm responsible. Come in, talk, and I'll decide if we're going to do it.". . .

. . . On really important matters, he usually did what was best for the students. Somehow he always seemed to find the money for new books or materials or field trips. She [Chris] thought Kelly's classes remained small partly because of Al's clever budgeting. She gathered that Al sometimes fell out of favor on Suffolk Street, school administration headquarters, but she thought it significant that during the first crucial year of desegregation, Suffolk Street had sent Al to Kelly to soothe the white parents who had demanded proof that their children would be safe down in the Flats. Al, with a great deal of help from the chief secretary, Lil, kept the school running smoothly. The office of the Director of Bilingual Education for the city was situated in Al's school. At least once a year Al would pick a fight with that department over some small administrative matter. The director insisted though, that he could easily forgive Al because of the way Al ran Kelly school.

—Tracy Kidder, *Among Schoolchildren*

When future teachers begin their formal training to become teachers, they focus primarily on the twenty-five children facing them in an elementary classroom or the 100 to 200 students that cycle through a secondary teacher's classroom in one day. Beginning teachers are concerned about lesson plans, materials, and the classroom management techniques that help them to get through the day-to-day teaching process. In doing this, they interact with experienced schoolteachers who serve as models, peers, and a critical source of support during their first classroom teaching experiences. Although it is important to understand the basics necessary to run a classroom, there is much more to being a teacher than what happens inside the classroom. School policies and organizational patterns continually impact the daily lives of teachers. In addition, various educational professionals influence the work of a beginning teacher.

One advantage of becoming a teacher in a field-based setting is that the experience provides immediate exposure to the whole context of a school and a

In addition to providing leadership for schools, principals play many roles during the school day. Charismatic principals such as Mario Chacon Soto are often recognized for creative and successful leadership.

school district. Preservice teachers in school-university partnership settings who are formulating their ideas about teaching will learn that teaching is more than an autonomous job with teachers and learners working behind classroom doors. They will learn about the organizational context, policy implications, leadership roles, and the multiple responsibilities of teachers that are routine in today's educational settings.

A modern view of a teacher features an expanded role that includes contributions as members of a learning community and responsibilities that extend beyond their classrooms. The constant changes and innovations in teacher roles place different expectations on everyone in the school setting. Teachers contribute to the learning communities by taking on various roles and responsibilities. Teachers are part of a collaborative team, and they work with peers and other school professionals to shape the professional culture of the schools and strengthen their school's curriculum, programs, and learning experiences. Within the structure of a professional development school setting, they also may be called upon to mentor future teachers. They are learners, subject matter specialists, instructional experts, and collaborators with a wide range of individuals who interact in the school context.

Other educators besides classroom teachers have an impact on schools, and their roles are changing, too. There are traditional expectations and require-

VOICE OF A TEACHER

When I first heard I would have a student teacher and an intern in my classroom, I was ecstatic! Imagine the one-on-one instruction, collaboration, and general productivity in my classroom! I am an organizer and planner, so I planned for weekly meetings during which the three of us would brainstorm and structure lessons together. I provided dialogue journals for each preservice teacher as a quick communication tool during our hectic school days. Each preservice teacher had his or her own teacher desk, decorated with welcome signs from my students. I was ready for what I thought would be the best semester of my educational career.

But when Holly, the intern, came into our classroom, she felt "behind" Jennifer, the student teacher, and a little left out. She let me know this and I attempted to explain to her that both she and Jennifer were equally important to our classroom, although they held different roles.

I felt relieved to clear up this problem only to be presented with another. Holly essentially did not feel more comfortable after our chat and she was not very friendly toward Jennifer. This in turn made Jennifer feel uncomfortable and she came to me with her concern. What a mess! I never thought about personality dynamics not working or jealous feelings coming out of this experience. I guess I had the logistics figured out but had not considered the human factors.

I finally realized I did not need to smooth things over between my student teacher and intern student. A feeling of mutual respect was fostered by being in a classroom where so much was happening and so many people were involved in the instruction. I feel that this is one of the greatest strengths of a Professional Development School. We learn from other educators and are exposed to other teaching styles and ideas. So many more solutions can be found by seeing actions rather than hearing words. Indeed, the semester turned out to be the greatest of my educational career, surprising me with wonderful learning experiences from the preservice teachers I worked with.

ments of superintendents, principals, and supervisors. The school reform efforts discussed later in this chapter have specifically defined the jobs that principals and teachers do. Roles and titles differ from school to school, but the changing expectations of various educators will impact the expectations of traditional roles and jobs. Every person who takes on the role of an educator will be responding to the traditional notions of his or her role, the new ideas and requirements of the many innovations in the school, the unique contexts of the school and community, the expectations of the school and district leadership team, and the skills and talents of the individuals involved.

One of the major changes in roles in recent years has been the requirement that educators collaborate with a wide range of professionals, parents, and community members. It has become important for everyone involved in the lives of young people to work together on educational processes and improvements in order to share resources and talents and to discover new ways to approach problems. Parents, businesspeople, police, social workers, and health and human service professionals, among others, can contribute to the daily activities of a school.

One of the important tasks of a preservice teacher is to learn about the context of schools, the policies that govern the profession, and the wide range of expertise and knowledge available in the school and community. This chapter illustrates that teachers' responsibilities go far beyond the walls of their own classrooms and the buildings the teachers and students occupy. An explanation of educators, professionals, and parents who become collaborators in the learning community is also presented. This chapter provides insights into the following questions:

- Do schools differ based on location?
- How are schools organized?
- What leaders take responsibility for schools?
- What is the difference between leadership and administration?
- What are some of the ways that teachers demonstrate leadership?
- How can preservice teachers demonstrate leadership?

Contexts of Today's Schools

The location of schools and the size of the community populations where schools are located affect teachers' day-to-day working conditions and environments. Schools are located in small districts serving fewer than 500 students as well as in large metropolitan districts such as New York City or Chicago that educate thousands of children. Smaller school districts may have only one superintendent and as few as one building for an entire Pre K-12 school. Large districts like New York City have multiple superintendents, school boards, and administrators, and hundreds of buildings to maintain. The different schools across our nation have different organizational, administrative, and leadership systems, but all work with children and families who have diverse experiences, talents, and concerns. Providing the best educational environments, meeting the challenges of a diverse society, and using available resources to their maximum benefit becomes the focus for any school setting no matter where it is located. Urban, suburban, and rural schools develop educational contexts that reflect the values and expectations of the surrounding communities. Size and contexts may separate the schools, but issues such as poverty, finance, and social problems establish commonalties in school settings (see Table 8.1).

Table 8.1
Selected Demographic, Economic, and Educational Factors, 1960–90

Factor	1960 Rural	1960 Metro	1970 Rural	1970 Metro	1980 Rural	1980 Metro	1990 Rural	1990 Metro
Demographic								
Percentage of the population living in nonmetro/metro areas	30.1	69.9	26.4	73.6	23.8	76.2	22.5	77.5
Percentage of the population age 18–64	52.2	56.3	53.3	56.4	57.5	61.5	58.6	62.8
Percentage of the population age 65 and older	10.1	8.6	11.7	9.3	13.0	10.7	14.7	11.9
Economic								
Median family income	$4,278	$6,211	$7,458	$9,962	$16,451	$21,104	$27,620	$37,933
Percentage of the population living in poverty	34.2	17.0	20.9	11.5	15.7	11.4	16.8	12.0
Percentage of children under 18 living in poverty	37.0	17.3	22.4	12.8	18.9	15.0	21.9	17.1
Percentage of the employed working in professional/managerial positions	14.3	21.4			19.9	27.4	22.6	32.0
Educational								
Percentage of the population completing high school or more	34.0	43.3	44.3	54.8	58.7	69.0	69.2	77.0
Percentage of the population completing college or more	5.1	8.5	7.0	11.8	11.0	17.9	13.0	22.5

Sources: *Rural Conditions and Trends*, Fall 1993; Fred K. Hines, David L. Brown, and John M. Zimmer, *Social and Economic Characteristics of the Population in Metro and Nonmetro Counties, 1970* (Washington, D.C.: U.S. Bureau of Agriculture, March 1975); *Statistical Abstracts of the United States, 1972* (Washington, D.C.: U.S. Bureau of the Census, 1972); and Economic Research Service, *Rural People in the American Economy* (Washington, D.C.: U.S. Department of Agriculture, 1966).
From Herzog, M. J. R., & Pittman, R. B. (1995) Home, family, and community: Ingredients in the rural education equation. *Phi Delta Kappan, 77*(2), 113–118.

Urban Schools

The schools in our large cities have been associated with crisis for many years, and the figures about their failures are overwhelming and depressing. Urban schools are perceived as dealing with insurmountable problems and being on the verge of failing the children and young people who attend. Many of the grim descriptions in Chapter 4 pertaining to the lives of students apply to the urban setting. Cities across the country report dismal academic results. In 1990 only 10 percent of the tenth-graders in Chicago were able to read; graduating seniors in New Orleans were reading at levels lower than 80 percent of the graduating seniors anywhere else in the United States; and over half of Houston's elementary students were repeating grades because of unsatisfactory progress (Englert, 1993). Not only are the problems complex, they are long-term. There is plenty of evidence to suggest that conditions in urban schools have worsened in the last twenty-five years (Englert, 1993). Test scores of urban students continue to be much lower than suburban students (Ornstein & Levine, 1989). Since the 1960s, students in city schools have continued to achieve at levels lower than those in suburban and rural schools (Wolf, 1978); city schools have reported terrible attendance records (Maeroff, 1988) and have been associated with hopelessness and high dropout rates (Kozol, 1967). Dropout rates continue to grow, and some cities report dropout rates as high as 75 to 80 percent (Hahn, Danzberger, & Lefkowitz, 1987).

Academic failure is compounded with the evidence that poor performance is concentrated in minority groups. A high percentage of minority students are educated in urban schools. Many students come from low-economic and single-parent homes, and their parents or family members often speak a language other than English (see Chapter 4 for a complete discussion).

Poverty has been identified as the basis for much of the crisis associated with education and other social institutions in inner cities. Poverty affects all aspects of inner-city children's lives. Transportation and housing become major issues in urban students' lives. Inner-city teachers report their students living on the streets or in cars. Low-income housing may not be accessible to families since credit is not as available to those who are living in low-income areas. Even when parents or caretakers are working, the availability of low-income housing prevents families from acquiring suitable living conditions.

Health and safety issues impact the children who attend inner-city schools. Inner-city young people tend to have greater health-related problems than young people in other areas do. The rate of infant mortality is higher, lead poisoning is elevated, asthmatic conditions are numerous, and poor dental care results in abscessed teeth and other painful ailments. Illegal drugs are more available, and violence is a common occurrence. Drug-related violence claims younger and younger victims each year. In 1990 a report estimated that "nationally, there are about 3 million incidents of street crime on school property annually and that about 338,000 students had carried a handgun to school at least once. . . ." (Englert, 1993, p. 27). Urban areas have difficulty identifying and retaining qualified teachers, particularly minority teachers. Salaries are not as high as they might be in suburban schools, and because of the conditions, city teachers must combat high turnover and morale problems. Even the inner-city school buildings create part of the problem: the physical facilities are housed in older buildings that need maintenance, and asbestos and lead paint may be present.

Despite the grim picture, there are some positive characteristics associated with schools in large cities. Urban cities have long been identified as locations of educational innovation and reform, and as a result, there have been miraculous and confirming success stories of improving school conditions. The diversity of inner cities offers a richness and tolerance for a wide range of behavior. Greater population increases the political power and special-interest group activity that allows for support of educational issues. Large cities also offer a great number of economic, cultural, financial, religious, and noneducational resources to educational institutions.

Even though inner-city schoolteacher has been identified as one of the most stressful career choices (Farris, 1996), some teachers feel that the rewards are great. Teachers who are socially oriented look forward to the challenges of inner-city schools. Curriculum is designed to encourage diversity of all kinds, allowing students to examine the social realities of their world and bring the richness of the urban setting into the classroom. Those who are successful in the inner-city schools experience challenges and rewards not as evident in other settings and have a fierce commitment to urban school reform.

One of the most hopeful signs that urban schools can meet the numerous demands of the settings is that educators are attempting to promote smaller and more personal schools (Pipho, 1995). New York City has been on the forefront of this trend and in the last four or five years has opened forty-six high schools whose attendance ranges from 110 to 600 students. The schools are characterized by a great deal of interaction among parents, teachers, and students, and these small, creative learning environments offer some hope for success. Los Angeles is also considering breaking up its large high schools into smaller schools and is reporting a new determination to make new arrangements work in large cities. Some inner cities are attempting to establish contracts with private companies to set up plans and programs to improve educational systems. Hartford, Connecticut, entered into agreement with a private company to operate thirty-two of its schools and improve its curriculum, technology infrastructure, and physical plant (Pipho, 1995).

Becoming a Teacher in a Field-Based Setting

Suburban Schools

Suburban districts are typically located outside of large cities. In many cases, urban dwellers have left the city and relocated in order to leave the problems associated with inner-city settings. This may result in the perception of more affluent neighborhoods and a school population coming from two-parent families, a mother in the home, and parents with more time and resources to spend with their children. But in reality, suburban schools vary in their makeup and approach to education. Some neighborhoods include low-income housing and others are upscale and very affluent. The greatest contrasts between school settings can be seen in suburban areas. The numbers of children and young people living in poverty, experiencing violence, and residing in dysfunctional homes may not be as great or as concentrated as in urban settings, but issues of poverty and violence are still present in suburban contexts.

Suburban schoolchildren have a prevalence of problems associated with middle-class families. In many households both parents work, and children either are in child care facilities or are latchkey children. There is a high percentage of single, working parents who leave for work before their children go to school and who arrive home long after school is out. Children and young people in suburban settings may change schools often as their mobile parents are transferred from job to job. Suburban children often have ample money but spend great amounts of time on their own and have parents who are stressed by work and financial obligations. Many schools offer before- and after-school programs so that children are not unattended when parents are out of the home.

Since suburban parents have higher incomes, the tax base provides resources and support not evident in inner-city schools. Suburban schools are able to build and repair physical facilities, equip their schools with up-to-date technology, and pay their teachers well. Suburban schools usually have more flexibility in their curriculum and will offer courses that prepare their students for postsecondary educational opportunities. Furthermore, there is generally a wide range of extracurricular activities to accompany basic coursework. Suburban teachers and administrators are more highly educated and better paid than their counterparts in urban and rural settings. Suburban schools are the settings that most beginning teachers imagine themselves teaching.

Rural Schools

Rural schools are defined by the U.S. government as nonmetropolitan communities with fewer than 2,500 inhabitants or fewer than 1,000 inhabitants per square mile (Herzog & Pittman, 1995). Since the 1800s, the population of the

United States has moved from rural locations to urban and suburban communities. Nevertheless, there are numerous small rural districts. Nationally, 51 percent of all school districts are small and rural (Schmuck & Schmuck, 1992).

Rural communities are changing as farming and other agriculture-related occupations continue to change. Large farming operations, fast-food, and nationally based retailers have changed the face of rural America. Job opportunities continue to decline, forcing many students of rural schools to seek training that will take them away from their homes to work in more populated areas. The loss of business and jobs results in fewer opportunities to raise taxes and revenues for schools (DeYoung & Lawrence, 1995). Farmland has a lower tax base than other businesses, factories, and homes, so economic environments in rural communities prevent educators from providing educational contexts that are offered by more affluent schools in cities and towns.

Rural communities offer a great deal of diversity and share many of the problems that urban and suburban schools have. Poverty, financial problems, and disenfranchised youth are all evident in small towns. Low achievement and failure to master basic literacy skills are also issues in rural areas. While poverty is traditionally associated with inner-city settings, a great amount of poverty is located in rural areas, particularly in Appalachia and other locations in the South. In 1986 the nonmetropolitan poverty rate was 50 percent higher than the urban poverty percentages, and more than one-third of rural Americans in poverty are children (Englert, 1993). Some families have remained in the same community for decades, but mobility and transit families are becoming more and more evident with the availability of low-rent housing and the lower living expenses in rural areas. Even though abuse and violent activity is evident in smaller communities, the level is much lower than in urban areas. Schools are often the center of the community, with Friday night football and basketball games the focus of the week's events (Farris, 1996).

FIELD-BASED ACTIVITY 8.1

Identify some of the salient characteristics of your school. What levels of socioeconomic status are represented in your school? What is the dropout rate in the district? Does your school have unique problems associated with its location? What are the percentages of cultural, ethnic, and religious diversity? Do the characteristics of your school reflect descriptions associated with urban, suburban, or rural locations described in this chapter?

Becoming a Teacher in a Field-Based Setting

Rural students have higher graduation rates than urban students, but fewer students from rural contexts attend postsecondary schools (De Young & Lawrence, 1995). Rural schools are smaller and poorer than nonrural schools (Herzog & Pittman, 1995). Historically, vocational and agriculture programs have been important in rural schools, but the decline in jobs associated with technical and agricultural professions have contributed to further disadvantaged rural youth.

One particularly unique cultural contribution to the rural educational issue is the ambivalence that adults have regarding educational experiences that educate their children for work in cities and large urban areas. Rural young people who are educated tend to leave their community to find work (DeYoung & Lawrence, 1995). Older community members believe that rural life is preferable to urban life and feel that education takes young people away from the rural contexts. This belief may cause them to reject referendums that would provide money and resources for schools.

Some of the positive stereotypes of rural communities, such as close connections with community and family, a slower pace of life, and close contact with agriculture and nature, suggest some of the strengths associated with small community contexts. A sense of community with small businesses and small settlements of people where everyone knows one another and watches out for their neighbors' welfare are also positive aspects of rural contexts. A close-knit family feeling characterizes schools in rural areas, even though students and parents may be critical of the facilities and resources (Herzog & Pittman, 1995).

Teachers and administrators in rural areas tend to be less experienced and lower paid than their counterparts in metropolitan areas (Herzog & Pittman, 1995). The slower lifestyle of rural communities and the isolation from cultural and recreational centers discourage beginning teachers from looking for jobs in small towns.

Organizational Contexts

Children and teachers are organized around developmental and curricular needs. There is no longer a standard arrangement for grade levels in elementary and secondary schools. Grade-level arrangements are often determined by physical space needs, community traditions, and administrative decisions.

Preschools

It is more and more common for schools to include programs for three-, four-, and five-year old children. The preschool curriculum is flexible and includes time for play, reading aloud, naps, nutrition, and social interaction. The focus of many preschool programs provides stimulating experiences and opportunities to develop language skills and other important concepts. The importance of a good preschool experience has been supported by research associated with Head Start programs, which were initially funded in the 1960s. Head Start was designed to provide preschool experiences that would help children from low-income families succeed when they entered school. Preschool teachers have different requirements from state to state, and there are some states where teachers do not meet the same certification requirements as kindergarten, elementary, middle, and high school teachers.

Elementary Schools

Our formal education usually begins in elementary schools. Elementary teachers have a great deal of responsibility for establishing the learning environment for young children. Most elementary schools are organized by grade level and are self-contained, with one teacher planning and delivering instruction for all subjects. Most early elementary years are devoted to reading, writing, spelling, and mathematics, with smaller amounts of time designated for social studies, science, art, and music. Schools are increasingly focusing on basic skills before moving on to other subjects.

The structure of elementary schools varies. Traditionally, elementary arrangements included kindergarten through sixth grade. It is not unusual to see primary school arrangements with preschool, kindergarten, and first and second grades in one building or with other structures and arrangements of different grade levels. Arrangements may be based on space and other special needs of the school. Preschool programs, middle school arrangements, and programs for at-risk students have expanded the complexity and offerings at elementary schools.

Upper Grades and Middle Schools

The more than 5,000 middle schools and junior high schools (Lewis, 1993) in our country educate preadolescents, aged eleven to fifteen. Upper grades may be self-contained or departmentalized, with teachers trained in specialty areas taking the responsibility for individual subjects.

Becoming a Teacher in a Field-Based Setting

Middle schools are usually defined as some combination of grades five through eight. The middle school concept focuses on the transition between elementary and high school environments. Teachers of older elementary children are highly student oriented and are trained and certified to teach students in grades one through eight. The focus is on the special needs of adolescents, and the teachers use elementary teaching methods to instruct specific content area material, preparing students for the subject-focused instruction of junior high and high school. The focus on content becomes greater with each successive middle school grade level. Most middle schools are departmentalized but encourage interrelationships and connections across subjects and encourage teachers to plan for instruction in an interdisciplinary manner.

Junior High and High Schools

Junior highs can include any combination of grades seven through nine. High schools commonly include grades nine through twelve, but some include only grades ten through twelve. The focus of junior high school and high school is on general subjects, college preparatory curriculum, and vocational training. A great deal of freedom is given to junior high and high school students to select courses. High schools are referred to as comprehensive because they offer not only a wide variety of course offerings but also programs for students who plan to attend college or vocational schools or enter the workforce after completing high school. There are also magnet high schools that offer students an emphasis in a particular area of study, such as science or the arts.

High school students have many social pressures and make decisions that impact the rest of their lives. Behaviors and attitudes related to smoking, drinking, dating, and driving are established during this time. They also begin to develop interests and abilities that will influence future career paths and lifestyles. Peer pressure is great for junior high and high school students. Students can legally drop out of high school at age sixteen, and students who drop out are a particularly troublesome issue for most high schools.

High school teachers are trained as subject matter and educational specialists. They usually major in a content area such as math, biology, or English. Their certification typically allows them to teach grades seven through twelve, but this may vary from state to state. Junior high and high school teachers are much more focused on the subject matter than their elementary and middle school colleagues are, and they may teach five or six daily classes in a specific content.

Leadership in Today's Schools

During the 1970s and 1980s, when many of us were in school, school leadership was viewed as an individual and personal activity, usually embodied in a principal, that led to a successful and effective school. In the traditional definition of leadership, the principal was the single leader in a school and the multiple followers were the teachers (Mendez-Morse, 1992). The principal had a great deal of the responsibility for setting goals and for establishing budgets and other activities that contributed to establishing long-term objectives and everyday processes in a school. In the past, definitions of school leadership implied that only administrators such as principals and superintendents were leaders in a school setting.

More recently, school reforms and changing views have contributed to a different view of leadership that is much more complex and requires collaboration and contributions from multiple viewpoints. The newer definition of leadership evolving in many schools requires leadership contributions from all educators and staff in the school setting, including principals, teachers, general staff, superintendents, school board members, parents, and the community. This view of leadership directly impacts teachers' roles, and in many schools teachers are required to participate in various decision-making processes related to teaching, learning, and policies. While traditional administrative roles are still present in schools, there are changes in the leadership processes.

State Policy Makers

State Governments State governments have a great deal of impact on the education available in individual districts. Often the state is responsible for the funding patterns that support its schools. Governors are often seen as leaders in developing educational reform. Both President Clinton, when he was governor of Arkansas, and Lamar Alexander, former governor of Tennessee, were viewed as strong educational supporters.

States continue to exert a strong amount of control over the schools. They can impact an individual school in several ways. They may develop and require competency tests for both students and teachers, establish teacher certification regulations, develop state-adopted curriculum and textbook selection processes, set school year schedules, oversee special needs accommodations, and make rulings about many aspects of school life.

In most cases, the state has a direct impact on teachers and on what happens in individual classrooms. This is particularly obvious in states that put a great deal of emphasis on mandated achievement tests. Most states develop standardized tests, establish test schedules, score and tabulate results, and respond to district performance on tests by awarding designations that indicate successful school achievement based on testing.

State Educational Agencies and School Boards State agencies and school boards have official authority over schools, particularly in areas of high school requirements, student achievement testing, curriculum guidelines, teacher certification, and professional development of teachers (Myers & Myers, 1995). State agencies are made up of professional educators who work on establishing state guidelines, implementing policies established by the state legislature and school boards. Their duties include assisting and assuring that schools comply with state requirements, maintaining high standards for students, and conducting research that informs the public about schooling. The state agency also assists local school districts in interpreting new laws that have been passed by the legislature.

Some states have a state agency and a state school board. Usually, the state agencies work closely with the state school boards. State school boards are most often comprised of elected citizens or those appointed by the governor. They meet regularly to discuss school policy, review curriculum, and select state-adopted textbooks. In several states, the school boards accredit the teacher preparation programs and encourage the professional development of experienced teachers. They may also grant waivers to schools who want to try innovations that may not concur with existing standards.

Teachers should be aware of the politics and policies established by state agencies and school boards because they can have a direct influence on important issues such as what and how teachers teach, when they teach, and how they and their students are evaluated.

Professional Organizations

Teachers share many of the same concerns and hold the same professional goals and responsibilities. There are many times that they need to work together to provide input and to influence the profession. Several organizations help teachers collect the power to deal with organizational, curricular, and personnel decisions that contribute to the context of teachers' professional lives.

Unions Unions are organized groups that advocate for teachers in relation to issues of hiring, benefits, working conditions, and pay. There are two major

School board meetings provide a forum for many ideas and opinions. An Austin school board meeting attracted a large audience that engaged in a debate about issues associated with sex education.

teachers unions in our country—the National Education Association (NEA) and the American Federation of Teachers (AFT). NEA was organized in 1857 and about two-thirds of the teachers in our country are members (Myers & Myers, 1995). Anyone who works for a public school is eligible to join NEA. A member of NEA may participate in a wide variety of activities sponsored by the association, including professional workshops, legislative sessions, and work on innovative programs. NEA has stated that it is changing its mission and focusing primarily on teaching conditions and pay, and that in the future it also will be involved in setting and assessing high standards for the teaching profession. The NEA's goal is to involve teachers in the profession's evaluation and promotion of excellence.

World Wide Web Site: You may learn more about the National Education
   Association at: http://www.nea.org/info/faq.html

Nearly one million educators belong to the American Federation of Teachers. Most of the membership of AFT is located in cities, and the activities of the federation focus on teacher employment concerns. AFT provides activities and support about job security, establishes standards, disseminates profes-

Becoming a Teacher in a Field-Based Setting

sional information, provides training programs, and works to make sure that teachers have affordable health care and fair employment opportunities. In the last few years, the NEA and AFT have considered how they might work closer together in establishing and implementing high standards for teaching.

World Wide Web Site: You may learn more about the American Federation of Teachers at: http://www.aft.org

Unions are organized at national, state, and local levels. They have different levels of influence depending on the state and region. In many states, the unions negotiate contracts between school boards and teachers. Unions in other states support teachers' rights to strike when certain situations exist. Most strikes occur during salary and working conditions disputes. However, unions do a great deal more than organize strikes and negotiate contracts. They also influence legislative and regulatory policy, protect teachers against legal action, provide personal support, set professional standards, and provide such things as insurance, investment programs, travel packages and book clubs for teachers (Myers & Myers, 1995). In some schools, identified teachers represent the union and will contact a new teacher soon after they join the faculty. They provide a new teacher with information about the union and encourage membership in it.

Specialized Organizations Several professional groups are closely tied to specialty areas, particular groups of children, or different educational professional roles. There are also groups of professionals who are brought together because they teach in a particular setting, region, or type of school. The specialty groups and associations attempt to influence decisions and advocate around their particular area of identification. These groups also publish journals, hold national meetings, conduct research, and provide staff development for their members. These organizations include, for example, the American Association for Gifted Children, the International Reading Association, the Association for Childhood Education International, the Council for Exceptional Children, and the National Council for Teachers of English.

FIELD-BASED ACTIVITY 8.2

Ask teachers in your school and education and other professors what professional groups they belong to and what activities and resources are associated with membership. Share your findings with your classmates.

In a recent school board interaction in a southern state, the school board and community became involved in a long, heated argument over naming an elementary school. The selected name—one of a famous state hero—represented an historical figure who was also a slave owner. One school board member objected, the community reacted, and the papers and nightly news in the small city became embroiled in the discussion. The discussions were very heated, and it wasn't long before state and national news agencies began to run the story.

Local Policy Makers and Administrators

The states make broad sweeping decisions about policy, curriculum, testing, and other issues related to education, but the state policies are enforced and interpreted by local policy makers and administrators. Local educational governance such as school boards, unions, and districtwide leadership directly impacts the day-to-day working conditions and environments in schools.

District School Boards The local school board is a group of elected citizens who oversee the total process of schooling in the community. Depending on the state and the community, the school board has a great deal of responsibility for leadership and advocacy for the educational process and young people (Cohen, 1990). It contributes to the development of long-range goals, attracts and retains high-quality personnel, and assures that resources are directed to students with the greatest need. It oversees the implementation of goals and policies and checks to make sure intended efforts are being accomplished.

A typical school board meeting addresses citizen and parental concerns as well as teacher and staff issues; approves building plans and budgets; and supports and suggests local educational efforts. Controversial issues such as sex education, role of prayer in schools, and censorship are often considered by the school board. The school board attempts to build policy consensus in school dis-

---

FIELD-BASED ACTIVITY 8.3

Attend a school board meeting. Make a chart or otherwise illustrate the patterns of interaction among those attending. Answer questions about who attended, who spoke, and their concerns. What topics were on the agenda and what decisions did the board make during the meeting?

---

tricts with factions and pluralistic differences. One of their big jobs is to interview, identify, evaluate, and supervise the superintendent. As a result, the superintendent's role can be greatly affected by the district's school board.

School boards offer a good example of the democratic process. School boards discuss and make decisions about issues that are reflections of societal concern. School boards that are attuned to their constituency listen to citizens and are impacted by what they hear. The most positive outcomes occur when decisions and solutions represent multiple constituency in the community. Their decisions are usually made quietly and without a great deal of fanfare, but sometimes the entire community can get involved. Controversial decisions can produce an appearance of television cameras at board meetings, newspaper reporters at the schools, and citizens' debates in newspapers.

Superintendents and the Central Office The superintendent is the chief executive of an entire school system. As in most leadership and administrative jobs, the superintendent's role reflects the personality of the individual who assumes the role. Approaches to the demands of the job vary dramatically. The influence of the superintendent is reflected in all aspects of schooling in a community. The superintendent is usually the point person for the community in regard to educational issues and is responsible for the public view of the school. The community holds him or her responsible for establishing and maintaining a shared vision that reflects the community values. In addition, the superintendent is responsible for overseeing the budget, conducting bond elections that raise money for the schools, working with the school boards, meeting state and local directives, and supervising and working closely with principals, curriculum directors, and other administrators in the district.

The amount of contact between teachers and superintendents will depend on the school setting. New teachers in a large city will probably seldom see their superintendent, whereas a small-town superintendent may know most of the teachers by name. There are, however, large-school superintendents who make it a point to walk the halls of their schools so that teachers are familiar with them and feel free to talk to them. The principal may serve as a liaison between the school and the superintendent, and in all but the very large districts, the superintendent and principal probably will know each other very well and have a strong working relationship.

A superintendent's office may be referred to as the central office or the central administration. The central office is usually the hub of the entire district operation. Central offices in large cities may be housed in multiple buildings. In small school districts, the superintendent and support professionals and staff are often located in one of the school buildings, but in most cases there will be a physical complex devoted to the administrative aspects of a school district. Central office administrators include curriculum directors, special program coordinators, teacher appraisal specialists, and personnel officers. Professionals in the central office assist schools and monitor compliance with state and federal requirements.

Teachers usually come in contact with the central office during professional development sessions and curriculum planning projects. Professional development sessions may be conducted in afternoons after school, during the week or so before school starts, or for longer periods of time during the summer. These sessions are usually planned by the central office to introduce a new teaching approach or to work on instructional areas (such as improving math scores on state achievement tests) targeted by school goals and objectives. Central office curriculum directors are responsible for guiding the development of new curriculum. They often identify representatives from individual schools and bring them together as a work group to design new guidelines for teaching and learning.

Supervisors One group of educators who may support teachers at either the school district level or on the school campus are the supervisors. Supervisors are usually assigned to oversee the instruction of a particular content or specialty area. They may be specialists in areas such as math, language arts, or fine arts who operate at the district level or who are assigned to a specific school. Schools also employ early childhood, special education, gifted and talented, and English as a second language supervisors who may be housed in the central office, visit school campuses regularly, establish professional development activities in their particular area, engage in problem solving with a teacher who is experiencing difficulty, or develop classroom innovations. Usually, supervisors have been outstanding teachers who have demonstrated a great deal of curriculum and instruction understanding and also possess leadership skills to offer needed guidance

---

FIELD-BASED ACTIVITY 8.4

Tour a district's central office. Arrange to have someone who works in the office explain what they do. Think about how a new teacher would depend on the support and resources offered by the office.

Note: Smaller schools may not have a central office. Find out how the services typically provided by the central office are offered in smaller districts.

---

and direction. They can be a great help to new teachers and will often be available to observe instruction and make suggestions for improvement. Some large school districts hire a supervisor for new teachers, and his or her job is to support beginning teachers during their first year.

School Administration and Leadership

Teachers work for and with many people—students, parents, school boards, communities—but principals and teachers often develop a very close working relationship. Principals are the most immediate supervisors of teachers and usually serve an important leadership function in any school. The principal's role includes many responsibilities and has been identified as the primary factor contributing to excellence in public schools, regardless of the unique ethic or socioeconomic factors of the school community (Task Force on Education for Economic Growth, 1983). Whether the principal's main job is to oversee the day-to-day operations of the school campus, he or she often performs a variety of other functions and extends leadership opportunities to others.

The Principal's Roles A simplistic review of a principal's day reveals the variety of activities that are a part of his or her job. The principal may arrive at the school before teachers. This may be the only quiet time he or she has in the day to go over budgets, write memos to the central office, or establish a schedule for the next school year. When teachers begin arriving for their day, they often stop by to talk to the principal about one of their students, an encounter with a parent in the grocery store the night before, or their progress on curriculum development. On other mornings, teachers might want to talk about conflicts between two teachers, ordering more paper, or requesting a substitute teacher for a personal day of leave. As the early morning continues, the principal's office begins to fill with children arriving at school. Parents often stop by the office to compliment, complain, request, or greet the principal. As more children begin to arrive, the principal begins to walk the halls greeting the children. He or she may stop to visit with students, interacting and commenting on their concerns. As the school day continues, the principal is often called to fix the heat, help with a sick child, monitor a group of children while a teacher returns an important phone call, or talk to a parent. Once the bell rings and the school day starts, the principal divides the time between attending meetings at the central office, dealing with parental phone calls, meeting with local community groups, writing reports for state requirements, balancing the budget, ordering supplies, and meeting with small groups of teachers. At lunch, he or she may make an attempt to be present in the lunchroom or appear at the bus stop or on the playground during

VOICE OF A PRINCIPAL

Last week, I was kicked, screamed at, bled on, and bitten, all in the course of doing my job. I'm not a doctor or a policeman. I'm not even a professional wrestler. I am a public school administrator. I work in an elementary school in a good neighborhood with parents that, for the most part, are very concerned and involved with their children's education. But even the "good" schools are not immune to the changing demands placed on our public schools today.

On Monday, I told a teacher to lock herself in her classroom with twenty-two four-year-olds. One of those four-year-olds was wearing the marks of an abusive parent—a parent who was on his way up to the school. I stood outside that locked door, between that large, angry man and those children, and prayed . . . prayed he didn't have a gun . . . prayed he wasn't going to hit me . . . prayed I would be brave. I never thought my profession as an educator might one day cost me my life. I thought about it a lot last Monday.

On Tuesday, I listened to parents. Bobby Miller's parents said the teacher doesn't understand him—he's not meeting Bobby's needs. Bobby is attention deficit and that's why he knocked out Suzy Johnson's two front teeth. Martha Wilson's parents said the teacher doesn't understand her either—she's not meeting Martha's needs. Martha's gifted and that's why she ate all the tape residue off the chalkboards. So many needs. How can we possibly meet them all?

On Wednesday, Joe Patterson busted his head open on the playground. Due to the budget cuts, we don't have a full-time nurse. I got there first. By the time I got him inside and calmed down, I was covered in blood. The counselor kept waving those plastic gloves in my face, but I couldn't stop. The child was hurt. The child was bleeding. I wasn't going to leave him to go inside for plastic gloves. Later, I washed the blood off my hands. It will never come out of that white dress.

On Thursday, Michael had a bad day. When Michael has a bad day, we all have a bad day. Michael was born addicted to crack. He bit me three times on the way back to the office. No one taught me the right way to carry a biting six-year-old out of a classroom so that others can learn. No one taught me about Michael.

On Friday, I listened to teachers. I listened to them teaching despite the distractions. I listened to them worrying in the teacher's lounge over children they couldn't reach. I listened to them crying in my office over the stress of the job. I listened. It was the least I could do.

On Saturday, I yelled at someone I loved. He had no way of knowing about Monday through Friday. He had no way of knowing it was not for him.

On Sunday, I was back at school—working quietly in a deserted office. And when the work was finally done, I walked those quiet halls on Sunday all alone. I didn't think about being kicked, or screamed at, or bled on, or bit. I thought about children—laughing children, reading children, learning children.

But on Monday . . .

recess. After the children leave, the principal may work or meet with teachers, conduct staff meetings, attend extracurricular activities associated with the school, or have an hour or two of paperwork to finish before the day is over. Often in the evening the principal attends school board meetings or other activities associated with the school.

While principals in secondary schools may have daily schedules that are similar to that described above, there are some differences. Their day starts early and ends late, but they may be working on larger budgets, ordering supplies for larger groups of teachers, and working closer with professionals from central administration. Secondary principals also work with assistant principals who supervise teachers and deal with individual student concerns. Supervisors and teacher team leaders take a great deal of responsibility for developing and implementing curriculum, but it is the principal's job to establish the vision, facilitate communication, and make sure standards are being met in all subject areas. Since the students are older, the parents are not as evident, and some of the discipline problems are much more serious. Teachers and principals in larger schools may not have the same close, working relationship common in smaller schools. In the evenings, the principal can be found supporting and attending sports events, concerts, drama productions, and other events that are part of the school's extracurricular activities.

Principals differ widely in the way they perceive their role (Leithwood, 1992), based on different personal philosophies, personalities, styles of operation, idiosyncrasies, and habits. Administrative styles, personal interactions, and beliefs about student development all contribute to the uniqueness of leadership style. Some principals may be very reserved, whereas others are accessible and easy to approach. A supportive principal will remove obstacles, provide material and emotional support, manage details, share in the professional comradeship, and help establish the goals for the school (Sergiovanni, 1992). Although there are numerous categories of tasks of the principal, the following are particularly important to new teachers or preservice teachers who are beginning their professional development.

• *Establishing vision.* Principals are responsible for maintaining the school vision and for implementing the practical steps to accomplish educational goals and objectives. They help establish a " . . . clear vision of short- and long-range goals for the school . . ." (Sergiovanni, 1992). A school's context and character reflect the goals and objectives established through the principal's facilitation. In one elementary school, the principal was the leader in recognizing the richness that accompanies the large numbers of international students in attendance at his school. The school hallways, curriculum, extracurricular activities, and pride became rooted in the focus on internationalism. They welcomed children from around the world and became known as a school that displayed a great deal of diversity. The same school faculty, under the leadership of the principal, accepted the preparation of new teachers as part of the vision. All the teachers in the school accepted the responsibility of preparing new teachers and becoming involved in a complex school-university partnership. The goals of internationalism and teacher education established a unique culture in the school that impacted every teacher in the school.

The most important goal of any school is the success of all students, teachers, and professionals in the school. The achievement and happiness of students comes first in the establishment of a vision for the school, and principals must also have high expectations for teachers and themselves. A principal's way of administrating and leading can have a great impact on the potential success of all who work and learn in the school. Successful principals have figured out how to balance their focus among teachers, children, and community.

- *Managing the school.* Principals are crucial contributors to the school and the way it operates. They manage the budget, oversee equipment purchases, hire teachers, and establish school schedules. Although they may distribute their managerial responsibilities to other professionals in the school, principals are ultimately responsible for administrative aspects. Some schools may enroll a large number of students and justify hiring assistant principals to be responsible for scheduling, student conduct, curriculum development, or other issues related to the complex process of school leadership. But when there is a problem to be solved, an issue to discuss, or teaching/learning expectations to uphold, it is the principal who must administer and guide the process.

- *Maintaining high standards for instruction.* The principal is seen as an important element in the implementation and maintenance of effective instructional programs within a school (Fullan, 1991; Hansen & Smith, 1989). Principals' beliefs about students' abilities to learn and teachers' ability to teach affects long-range and everyday teaching and learning processes (Greenfield, 1991). They are actively involved in decision making relative to instruction and must attend to instructional objectives as well as instruction strategies. The principal is also responsible for collecting information and using data in a manner that keeps everyone in the school well informed about the performance of teachers and students.

Principals have a great influence on the work of teachers. The way that a principal interprets what a teacher does is of primary importance in the life of a teacher. Two examples of their direct impact on a teacher's career are instructional assessment and professional development activities. Consider that principals are responsible for observing and assessing teachers' classroom instructional behaviors. They provide feedback on teachers' instruction, interactions with children, and other important classroom procedures. They are responsible for providing ongoing professional development for teachers at their school. Effective principals work hard to build up the capacities of teachers and others so that they can take on some of the leadership in a school (Sergiovanni, 1992).

Schools often provide teachers a common time so they can collaborate and plan together. Planning times can be scheduled for teachers in same or related subject areas or across grade levels.

They keep in touch with beginning teachers and provide support and advice for them. The principalship is a demanding and important role and one that influences and impacts each new teacher's professional development.

• *Facilitating decision making.* Effective principals involve teachers in decision making, however, they often provide the background information related to particular decisions (Sergiovanni, 1992). In addition, they establish the parameters and processes that facilitate the decision-making process. Principals may use many different methods to involve teachers and other school professionals in decisions and once decisions are made, they aggressively seek support for resources within and outside the school to foster the goals of the school (Rutherford et al. 1983).

FIELD-BASED ACTIVITY 8.5

Ask the principal or an assistant principal to talk with you about some of the events or activities that occur during her work day. As she talks, try to determine which of the categories described in the previous text section are taking most of her time. Build a chart or graph that illustrates the principal's responsibilities.

- *Site-based decision making.* One impact of the reform movement of the last ten years is to involve as many people as possible in local school decision making. Site-based decision making reflects a less centralized approach to school leadership and requires a great deal of collaboration and trust (Midgely & Wood, 1993). Site-based decision making means many things and takes many forms depending upon the people involved in the process. It usually means placing as much decision-making authority as possible with the teachers, counselors, parents, and other professionals at individual school buildings (Myers & Myers, 1995). The knowledge and expertise of teachers is used to help make informed decisions and provide crucial insights into the teaching/learning process.

Usually, a team of decision makers includes the principal, teachers, other school staff, community representatives, and parents who work together to make decisions. These site-based leadership teams can have an impact on who is employed at a school, what curriculum is implemented, and what textbooks are published. There are many ways of interpreting what site-based decision making involves since so many schools and school districts have their own versions of the process.

One of the most common issues that arises with a site-based decision-making process is the sharing of power by those who have traditional leadership roles. Superintendents and principals must make dramatic shifts in their ideas about leadership to support the site-based management concept. Likewise, parents and others may not be familiar with decision-making responsibilities and may not possess the skills and time required to make good decisions about the school. Many districts are still experimenting with this concept, and as you begin your career, you may see many levels of success with this process.

One of the most ambitious site-based management systems was implemented in Chicago in the early 1990s. The school district completely reorganized the administrative organization to include parents in the decision-making process. Each individual school established an administrative board that provided governance and made administrative decisions. The board membership consisted of school administrators and teachers and at least half of the board was made up of parents. After nearly five years, the reorganization reports uneven results, with some of the schools improving their educational processes and others not achieving success.

Training to engage in collaborative decision making is necessary to promote the effectiveness of the site-based management process. Many teachers and administrators have been trained to understand the process in the traditional sense in which the superintendent, principal, and curriculum leaders make the decisions. But special skills are required to participate in collaborative processes. The following list of skills needed to work in collaborative decision making was compiled by the Danforth Foundation and the National Foundation for the Improvement of Education (Wallace & Wilson, 1994).

group process	honoring dissenters	goal setting
visioning	consensus building	budgeting
advocacy	cultural sensitivity	network building
conflict management	running meetings	collaboration
listening	enabling	giving away power
action research	facilitation	feedback

Many of the skills are associated with teaching, but not enough is known about the best way to help teachers become able to develop the skills to use in site-based decision-making processes. This list of skills also suggests that site-based decision-making procedures may have a great impact on the role of a teacher. The process puts a great deal of responsibility on teachers for making decisions about what occurs in their classrooms. In schools that use site-based decision-making processes, teachers can be involved in many of the decisions that have traditionally been a principal's responsibility. When there are changes in the roles and locus of authority in schools, as in Chicago, leadership responsibilities for the entire school may change quite dramatically.

A school-university partnership usually illustrates a site-based management process. In most cases there is a leadership team that makes decisions about the teacher education process. School administrators, teachers, and university faculty are involved in making decisions for the students in the teacher education program.

Perspectives of School Leadership

Educators' roles have become so complex that leadership can come from professionals who have not always been seen as facilitators, decision makers, and problem solvers. Leadership is shared among and between those in the schools (Bolman & Deal, 1994), and many must make contributions to establish and maintain vision, missions, and goals. No role has changed as dramatically during the last ten years as the responsibilities of the teachers who believe that leadership is an important part of their contribution and who take day-to-day responsibility to make leadership contributions.

There are multiple views of leadership and each school staff must interpret what leadership is and how it is best implemented in their school. A new definition of leadership that requires new skills and strategies that focus on collaboration and communication is emerging. Principals, teachers, and others in the school share decision-making processes and work together to solve problems. At times, students in the school are involved in the process. Many who accept this view of leadership believe that the process is strengthened when there is a way to hear and accept different views and perspectives.

Teachers as Leaders

Teacher leadership has been seen in traditional roles such as department heads, textbook selection committees, and union representatives. These traditional roles are limited compared to the teacher leadership opportunities that are emerging. Reforms such as site-based management and other restructuring efforts include a broader role for teacher participation and leadership. Teacher leadership roles involve teachers as mentors, team leaders, and curriculum developers. More innovative involvement in teacher leadership can come about as a result of participation in teacher-as-researcher or action research projects, instructional leadership, teacher education activities, and staff development sessions (Mendez-Morse, 1992). Educators who work with instruction and learning in the classroom are probably the best qualified to make decisions and provide solutions to many related issues. Teachers can provide leadership in curriculum, student grouping patterns, and instructional strategies. Teacher leadership is being developed in this broader sense in order to provide teachers with the opportunities to improve the quality of public education (Wasley, 1991).

The new roles that teachers are assuming involve them in the decision-making process, and they begin making direct contributions to the change that is occurring in the schools. A good example of this exists in schools that are part of a school-university partnership. Teachers' responsibilities can be very different in a school that has a mission of involvement in teacher preparation. Teachers serve as members of committees that make decisions about the preservice activities, and they assume roles as mentors, university course instructors, or internship supervisors. Sometimes teachers take strong leadership roles in planning and developing research and inquiry projects. For example, one group of teachers in a school-university partnership conducted a three-year study of the impact of interns in the school on the learning of the children in the school.

Teachers also have a great deal of insight and responsibility in decisions about teaching and can provide an important role in providing instructional

VOICE OF A TEACHER

Some families are made up of doctors, lawyers, or dentists, and people who make money. My family has chosen a lifetime of poverty in exchange for the rewards of teaching. I'm the twelfth teacher in three generations. Most of my relatives have taught elementary school, with an occasional coach or high school math teacher thrown in. My mother has even taught special education classes in the Texas prison system. During my high school years, I fought the urging of my family. I was determined to be different, but after graduation I gave in to my destiny. I love teaching elementary children and have never regretted my decision. I would have been perfectly satisfied to teach third-graders for the rest of my life, not knowing that anything else was possible, but thanks to the Professional Development School program, I have experienced types of teaching that were never dreamed of by the previous teachers in my family.

Recently, I applied and received a position as a co-teacher for a math methods course that was made available by the Professional Development School program. I wanted to teach this course because I knew that math was a weak area for me and I wanted to challenge myself as a teacher. I've been surprised by the changes I felt as a result.

Teaching this course, and working with college students, has helped me to acquire more information. I am a learner as well as a teacher. I feel more pride in what I do, which causes me to perceive myself differently. My role as a teacher has changed and expanded. I feel that my colleagues' perceptions of me have changed also, which increases my self-esteem. Whether these feelings are real or imagined on my part, the result remains the same. My teaching has improved.

It's a wonderful change of pace to work with college students. I feel the same joys when they succeed or learn a new concept that I do with my elementary students. The difference is the level of learning. We can deal with concepts and discuss topics that are far above my third-grade students. One of my favorite aspects of this class is when they come to me to discuss a problem or an idea that they have for a lesson. Many of their ideas are creative, and they are so enthusiastic about teaching that it's contagious. I've always felt that I touch the future when I work with my eight-year-old students, but now I also touch the future of all those children my college students will teach. What a phenomenal responsibility!

Teaching this math methods course and participating in the Professional Development School program has opened up a whole new world for me. It satisfies that part of me that needs to be different in a family of teachers and also that part of me that needs to teach.

leadership. Instructional leadership focuses on decisions related to students and their learning and is guided by high expectations of students and teachers and an emphasis on instruction (Heck, Larsen, & Marcoulides, 1990). Instructional leaders also use the results of students' achievement, strengths, and challenges to make decisions about instruction. For example, in the role of instructional leader, teachers may identify the writing process as an area that needs strengthening in their school. They may recognize this need because of their students' test scores or because teachers have expressed a desire to become more knowledgeable in this area. The teacher leaders may arrange for a consultant to come to the school and work with small groups of teachers, present model lessons in classrooms, and expose teachers to innovative methods for teaching writing. The consultant and the teacher leaders might provide opportunities for teachers to participate in process writing workshops during the summer and work with groups of teachers to develop lesson plans for the coming year. As they implement their plans, they continue to monitor their students' writing development through test scores and the authentic assessment of portfolios.

Instructional leadership can be interpreted as other than planning good instructional procedures for the classroom. There are several other ways that teachers can exercise their talents in leadership or can take part in activities that offer leadership opportunities. Teachers demonstrate instructional leadership when they become involved in planning and delivering continuing education for their colleagues. Successful teachers can share their favorite strategies and innovative techniques with other teachers. When teachers plan, design, and deliver learning plans or activities for their school's professional development, the activities and processes they plan reflect concerns and interests of their colleagues and are more meaningful.

There are also opportunities for teacher leaders to facilitate the organization and management of their schools. Teachers in larger schools are organized within small groups based on the grade level or subject area they teach. Schools with more than one or two teachers at each grade level or within content areas usually have team leaders that are responsible for communication, announcements, decision making, and planning. Team leaders are appointed by the principal or their fellow teachers. The small-group arrangement facilitates participation in decision making and provides a greater opportunity for all teachers to express their opinions.

The number of opportunities for teacher leadership is increasing and requires the modern teacher to consider tasks related to the profession. Individuals in schools that work in a shared leadership manner must possess strong communication and listening skills (Mendez-Morse, 1992). It is not easy to assume new roles, and teachers who are in these roles must know how to deal

---

FIELD-BASED ACTIVITY 8.6

Attend at least one team meeting or professional development session. Note the roles of the teachers that work at your school. Using the list on page 243 as a guide, determine which skills were most apparent.

Becoming a Teacher in a Field-Based Setting

with change, persuasion, and conflicts. But most of all, teachers who take on new roles must learn how to use their time differently. Even with help, it is difficult not to feel stressed as the roles of a teacher are expanded and changed (Wasley, 1991).

Experienced teachers seldom view themselves as leaders (Bellon & Beaudry, 1992; Wasley, 1991). It is, however, becoming an increasingly important part of a teacher's career. There are a growing number of opportunities and situations in which teachers can become leaders. As this trend continues, teachers may have many choices in exercising their instructional leadership capabilities.

Issues of Leadership and Authority

Preservice teachers rarely consider the aspects of leadership during their training and in fact may be unconcerned about leadership roles because they view school leadership as the responsibility of superintendents, principals, and experienced teachers. Recognizing leadership responsibilities, taking part in activities that encourage leadership, and understanding the challenges of leadership in today's schools should be a component of the preservice teachers' experiences.

Recognizing that leadership is part of the teacher's role is the first step to becoming a teacher leader. Teaching and leading are not necessarily separate processes. There are several common defining elements and common skills in teaching and leading. "Passion, meaning, and purpose" are the foundation for both leadership and teaching (Bolman & Deal, 1994, p.3) and as a person learns to be a good teacher, he or she also learns to be a good leader (Gardner, 1989, p. 18). Daily classroom interactions require leadership skills. Teachers use skills related to problem solving, persuasion, and conflict resolution in dealing with children and young people. Additionally, the teaching and learning situations offer numerous opportunities for achieving goals set for oneself and for helping students achieve their goals. The day-to-day classroom routines require leadership skills. A teacher constantly assesses situations, develops strategies, and implements plans that solve problems.

Preservice training offers methods, concepts, and ideas to help you develop into a successful classroom leader. While it is easy to understand the connections between leadership and teaching, it is not always easy to recognize some of the more subtle aspects of leadership that exist in schools. Understanding the roles and differing perspectives can provide insights into the complexity of leadership in most of our schools.

PORTFOLIO REFLECTIONS AND EXHIBITS

Prepare a portfolio exhibit. Adapt one of the field activities completed in this chapter, create your own exhibit, or complete Suggested Exhibit 8 to represent the learnings and understandings developed in this chapter.

Suggested Exhibit 8: School Leadership
Your portfolio representation for this chapter should include:
1. A summary of the field-based activities you completed for this chapter.

2. The selection and explanation of the activity that was most important to your learning.

3. Development of a graphic (a web or some other relational graphic) that illustrates all the different types of leadership that teachers can demonstrate. Use the text or other readings to support your observations. Describe each leadership role and some of the impacts of teacher leadership. Note which leadership roles can be developed during your preservice experience.

Related Readings

McIntyre, D. J., & O'Hair, M. J. (1996). *The reflective roles of the classroom teacher.* Belmont, CA: Wadsworth.

> *This book presents the many roles of the teacher and encourages each teacher to develop the capacities. Leadership is one teacher's role described by presenting realistic classroom scenes.*

Sergiovanni, T. J. (1992). *Moral leadership: Getting to the heart of school improvement.* San Francisco: Jossey-Bass.

> *This book describes school leaders who understand that attending to "people" will create more effective and successful schools.*

References

Bellon, T., & Beaudry, J. (1992, April). *Teachers' perceptions of their leadership roles in site-based decision making.* Paper presented at the Annual Meeting of the American Educational Research Association, San Francisco.

Bolman, L. G., & Deal, T. E. (1994). *Becoming a teacher leader: From isolation to collaboration.* Thousand Oaks, CA: Corwin Press.

Cohen, M. (1990). Key issues confronting state policy makers. In R. F. Elmore (Ed.), *Restructuring schools: The next generation of educational reform* (pp. 251–288). San Francisco: Jossey-Bass.

DeYoung, A. J., & Lawrence, B. K. (1995). On hoosiers, yankees, and mountaineers. *Phi Delta Kappan, 77*(2), 105–112.

Englert, R. M. (1993). Understanding the urban context and conditions of practice of school administration. In P. Forsyth & M. Tallerico (Eds.), *City schools: Leading the way.* Newbury Park, CA: Sage.

Farris, P. J. (1996). *Teaching, bearing the torch.* Dubuque, IA: Brown & Benchmark.

Fullen, M. G. (1991). *The new meaning of educational change.* New York: Teachers College Press.

Gardner, J. (1989). *On leadership.* New York: Free Press.

Greenfield, W. D. (1991). *The micropolitics of leadership in an urban elementary school.* Paper presented at the Annual Meeting of the American Educational Research Association, Chicago, IL.

Hahn, A., Danzberger, J., & Lefkowitz, B. (1987). *Dropouts in America: Enough is known for action.* Washington, DC: Institute for Educational Leadership.

Hansen, J. M., & Smith, R. (1989). Building-based instructional improvement: The principal as an instructional leader. *NASSP Bulletin, 73*(518), 10–16.

Heck, R. H., Larsen, T. J., & Marcoulides, G. A. (1990). Instructional leadership and school achievement: Validation of a causal model. *Educational Administration Quarterly, 26*(2), 94–125.

Herzog, M. J. R., & Pittman, R. B. (1995). Home, family, and community: Ingredients in the rural education equation. *Phi Delta Kappan, 77*(2), 113–118.

Kozol, J. (1967). *Death at an early age: The destruction of the hearts and minds of Negro children in the Boston public schools.* New York: Bantam.

Leithwood, K. A. (1992). The principal's role in teacher development. In M. Fullen & A. Hargreaves (Eds.), *Teacher development and educational change* (pp. 86–103). London: Falmer Press.

Lewis, A. C. (1993). *Changing the odds: Middle school reform in progress, 1991–1993.* New York: The Edna McConnell Clark Foundation.

Maeroff, G. I. (1988). *The empowerment of teachers.* New York: Teachers College Press.

Mendez-Morse, S. (1992). *Leadership characteristics that facilitate school change.* Austin: Southwest Educational Development Laboratory.

Myers, C. B., & Myers, L. K. (1995). *The professional educator.* Belmont, CA: Wadsworth.

Midgely, C., & Wood, S. (1993). Beyond site-based management: Empowering teachers to reform schools. *Phi Delta Kappan, 75*(2), 187–194.

Ornstein, A. C., & Levine, D. U. (1989). Social class race and school achievement: Problems and prospects. *Journal of Teacher Education, 40*(5), 17–23.

Pipho, C. (1995). Urban school problems and solutions. *Phi Delta Kappan, 77*(2), 102–103.

Rutherford, W. L., Hord, S. M., Huling, L., & Hall, G. E. (1983). *Change facilitators: In search of understanding their role.* Austin: The University of Texas, Research and Development Center for Teacher Education.

Schmuck, R. A., & Schmuck, P. A. (1992). *Small districts, big problems: Making school everybody's house.* Newbury Park, CA: Corwin.

Sergiovanni, T. J. (1992). *Moral leadership: Getting to the heart of school improvement.* San Francisco: Jossey-Bass.

Task Force on Education for Economic Growth. (1983). *Action for excellence: A comprehensive plan to improve our nation's schools.* Denver: Education Commission of the States.

Wallace, D., & Wilson, P. (1994, unpublished paper). *Teacher leadership.* A report from the Danforth Foundation and the National Foundation for the Improvement of Education.

Wasley, P. A. (1991). *Teachers who lead: The rhetoric of reform and the realities of practice.* New York: Teachers College Press.

Wolf, A. (1978, July). The state of urban schools: New data on an old problem. *Urban Education, 13*(2), 179–194.

9
Schools and Their Partners

In this chapter
- Families as Partners in Education
- Community Involvement
- Business Partners
- Interprofessional Partners
- Churches and Religious Groups
- Challenges of Collaboration

There were plenty of other caring, responsible adults who did their best to see that all the children in the community were getting the attention they needed. From librarians to crossing guards to Scout leaders, adults looked out for us, made sure we had enough to do and a place to do it.

There was consensus among adults that they need to present a united front when dealing with children. Adult authority gave us both a structure to our lives and a target to rebel against . . .

Community resources were managed for the benefit of children. The land surrounding each school served as a park and playing field for kids all year round. The schools were open summer mornings for sports and arts-and-crafts programs run by teenagers . . .

For good or ill, our families and the environments in which we live are the back-drop against which we play out our entire lives. Families shape our futures; our early family experiences heavily influence, and to a degree determine, how we for-ever after think and behave. At the same time, our families are shaped by the forces at work in the larger society—and by the village, whether it is a suburb or a ghet-to, in which the family lives. That is why it is important for us to try to understand the personal and social forces that formed our own families, and how they shaped—and continued to shape—both our lives and the village around us.

—Hillary Rodham Clinton, *It Takes a Village*

A teacher's work typically occurs in a single classroom characterized by daily lessons and learning activities. However, schooling goes far beyond the walls of classrooms and the buildings of the school. Potential partners from noneducational settings can create an expanded educational context. When school is a collaborative endeavor, successful practices evolve from the team effort of many potential partners.

Working with multiple partners may make the educational process more complex, but student success and achievement increases with additional partners. Depending on their roles, partners support teachers' daily work in different ways. Perhaps the most obvious, but also the most important partnership is between school and family. Children, teachers, and schools all benefit when parents or other caretakers show an interest in their child's education. Other potential partners include professionals who work regularly with children and parents, health and human service professionals, businesspeople, community members, and university or other educational partners.

A teacher who is aware of the importance of home, community, agency, and business involvement plans and encourages activities that naturally involve partners. Some traditional partnerships, such as parents and schools, are expected; other collaborations, such as those between social workers and teachers, are less common but also beneficial. This chapter discusses the importance of collaboration and support in young people's school achievement and suggests benefits, barriers, methods, and techniques that encourage the involvement of parents,

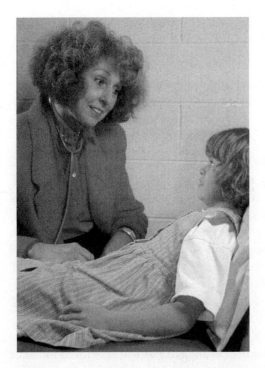

The school nurse is one of several professionals who contribute to students' well-being. A well-informed teacher will understand the contributions of the nonteaching professionals who work in the school building.

community, business, and health and human service professionals. The chapter answers the following questions:

- Who are the different partners that have the potential to impact the school achievement of children and young people?

- How can multiple partners be used to help children in today's schools, and what are the benefits of collaborative educational efforts?

- What is the school's and the teacher's role in encouraging collaboration with parents and others?

- How can beginning teachers involve others to improve the success of children in individual classrooms?

- How do other professionals associated with children and young people see their connections to the schools?

The task of collaborating with educational partners is difficult. It takes time, commitment, and skillful interpersonal skills to collaborate with partners to develop innovative and creative approaches to common problems. Connections to groups outside the school contribute to an expanded support system for children and to the likelihood that they will be able to reach the highest possible standards and successes.

Families as Partners in Education

Parents, family members, and other caretakers who provide the primary care to students make important contributions to their children's educational process. Recent suggestions that parental involvement in schools is of vital importance comes from many different sources. During the past decade, the federal government has advocated family involvement. The National Goals 2000 puts a great deal of responsibility on parent partners in educational activities. The national education goal on parent involvement states that "by the year 2000, every school will promote partnerships that will increase parental involvement and participation in promoting the social, emotional, and academic growth of children" (U.S. Department of Education, 1994, p. 2). This emphasis has remained through the presidential terms of Reagan, Bush, and Clinton, indicating that parents as partners in the educational process is not a fleeting fad and will be with us for some time to come. The National Board for Professional Teaching Standards (1994), which seeks to create common standards for teachers throughout the United States, proposes that "highly accomplished teachers work to create positive relationships with families as they participate in the education of their children."

Evidence supports the importance of parent and family participation. Getting parents and other significant adults involved in school improves young people's attitudes toward school and contributes to their overall school success (Rasinski & Fredericks, 1989). Parental involvement in school results in clear gains in the achievement of children (Henderson, 1988). Involved parents have children with more positive attitudes about school and higher aspirations for the future (Epstein, 1993; 1995).

Parental and family involvement results in achievement gains and improved attitudes toward education for several reasons (Scott-Jones, 1988). Parents and primary caregivers are children's first teachers and have worked with children for five or six years before teachers become involved. Parents know their children and continue to have a powerful influence on their attitudes and learning (Lortie, 1975). Nevertheless, adult support does not provide the same influence in all situations. Parental attitudes toward their children can cover a wide range of responses from helpful and supportive to domineering and intimidating, to displaying indifference, or to demonstrating open hostility.

Family involvement tends to decline as children get older. For the most part, parents of elementary age children control the environment and resources available to their children and have a great influence on children throughout the decisions and choices they make. While not as obvious and direct, families continue to impact young people even as they begin to exercise their own independence in middle school and high school. A change in relationship between families and their older children requires adjustment of expectations and requirements throughout school years as students take more responsibility for decision making.

The common decline in parental involvement at middle and high school can be avoided if parents and teachers consider and plan for changing needs of students. All students, no matter what level, want their families to understand and be more knowledgeable about school (Epstein, 1995). When children are younger, they are usually delighted to see parents and other family members at school. Later, in middle school and high school, parental and family involvement may not be as explicit and may take different forms, but it is equally as important as it was in earlier years. As students get older, they can become responsible for engaging their family in school activities and communicating with them about school activities, homework, and school decisions.

There are benefits for teachers, family members, and children when parental involvement is successful (Spaulding, 1996). Each time family members and educators interact with each other, more understanding and acceptance develop among all involved. Parents' observations provide teachers with insights into the lives of students and give a different perspective on school behaviors. Sharing information about the child's situation at home or at school supports the development of successful learning that contributes to more effective classroom interactions and planning. Likewise, when families understand what is occurring at school they can support students and become involved in school activities. Parents and family members involved in school activities perceive that teachers

---

FIELD-BASED ACTIVITY 9.1

Write a short narrative about your memory of your own family members' experiences with the schools. What did they do? When did they come to school? Were they interested and involved with your school experiences? Did their involvement change as you entered middle school and high school? If possible, contact your parents or other family members to determine what they remember about your own family's involvement in your education. Share this information with your peers.

---

understand their children, know about their backgrounds, including special circumstances in their history. Teacher expectations of the child are related to adult family members' involvement in school activities. Adults who work closely with the schools almost always perceive that teachers believe each child will succeed in school (Spaulding, 1996).

In addition to providing teachers with information about students, family members can become involved by visiting, volunteering, or working on projects at the school. The school can receive additional support from parents and family members when they add extra hands, additional ideas, untapped resources, and different perspectives to ongoing activities in the school. The presence of family members in the school and classrooms also means that community values are represented in the school. Family involvement in schools is one way to take advantage of a diversity of cultures in some areas and have the diversity represented in hallways, committee meetings, and school functions. At the same time, family involvement sends a signal to children and young people that learning and schools are important aspects in the community and in the lives of significant people in their families.

Characteristics of Family Involvement

Rioux and Berla (1994) and Flaxman and Inger (1992) point out that family involvement can take many forms, but certain elements of involvement characterize programs that are successful. Schools with successful family involvement programs share the basic assumption that collaboration with others provides benefits for children from elementary grades to high school. These schools encourage and nurture involvement and collaboration.

Children from low-income and minority families have the most to gain from parental involvement in the schools. Family participation in the education of these children enhances their achievement (Henderson, 1987). Despite this outcome, most collaborative programs have attracted primarily white, middle-class, English-speaking family members. Parents and other family members from all socioeconomic levels, but particularly from low income and minority groups, may be intimidated by interactions with school personnel, afraid the problems their child is encountering in school will ultimately be blamed on their inability to raise the child properly. In this manner, a child's difficulty in school can add to an already stressful home situation, leaving parents feeling like failures (Comer, 1994). In addition, some parents may relate school to their own past learning problems or bad experiences with school personnel.

Factors That Encourage Family Involvement

Parental involvement in schools can depend on the age and needs of the children. Family members may have every intention of being a partner with their teachers, and for some this comes naturally. Other family members may need to be encouraged and instructed on what will help their children and their teachers. Family involvement can be encouraged by district or school administration or by individual teachers. More than any other strategy the school may employ, the teachers' interactions and encouragement build successful relationships between homes and schools. Teachers and schools foster positive involvement by employing the following strategies (Epstein, 1993; Fredericks & Rasinski, 1990).

- *Fulfillment of basic needs.* One of the first ways that families can be involved in the schooling of their children is to provide the basic needs for their children. A secure home that provides food, clothing, shelter, and school supplies contributes a great deal to school success. Teachers may take this obligation for granted, but some families struggle to meet even basic requirements. Teachers may need to obtain help in meeting student needs from other professionals, social workers, community health professionals, or others. When it appears that families are having a difficult time providing basic needs to their children, teachers can be catalysts for involving other professionals who can help the families.

- *Home-school communication.* Family involvement is encouraged when effective communication processes are established between home and school. Teachers and schools assume a great deal of responsibility for establishing lines of communication to parents. Positive communication helps family members learn about the nature of the school and the daily routines. When family members do not respond to school queries, teachers and administrators should investigate the reasons for communication failures and apply problem-solving strategies to encourage parental response.

- *Recognition of family differences.* Families demonstrate a wide range of comfort with school involvement. Many parents and family members take for granted that they will become involved in the ongoing activities of the school. They visit classrooms, attend school plays, volunteer for specific jobs, and participate in instructional activities or as guest speakers. Mothers, fathers, and other family members become involved through organized volunteer programs, which encourage individuals outside the school to become involved in school activities. Some family members may become familiar with the school and know the names of many children in the school. Other family members are more hesitant because they do not know how to become involved, need a great deal of encouragement to participate, or perceive that they lack the resources or time for involvement.

Parental involvement in school activities has the potential to improve the school environment and student achievement. Schools should provide numerous ways for parents to take part in their children's education.

- *Home-based involvement.* Teachers may need to change their own definitions of family involvement. Involvement does not always mean that family members are visible at the school and participate in every opportunity available. Another way that busy family members can demonstrate their support of schools and the learning process is to participate in instruction at home. Well-planned, home-based activities provide a way for working parents and other family members to stay connected with school activities. While homework assignments provide one means, a creative teacher might use television watching, Internet research, and reading together as part of a plan to encourage students and family members to work together on school-related activities.

- *Schoolwide goals and objectives.* Schools that are most effective in involving parents have school goals and plans for regular parental involvement. Teachers might provide individual opportunities in single classrooms, but when family involvement is an overall goal of the school and accompanies a larger plan for increasing and maintaining parental involvement, it has more chances to be successful and long-term.

- *Multiple methods of involvement.* There should be several ways to involve parents and family members. When families have several options for involvement, they can select ways to work with their schools that best suit their comfort, work schedule, talents, and abilities. Activities, meetings, and parent-teacher conferences should be planned at different times of the day so that parents who work can arrange schedules and care for their younger children. Different family values, abilities, and schedules should be considered when teachers and schools plan home-school connections. Providing interpreters for multilingual family members is another way to provide a comfortable and welcoming environment.

• *Recognition.* Everyone likes to be recognized for contributing in a positive way. Family members who are recognized for a variety of activities indicating their involvement in schools and classrooms respond positively and enthusiastically. Positive reinforcement can result in parents who view their part in school activities as valued and recognized contributions to the child's academic career.

• *Children as recruiters.* Most parents will respond to requests of their children, particularly if children register a great deal of excitement and enthusiasm about their parents' involvement in school.

• *Inclusion of all significant adults.* Parental involvement can include other family or community members. Brothers and sisters, aunts, uncles, grandparents, regular caretakers, and good friends can take part in classroom events. Families take many different forms and do not always reflect traditional mother-father-children units, but can include aunts, uncles, grandmothers, and close family friends. Parental involvement activities should be flexible in nature to include all definitions of families.

• *Collaboration among families.* Involved families can work to recruit other families to participate in the classroom. Once family members understand routines in the schools, they can take over training of new classroom volunteers. When a teacher forms teams of regular classroom supporters, they can be engaged to explain to other parents how to read aloud and how to help children with their math and can demonstrate other learning tasks.

• *Child care provisions.* One way to encourage family involvement is to provide for child care for young children who are not yet in school. This encourages greater participation of family members who are caretakers to young children and assures that everyone who wishes to be involved in the school has the opportunity to do so.

In addition to the strategies described above, some schools use unique techniques to make parents feel welcome. Employing volunteers from the community to serve as greeters of school visitors is one way to make parents feel more welcome. One school in Washington hired a parent to greet all visitors to the school. She was a member of the neighborhood, and almost all the parents recognized her and felt comfortable walking in the school when she was there to greet them. This particular greeter didn't stay a stranger to anyone, and even people who had never visited the school in the past were greeted with a big hug and a warm hello. Everyone felt welcome to the school, and the school has become a gathering point for the community.

Schools can develop a family-friendly attitude by providing physical space for families. Some schools provide a room for parents to gather. The family room becomes the hub of involvement activities and provides a community meeting place, a training center for parent and family education, and a place for families to meet their children. When schools provide a comfortable place for family members, it signifies a concrete commitment to the importance of partnerships in students' learning and school success. At the very least, the routine for parents and family members who visit the school to take part in activities should be readily recognizable so that they feel a part of the school instead of feeling left out.

Family Involvement in Elementary and Secondary Schools

Most family involvement techniques are appropriate for elementary school, but there is less experience with the family-centered approach with older students. While it is most common in the elementary years, communication with schools continues to be a high priority at the secondary level with many positive results and benefits. Some of the most accepted practices associated with family involvement need to be reconstructed when adapting to middle school and high school. By the time children are in middle school, visits by parents must be carefully planned to support children who are generally pulling away from their parents and focusing on relationships with their peers. A parent's appearance in the hallway can cause extreme embarrassment, but at the same time a parent's absence

---

FIELD-BASED ACTIVITY 9.2

Talk to students in your classrooms about how they feel when members of their family visit the school or volunteer to work with school activities. Begin a list of tips and guidelines that reflect what students, family members, and teachers relate to your class about family involvement.

Becoming a Teacher in a Field-Based Setting

at a sports event can be terribly upsetting. Middle school children like to know that their parents help plan behind the scenes and support them at home, but they don't necessarily want their parents' involvement to be obvious. By high school age, parental involvement is very different than it is with younger children. Older children want their parents to work with them to gain information, discuss important topics brought up at school, and help them make decisions about careers and college. High school students are usually comfortable having their parents attend a seminar on career choices or a band concert. They may feel very uncomfortable having parents show up during the school day to observe in their classrooms. Many high schools plan open-house events and allow the high school student and the parent to go through the daily schedule together so that parents can have a better understanding of their child's school day.

Classroom Visits One way to encourage parental involvement at the elementary level is to invite them to visit the classroom. Having their parent or someone they know in the classroom to read, tutor, or help with a bulletin board can be exciting and comforting. The classroom should be open to parents, and each parent should feel comfortable visiting during instruction. Classroom visits could be arranged in several different ways and for differing purposes.

Observation of classroom instruction is the minimum level of parental activity in the classroom. A teacher can have a set time when family members are welcome to visit. They can observe specific teaching and learning activities. Visits that have no obligations other than observing in a friendly welcoming classroom encourage later involvement by the parent in other activities.

Classroom visits help familiarize family members with routines and procedures associated with teaching and learning activities. One of the simplest things for visitors to do when they visit elementary classrooms is to share favorite stories or reading material. Family members can be included in daily read-aloud sessions and can share their favorite books. Tutoring in math, helping with writing, or working with individuals and small groups are other things that can be accomplished during parent visits to the classroom.

Classroom visits with older children might not occur as regularly and might only involve very special occasions when there is a performance or guest speaker to which groups of parents attend. Classroom visits in middle school and high school are best planned and organized with a great deal of student input.

Family Members as Volunteers The roles that parents as volunteers can take are endless. Many schools have parent volunteer programs that are regular support systems for school involvement. Family members may be responsible for an ongoing specific job or responsibility associated with school routines. They can assist in elementary classrooms by listening to children read aloud, working as scribes for children, or helping children learn math facts. Family members can help in secondary schools by accompanying groups on field trips, selling tickets at sports events, and tutoring children who might be having trouble in content areas. In some schools, parents are morning greeters as the older children arrive at school, and they also walk the halls during class changes. The presence of family members provides teachers and administrators with needed assistance, and the practice has noticeably decreased rowdiness and negative behavior.

School Conferences Teachers and family members interact about individual children during school conferences. Conferences are one way that teachers measure the level of involvement by their students' parents. Teachers get frustrated when family members don't appear, and they assume that families do not care for their own children when they don't respond to school invitations. Ladson-Billings (1994) provides some insights about parental response from another perspective:

> *One of the persistent complaints among today's teachers is that parents are not involved enough in the schools. Teachers lament the fact that more and more children come from households where both parents work. One statistic suggests that 75 percent of parents never visit their children's schools. I don't recall my parents going out of their way to come to school. Perhaps once a year they came for a conference or a student performance, but neither my mother nor my father was very visible. They were too busy working. They expected me to do what the teacher told me to do. However, if my teachers needed my parents for something, all they had to do was call. (pp. 39–40)*

Teachers would do well to remember that perceptions of parents and family members may be very different than their own and that there may be numerous reasons why they do not respond to invitations to conferences and involvement.

Often conferences are required by school districts to maintain contact with parents and/or family members and to communicate how children are doing at school. Unfortunately, most conferences usually occur as a result of children doing poorly at school. Because of this, family members often feel very insecure when they are scheduled to discuss their child's work with a teacher. If teachers also arrange contacts with family members to talk about positive events and behaviors, conferences will not be dreaded. Most family members enjoy talking with others about their children, and conferences give them an opportunity to discuss progress, strengths, and potential problems. Conferences provide information to both parents and teachers, making their respective jobs somewhat easier.

When family members arrive at school, the conference atmosphere should be comfortable and relaxed. It is good to have something concrete to discuss during the first moments of the conference. Work samples, writing folders, records of progress in content areas, and portfolios can guide the discussions, providing samples of work and anecdotes of classroom activity. Conferences provide an opportunity to interpret tests and help parents and others understand the results. Teachers alleviate many fears by discussing children's classroom responses and behaviors. Not only can the teacher share information about the students' classroom and school behavior, but parents can provide information about home behavior that will provide the teacher with important information about the child.

Telephone conferences and home visits can also provide an important time to talk to a teacher in a more comfortable, less threatening environment for the parent. These contacts are most reasonable for working family members who cannot get off work to visit the school during the day.

Many levels of involvement can be expected from families. But the ultimate goal is to gain family commitment to the importance of active home-school cooperation. This is the level at which parents, family members, and teachers plan together for home-school involvement and work together to implement the plans (Rasinski & Fredericks, 1989). Very few programs of family involvement ever achieve this level of cooperation, and once achieved, it is very difficult to maintain. Even so, this level of parental involvement should be the goal and desired outcome of each effort. An excellent checklist provided on the World Wide Web by the Center on Families, Communities, Schools, and Children's Learning can help you identify effective parent-school partnerships.

World Wide Web Site: You may learn more about the Five Types of Parental Involvement at:
http://ericps.ed.uiuc.edu/npin/respar/texts/parschoo/fivetype.html

Challenges of Family Involvement

Family involvement in school activities makes sense, but it isn't always as simple as it sounds. Parents and other family members do not always feel comfortable in schools, and educators often dismiss their views as important to the educational task (Ayers, 1993). Certain attitudes and situations can interfere with interactions between parents and teachers. Sometimes school has a particular emotional impact on parents and family members. For example, they may have experienced school failure and feel uneasy when asked to be involved with their children's classroom activities (Wilson & Wilson, 1994). If parents have not finished school, do not speak English, or feel inferior to the teacher and other school personnel, it may be extremely difficult for them to work in the school setting and feel comfortable with their children's teacher. Parents' discomfort can increase if they do not understand what they are to do or if they feel they have nothing to offer in the school setting.

Parents and family members can also feel uncomfortable talking about their parenting skills, particularly if they are having difficulty providing some of the basic needs for their children. Family members may be embarrassed when they cannot provide basic supplies or pay for school lunches. When their children are exhibiting behavior problems or are not progressing in their schoolwork, parents feel that they are not successful. Teachers will need to understand that caretakers may be very worried about their children but may not understand how to respond to the children's actions and behaviors that are causing concerns in school. If family members feel schools are being judgmental, they may avoid contact or may view teachers' queries about children's progress as attacks on their own competence as parents (Hamilton & Osborne, 1994).

Sometimes communication difficulties between the home and school create serious family and school discontinuities, discouraging parent-school linkages and providing limited support systems for students with limited English proficiency (Chiang, 1994). Immigrant parents who work long hours, encounter linguistic and cultural barriers, and lack familiarity with the American education system will often avoid coming to schools and talking to teachers. Parents need to understand what to do and how to collaborate with the teacher to help their children succeed at school (Flores, Cousin, & Diaz, 1991). Unless parents, families, teachers, and administrators work together to build a supportive learning environment, students will not receive all the benefits available to them.

Family members may find it difficult to manage their time and energy in order to come to school and meet with parents or work on projects. Transpor-

---

FIELD-BASED ACTIVITY 9.3

Volunteer to work in an activity or project that includes parents and other family members. In the elementary schools, it might be decorating the school for a carnival or family night. In the middle or high schools, it might be working in a concession stand during a sports event or chaperoning a dance on Friday night. Share some things you learned about parents and families with your classmates.

---

tation, time, and child care are all barriers for parents. Barriers are particularly troublesome for low-socioeconomic-status families since they may have few resources and less flexible job schedules (Hamilton & Osborne, 1994). At the same time low-income families are in particular need of support and interactions that contribute to the education of their children. A good education is one way they can help their children have successful adult lives.

Teachers may contribute to noninvolvement of families by not understanding how to include them in the education of their children. Teachers may not have the skills or exposure to the benefits of working with parents and families. Many teacher education programs do not emphasize working with families. Teachers may feel uncomfortable talking with families, and this may be more problematic for new teachers. If the benefits are not explicitly emphasized or if the entire school does not encourage outside involvement, a teacher who has many tasks to complete may feel that parental involvement is an intrusion and represents yet another time-consuming task. But since research demonstrates that children's achievement and attitude about school can be influenced by parental involvement, it makes sense to find ways to include parents as partners.

Teachers' Roles

Working with parents requires good interpersonal skills, and when conducted with respect, interactions with families will be successful in establishing the contact necessary for helping children do their best. Teachers need to develop skills and understandings to foster collaborative relationships between school and family. Basic interpersonal skills of communication and respect go a long way in establishing school-family relationships. Parents respond positively to reinforcement of their attempts to increase their child's well-being. Teachers who attempt to understand parents' actions will increase the number of positive interactions with parents and will enhance parents and family members' perceptions of their own abilities. However, there are times that conversations with family members involve difficult issues. Teachers should be honest and direct when talking to parents, praising children and their efforts with sincerity.

One way to ensure that all voices are heard is to institute a school-based governance team with representatives from school and family groups. Together, this team, guided by the school principal, works to develop a school plan that includes strategies for a positive school climate and academic goals for all students. When a positive, inviting school climate is the goal of all participants, parent involvement can be built in as an integral, necessary activity (Comer, 1994). When the entire school supports and encourages parental involvement, it becomes easier for each individual teacher to work with parents in productive ways.

Community Involvement

Education should be everybody's business—"a common enterprise in which all adults of the community unite to protect, nurture, guide, and educate the young" (Hindle, 1993, p. 34). The community as a whole impacts the way children feel about themselves and their attitudes toward education and is linked to student success in schools (Mattox & Rich, 1977). Explicit connections between schools and communities will affect children. Role models from all aspects of life demonstrate the importance of learning and the value of an education. If school students can see that everyone around them cares about what and how they do in school, it can impact self-confidence, attitude, and achievement.

Accomplished teachers understand their school's community and use it as a powerful resource for learning by taking advantage of the many available resources and opportunities for enrichment and exploration. The community serves as a learning and resource lab for developing tolerance and civic responsibility and for understanding about human differences. Activities and events in the community can serve as examples or starting points for discussions and classroom lessons. Experienced teachers will find community events and opportunities that are important to students and use them to build curriculum and classroom lessons.

Teachers effectively use available resources by understanding the community and how the environment impacts the students and the school. The community's context, culture, and personality makes up the fabric of its schools. The ethnic, religious, and cultural diversity; the economic and business settings; as well as the religious and historical values are all important parts of the school. Using that knowledge to build classroom projects, activities, and lessons provides a relevancy needed for good teaching and learning.

There are many valuable resources offered by individuals in the community. Important community organizations, such as churches, women's clubs, the NAACP, and fraternal groups, can provide important alliances to bring people and resources into the schools. Volunteers from such organizations can serve as mentors, tutors, and resources for lessons on specific cultural groups. More important, they can give critical advice on curriculum content. Senior citizens, parents, businesspeople, and local organizations can enhance and supplement teaching and learning activities. They can visit classrooms, tutor children, provide emotional support, and provide examples of participation in governance and administrative activities. They volunteer in the school and support school sports, music, and theater by attending events.

Involving the community in school activities produces citizens who understand and are supportive of schools and encourages good public relations between education professionals and those outside the educational setting. Informed and supportive citizens influence decisions in the schools through voting in school issues, participating on school boards, and supporting education experiences with their own work and leisure time. When schools involve and consider the community in educational endeavors, they receive needed support in times of bond elections and other endeavors that take resources to improve educational environments. Citizens who are familiar with the children and school in a community support the efforts of educators. When it appears that schools have lost the support of their citizens, then they suffer economically and fail to receive the support they need for continued growth and progress.

Partnerships between schools and communities also are effective in working against some of our most difficult social problems. Communities and schools work together to curb violence, drugs, teen pregnancies, and other tough problems. Many effective community collaborations result in improved educational programs, changes in school climate, and an increase in family support systems (Epstein, 1995).

Communities include families and children, but also businesses, community services, health and human social services, city government, juvenile workers, and others. Educational experiences are enhanced when others who come from community settings become involved in the welfare and education of young people. Communities that encourage their agencies and institutions to collaborate and assist children and families are capable of building an effective support system that has the potential to impact educational experiences. To develop an educated person, efforts must go far beyond the classroom. Without the help of those outside the classroom, even the best teachers will have difficulty in educating their students.

Business Partners

The collaboration between business and education focusing on helping schools succeed is developed in several different ways (Hindle, 1993). Business and public schools often collaborate to offer special programs to particular schools or to sponsor students for career exploration. Sometimes a three-way partnership is formed between businesses, universities, and public schools. Business/educational collaborations are almost always formed believing that broad-based alliance involving many sectors of the community is necessary for providing the best schools possible. Here are some ways that business supports education:

- Businesses can provide resources that go beyond the basic expectations of school support (Hindle, 1993). Often business provides money and equipment to support special programs such as summer tutoring, field trips, or college/career exploration. In the past few years, technology-based business has regularly supported school programs that feature technology. Computer companies provide computers, scientific companies have donated lab equipment, and even school libraries have been stocked by companies.

- Business supports supplementary programs that enhance students' educational experiences (Hindle, 1993). Special programs encouraging students' interest in math and science are one focus of business-oriented programs. Business-sponsored programs may occur in the summer, on Saturdays, or after normal school hours. Activities are planned to provide students the opportunities to serve as junior interns, office helpers, or lab assistants. Businesspeople develop mentoring relationships with individual students and have a great influence on attitudes about schools and career.

- Businesspeople also offer their expertise to education professionals (Hindle, 1993). Specialists who use a particular group process or management technique work with schools to suggest ways to improve decision-making processes, organizational approaches, and management. Total Quality Management is an example of a decision-making technique similar to site-based management that was adopted by many schools in the early 1990s. (See Chapter 4 for a complete discussion of site-based management.)

- Places of business provide students a concrete lesson in understanding about possibilities, skills, and requirements of potential jobs and occupations (Hindle, 1993). Summer internships for high school students, field trips to particular sites, and guest speakers provide needed information as young people make decisions about their future occupations.

- Businesspeople may be encouraged to become actively involved in school projects. Just as people from other walks of life, people who manage and work in business volunteer, become partners, and work directly with schools to change and enhance educational programs. Some places of business give employees time off to help schools with activities.

Many of the activities sponsored by business and industry are specifically related to the focus of their work. The hope is that they will produce future workers who are prepared for their business. In other cases, business will partner with a school as a reflection of civic duty in the hopes that they can support the community. Often there is a very good match between the emphasis of particular businesses and the goals of schooling.

School-to-Work Programs

Business has recently been involved in school reform that supports changes in curriculum. Because of business' interest in education, a great deal of discussion about the nature and outcomes of schools occurred during the early part of this decade. As a result, the School-to-Work Opportunities Act established a national framework to broaden the educational, career, and economic opportunities for all youth through partnerships between businesses, schools, community-based organizations, and state and local governments. The intention of school-to-work programs is to change the way teachers teach and children learn in schools. The basis of the change is to focus on identifying and classifying the skills workers need to perform successfully in the workplace and to coordinate curriculum developed from the skills of workers with school curriculum. Federal funds were allocated to help establish these programs throughout the nation.

School-to-work programs encourage the involvement of state and national government, employers, educators, parents, labor unions, communities, and others to become involved in designing curriculum that will meet the specific needs of local areas. Proponents of the plan believe that all young people—whether they are college bound, career bound, or out of school, or whether they possess disabilities or are culturally and linguistically different—will benefit from collaboration between business, industry, and schools.

The school-to-work plan contains three core elements:

1. Classroom-based learning that integrates work and school-based learning. This learning incorporates knowledge or skills associated with certain jobs or occupations into the regular school curriculum.

2. Work experience that includes training and mentoring at job sites. This component will usually encourage high school students to work in business and industry during the summer, in the evening, or on weekends.

FIELD-BASED ACTIVITIES 9.4

Find out about the school-to-work efforts in your community. Take a field trip to where the efforts are located or bring in an individual who is involved to describe some of the activities. Identify the concerns and issues.

---

3. Activities that interconnect school and work. This component may involve the business or industry in the school day. Students attend class during the morning, studying a curriculum related to a particular type of work, and then work on-site at the business during the afternoon.

The school-to-work opportunities systems were designed to create a transition between classrooms and the workplace or other educational settings. Creative transition programs which many people are already familiar with (such as youth apprenticeship, cooperative education, and career academies) are the primary foundations on which school-to-work systems will be built.

Influences of Business

Business tends to have a greater influence over educational changes than other groups have (Myers & Myers, 1995). Business people are usually more active in government and have power in local and state decisions. During the last decade, the influence of business has had a great influence on the educational curriculum and evaluation. Business directly impacts how schools spend tax money and the attitudes of the public toward education.

During the past decade, business and labor have paid particularly close attention to educational reform (Farris, 1996). There are many who believe that businesses have the authority as prominent community institutions and the expertise to reform and work in school reform efforts (Hindle, 1993). In some instances, business has leveled particularly harsh criticism at education, schools, and teaching. In particular, those in business question the effectiveness of school management and operations. They also support better teaching of basic skills. Most people associated with business believe that it is in their best interest that teaching and learning produce students that are proficient, knowledgeable, and able to be successful in the workforce upon graduation from high school.

Interprofessional Partners

There is no great mystery about what it takes to help a troubled child or family. In study after study, we find that two things stand out in the histories of kids who make it against the odds . . . The first fact is access to a second chance to succeed at something the person failed at before—going back to school, being helped to pass a class (as opposed to being either punished or excused for it), . . . The second is the intervention of just one caring person from outside the family

. . . that person's role is . . . to get involved in the child's life. (Coontz, 1995, p. K16)

Children and young people often face personal and social difficulties that impact their academic achievement. Teachers commonly mention that the toughest problems they face when working with children and young people are related to social, personal, and health issues. Issues of poverty, violence, drugs, and homelessness become major factors in schools that even the best teachers and the most well planned curriculum can't overcome. One way to combat social issues and the many demands that children and families face is to develop collaborative relationships between education and health and human services professionals. Nurses, doctors, social workers, community health professionals, and others are partners who focus on the welfare of children and can provide a wide range of social service activities and programs that help parents help their children. A collaborative effort between professionals who care about children is one of the best ways to offset at-risk behavior. There are many who feel that the collaboration of professionals who work with children and families, called interprofessional collaboration, is one trend of the future that holds a great deal of promise for improving the lives of children and young people.

Many of the 17,000 organizations that offer community-based programs for children and youth are fragmented and address only one specific problem (Carnegie, 1992). The services designed to help troubled children and families and the red tape associated with support are overwhelming to even the most savvy person. When children and families need help, there may be several agencies that need to be contacted before they can receive the help they need. The offices where the families could get help are often located in different parts of town and in areas that are unfamiliar to the adults and the children who need to access the services. Once individuals find where help can be provided, there are many forms to be completed, questions to be answered, and documents to be provided. The health clinic requires one form that asks a multitude of questions, the social worker asks for another form, the social security office requests still another, and so on. These documents and instructions are usually written in English that is difficult even for native speakers, much less for families who speak little or no English. Even when families finally access services, the services may be limited and may not accomplish what is needed or may require repeated visits. It is no wonder that children do not receive the services they need to do well in school.

Parents, especially those in low-income, high-risk neighborhoods, are often unaware of the array of social services available to them through the many different organizations working in the community. A school that strives to link social services and academic programs can meet many needs that can potential-

VOICE OF A PARENT

I am Maria Sanchez. I live with my husband and two children just up the block from the Family Center. I want to tell you about my experience.

I've been coming here [to the Family Center] for a year now. It is a great place to come and learn about resources around the community. Everything is in one place.

Let me tell you how I got started coming here. I used to walk my boys to the school cafeteria (adjacent to the Family Center) for free lunch during the summer. I had to walk by here and I noticed things going on. I peeked in and saw flyers telling about activities and meetings that were planned here in the Family Center. To be honest, I was bored and spent much of my time sitting in my apartment in front of the TV. It was summertime and it was hot. I had no air conditioning, and this was a cool place to bring my children. I would bring my children here to the programs or to play with toys or read books or just to talk to people. I started coming a lot in the daytime. I came to CPR classes, jewelry classes, and the one I liked best was taught by the School District Parent Educator. It was a program about how to buy a house from the city. It raised my hopes for the future.

I am thirty years old now and I have been out of school for fourteen years. I don't know why I have not thought about doing anything much to improve myself, but I guess I just lacked the drive. Now I have completed and passed my GED and I have a job with the Family Literacy Program where I get to work with and help other parents.

If it hadn't been for the Family Center, I would not have my job. The Family Center Program Manager knew my capabilities and she recommended me to the Family Literacy people for this job. At the time I didn't have any intention to get my GED, but since it was a requirement for the job I went ahead and took the GED test. I passed right away. Now I plan to go back to school. I want to take courses at the community college.

I love my job. As I said, I like working with parents. I get to plan trips to the library for parents. Let me tell you about one mother who had never had a library card before me. It was a very exciting thing for her to get a library card. I made a xerox copy of her library card to keep in her file so that she could have a memento. It was so special.

And since I know about the Family Center, I bring new people from the Literacy Program down here to see what's going on.

I want to add that since I have been coming here to the Family Center, and since I have joined Community Voices (neighborhood action group that meets at the Family Center), I have become more involved with my children's school. I feel more confident about just going to see what is happening.

ly impact the academic achievement in the classroom. Through this link with family support services, schools can address not only the academic problems of students, but also the social, psychological, and health problems. Such a school might offer, by serving as a center for other social programs, after-school care for school-age children, day care for three- to five-year-olds, adult literacy classes, teen pregnancy prevention classes, and other services that address the needs of the community they serve.

Becoming a Teacher in a Field-Based Setting

Efforts that connect social programs and educational outcomes report success stories for children. "Schools, social programs, and caring individuals can compensate for stressful environments and troubled families" (Coontz, 1995, p. K17). Problems facing children and families seem overwhelming to parents and teachers. At the same time that parents are faced with troubled children, they may be having their own crises and can't find the energy or resources to focus on their children's issues.

Interprofessional programs and activities provide needed support to children and families who find themselves in crisis. Teachers, social workers, community nurses, doctors, dentists, and juvenile workers are among those who generally collaborate to simplify processes. In some cases, police and judges are also involved in these endeavors. These professionals have various objectives, but improvement of children and family situations is at the center of their professional mission. Collaboration can begin by talking together. Collaboration among these groups must be learned, and often simple tasks between health and human service agencies take a great deal of time. In one town in Texas, professionals worked together for a year and a half to devise a single form that could be used in several social services. The result was that families and children could access services with a bit more ease than before the professionals sat down to talk

The physical facilities supporting interprofessional activities may be based in schools or housing projects, community development corporations, and child care centers. Sometimes collaborative efforts result in school-based clinics or family centers designed to encourage interprofessional collaboration. The results of these efforts help parents and other interested adults promote their children's learning and give parents training and self-confidence to be involved in their children's educational processes.

Interprofessional activities such as job counseling and training, health care, substance abuse treatment, nutrition, housing, transportation, referral centers for family social services, and before- and after-school programs for working parents are examples of support systems that can impact learning and teaching. Several labels and terms are used to describe activities that occur as a result of individuals from different professions collaborating together to provide integrated services, which are also called community-based services, school-based services, "one-stop shopping," or interprofessional activities.

Interprofessional collaborations focus on three major activities:

1. Parent education and parent involvement in the education of their children. Programs focusing on schools include the family, the school, child care and youth programs, and health care agencies.

2. Intersections between health and human service possibilities services. The focus of these programs is to encourage parents to take greater responsi-

bility for the primary health care of their children. Parents learn more about health care services, how to gain access to services, and how to make them work for the betterment of their children's lives. Efforts in this area work to assess health needs of children and youth, link families and health care providers, and help improve health education in the school.

3. Professional training of teachers and other professionals. The professional development of individuals who are trained to work across professions is crucial. University faculty involved in professional training of teachers, social workers, and other health and human service professions design curriculum and develop field experiences that allow future professionals to learn about this work.

Interprofessional work does not need to be large complicated programs. Answers to some problems may not reside in big programs designed to solve all problems at once. Intervention and help for children and their families occurs when a teacher, a social worker, a community nurse, or a police officer talk and work together on one issue. In other cases, professionals may collaborate to share needed information.

The importance of interprofessional support is that public and private community resources and public school resources can be combined to focus on prevention and early interventions that address the needs of all students. Different professional groups work together to identify and remove unnecessary regulations and obstacles to coordinating efforts and providing a strong support system to children. Professional collaboration increases the students' access to social services, health care, nutrition, related services, and child care services. The partnerships can help parents and families by locating such services in schools, cooperating service agencies, community-based centers, or other convenient sites designed to provide "one-stop shopping" for parents and students (U.S. Department of Education, 1994).

Three Examples of Interprofessional Collaboration

Healthy Learners One of the best known examples of interprofessional collaboration is Healthy Learners (Briar, 1993), a community-based program in Miami, Florida. The program is a joint effort of Florida's public schools, a university, and the state's department of health and rehabilitative services. One of the most effective and critical components of the program is the Referral and Information Network (RAIN). Composed of a family advocate and a group of mothers and calling themselves the Rainmakers, they visit families and children in the community and hold community meetings that help parents understand how they can better access the services offered in the community. Although it is difficult to assess the results of their work directly, there are positive indicators in the community that demonstrate that changes for the better are taking place. Some of the indicators are fewer police sweeps, less graffiti, higher attendance in the schools, and fewer evictions from housing in the community (Corrigan & Udas, 1996).

Corridor of Success Educators from Bronx Community College teamed up with local schools and began to develop collaborative relationships with city health and human services. The objective of the collaboration was to take back one school at a time and to develop a corridor of success in schools that were linked together by common neighborhoods and children. The initiative focuses on an evolving partnership among Bronx Community College (BCC), IS 82, and School District 9, and includes human service people and other schools. BCC and IS 82 have served as a hub for the expanding efforts related to developing a Corridor of Success for children in District 9. Parents, teachers, school administrators, and health and human service professionals are collaborating together to open lines of communication and link child and family services. The effort that began as a collaboration between BCC and IS 82 now includes schools that feed to IS 82 and a high school where many of the IS 82 children attend. A cornerstone activity of the Bronx initiative is "Friday on the Campus," in which fifth-grade students spend their day at BCC being taught by university professors, working in science laboratories, and becoming familiar with the campus.

School Families A middle school and university in Texas developed a program to involve community volunteers, university professors, and teachers in a mentoring relationship that provided middle school children support during the school day. A cornerstone activity at the Texas site has been the School Families program, which provides an academic and social support system for middle school

---

FIELD-BASED ACTIVITY 9.5

Locate a community facility that has more than one service (i.e., social services, law officials, community health facilities) in one place. It will probably be a community or family center. Choose one of the following activities to help you learn about the activities in the center: (1) Interview the professionals and/or the children and families, (2) volunteer to help with a project, or (3) sit in the reception area of the facility and take field notes.

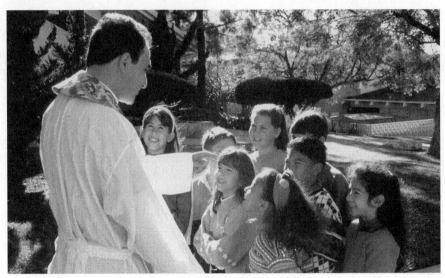

Schools are part of the larger community in which individuals and organizations outside of school contribute to students' personal, social, and academic development. Religious leaders may serve as role models, teachers, and counselors for students.

children and provides opportunities for preservice and inservice teachers, school counselors, administrators, and community volunteers to collaborate. Once a week, five adults meet with one classroom, beginning with whole class discussion and breaking apart into small groups where students and adults can discuss social, academic, and personal issues.

Accomplished teachers participate in the coordination of services to students. They understand what is available to assist children and families who are under stress, and they know how to access support systems that will contribute to their students' classroom success.

Churches and Religious Groups

Even though there is separation between church and schools, students do arrive at the classroom with different ideas about how to act on their religious faith in the school settings. Teachers and administrators must understand the law and decide the application of the law in their unique setting (Myers & Myers, 1995).

The role of the church as a partner in education is an issue in almost all school settings at one time or another. Churches provide an important community link. For many groups represented in classrooms, the church is an important component of family life. Church ministers are often considered members of the extended family and can be valuable in making school-home connections. In some communities, churches and schools are working together to provide day care and after-school programs, organize parent support groups, and improve education for their children (Freedman & Negroni, 1992; Lawson & Briar-Lawson, 1997). Constitutional law may prohibit churches from influencing public school curricular decisions, but their impact on families and their children must be considered as part of the context of schooling.

Challenges of Collaboration

There are many potential partners that can be involved in the complex job of educating our children. Collaboration is difficult, but when it is successful, there typically are payoffs to students. The challenges to developing broad-based community collaboration are many.

One of the factors that keeps this wide range of collaboration occurring is the role-specialization of all professionals in our society. Professional specialists from nurses to librarians are trained to understand a particular area and to control and manage different parts of the school system. The collaborative work between schools, families, and communities involves a great deal of negotiating to ensure that a level of cooperation between professionals will occur.

There is not a precedent for interdependence of roles in schools. Educators' roles usually are based on specialization and on understanding certain parts of the educational processes. Science teachers want to teach science, nurses are trained to provide health services, and social workers are experienced in social services. These professionals have not been exposed to ways of working together and connecting the work across professions. To begin this work, professionals will often have to learn how to work collaboratively, not worry about their own turf, and take the time to understand the context of other people and professional lives.

It takes time to see differences from interventions that involve collaboration, and schools and business don't often have the patience to support an initiative for the five to seven years it may take to note any differences.

The involvement of parents, family members, community, and health and human service professional personnel in the schools adds to the existing complexities and ambiguities that already exist. Involving others in the educational experience may seem an overwhelming task at first. However, if teachers and administrators can view the involvement of others in the day-to-day routine of schools as vital to their mission and as a resource to supplement ongoing school activities, attitudes and approaches to collaboration with available partners will be viewed positively. The results of involving the community in children's learning are recognizable yet difficult to measure. No matter what level of family, business, and community involvement a school enjoys and encourages, there will be obvious and unexpected benefits.

Beginning teachers can probably be convinced that working with families, the community, businesses, and other professionals is a good idea. How to go about getting involved in collaborative efforts is quite another matter. It may take several years of teaching before you understand how you might develop your contributions in this area. The first step for beginning educators is to become comfortable with the families and learn about the community where you work. Volunteer in community projects, serve on a citywide committee, or visit boys' clubs and girls' clubs in which your students participate.

A second step that you can take is to understand the potential and be open and flexible to ideas that involve partners outside the school walls. Learning to talk and communicate with individuals from other professions and other walks of life is a first step to developing the capacity for understanding how to work with communities. Participating in ongoing discussions and planning already occurring at the school will help a new teacher understand the potential of the partnerships. Finally, when new teachers see a way that they can become involved, they can make themselves available to participate in activities in a way that seems appropriate in their own lives.

Understand the skills associated with good collaboration. They are simple skills that are useful in all that you do and are ones that teachers usually possess. Listening to others, rephrasing what others have said, remaining flexible and accepting when hearing new ideas, and realizing conflict will emerge when people work together are just a few of the valuable skills needed to collaborate with others inside and outside the school walls.

It will be difficult to become involved with other professions when you are learning about your own role as a teacher. But there are certain options for beginning teachers that will help them work in an interprofessional manner. This goal will be much easier if it is done from the school level. Try to learn about the different social and human and health agencies that impact children's welfare. In particular, new teachers should be aware of the way to access services when their students are in need of support. Often additional support will alleviate classroom problems, and when a child needing help gets needed support it will make a new teachers' job somewhat easier. Once new teachers gain information about what is available, then they can begin helping plan cooperative ventures and participating with health and human service professionals.

Although a teacher can't always single-handedly marshal resources on the behalf of his or her children, there will be opportunities for new teachers to take part in discussions and encourage the involvement of their students in the community and look for ways for the community to become involved with them.

Related Readings

Clinton, H. R. (1995). *It takes a village to raise a child.* New York: Simon & Schuster.

> *Mrs. Clinton describes her own upbringing and her view of raising children. She describes the responsibilities of communities and how it takes more than families to watch after children.*

Hechinger, F. M. (1992). *Fateful choices: Healthy youth for the 21st century.* Carnegie
Corporation of New York: Carnegie Council on Adolescent Development.
This book provides a sense of the complexity of the risks and opportunities of the
adolescent years. The author believes that if adolescents are to make wise choices, then
families and communities must provide support while they are making the transition
from childhood to adulthood.

References

Ayers, W. (1993). *To teach: The journey of a teacher.* New York: Teachers College
Press.
Briar, K. (1993). *Response sheet: Program information on integrated services and inter-*
professional education. Unpublished raw data. Florida International University,
Miami.
Carnegie Corporation. (1992). *Matter of time: Risk and opportunity in the nonschool*
hours. New York: Carnegie.
Chiang, R. A. (1994). Home-school communication for Asian students with limited
English proficiency. *Kappa Delta Pi Record, 30*(4), 159–163.
Comer, J. (1994). Home, school, and academic learning. In J. I. Goodlad &
P. Keating (Eds.), *Access to knowledge: The continuing agenda for our nation's*
schools (pp. 23–42). New York: The College Board.
Coontz, S. (1995). The American family and the nostalgia trap: *Kappan* special
report. *Phi Delta Kappan, 76*(7), K1–K21.
Corrigan, D. C., & Udas, K. (1996). Creating collaborative, child- and family-
centered education, health, and human service systems. In J. Sikula (Ed.),
Handbook of research on teacher education (pp. 893–921). New York: Macmillan.
Epstein, J. (April 1993). Make parents your partners. *Instructor, 103*(1), 73–76.
Epstein, J. (1995). School/family/community partnerships: Caring for the children
we share. *Phi Delta Kappan, 76*(9), 701–712.
Farris, P. J. (1996). *Teaching, bearing the torch.* Dubuque, IA: Brown & Benchmark.
Flaxman, E., & Inger, M. (1992). Parents and schooling in the 1990s. *Education*
Digest, 57, 3–7.
Flores, B., Cousin, P. T., Diaz, E. (1991). Transforming deficit myths about learn-
ing, language, and culture. *Language Arts, 68*(5), 369–386.
Freedman, S., & Negroni, P. J. (1992). School and community working together:
Community education in Springfield. In L. E. Decker & V. A. Romney (Eds.),
Educational restructuring and the community education process (pp. 11–120).
Charlottesville: University of Virginia.
Hamilton, D., & Osborne, S. (1994). Overcoming barriers to parent involvement
in public schools. *Kappa Delta Pi Record, 30*(4), 148–152.
Henderson, A. (1987). *The evidence continues to grow: Parent involvement improves*
student achievement. Columbia, MD: National Committee for Citizens in
Education.
Henderson, A. T. (1988). Parents are a school's best friends. *Phi Delta Kappan,*
70(2), 148–153.

Hindle, W. R. (1993). The business-higher education link: Consider the possibilities. *Educational Record* (Summer), 33–38.

Ladson-Billings, G. (1994). *The dreamkeepers.* San Francisco: Jossey-Bass.

Lawson, H., & Briar-Lawson, G. (1997). *Connecting the dots: Progress toward the integration of school reform, school-linked services, parent involvement and community schools.* Oxford, OH: The Danforth Foundation and the Institute for Educational Renewal at Miami University.

Lortie, D. C. (1975). *Schoolteacher: A sociological study.* Chicago: University of Chicago.

Mattox, B., & Rich, D. (1977). Community involvement activities: Research into action. *Theory Into Practice, 16*(1), 29–34.

Myers, C. B., & Myers, L. K. (1995). *The professional educator.* Belmont, CA: Wadsworth.

National Board for Professional Teaching Standards (1994). *What teachers should know and be able to do.* Detroit: National Board for Professional Teaching Standards.

Rasinski, T. V., & Fredericks, A. D. (1989). Dimensions of parent involvement. *The Reading Teacher, 42*(2), 68–69.

Rioux, W., & Berla, N. (1994). The necessary partners. *Education Week, 13*(17), 31.

Scott-Jones, D. (1988). Families as educators: The transition from informal to formal school learning. *Educational Horizons, 66*(2), 66–69.

Spaulding, A. M. (1996). The politics of primaries. In A. Pollard, A. Flier, & D. Thiessen (Eds.), *Children and the curriculum: The perspectives of primary and elementary school pupils* (pp. 132–148). London: Falmer Press.

U.S. Department of Education (1994). *Changing education: Resources for systemic change.* Washington, DC: U.S. Department of Education.

Wilson, S. M., & Wilson, J. D. (1994). Kentucky parents respond to primary education reform. *Dimensions of Early Childhood, 22*(2), 28–31.

Photo Credits

Page 253 © Richard T. Nowitz/Corbis
Page 258 © Austin MacRae
Page 276 © Myrleen Ferguson/PhotoEdit

Index

International Reading Association (IRA), 233
Internet, 177
Interpersonal relationships between teachers and students, 158–160
Interprofessional collaboration, 273–274
Involuntary minorities, 88

J

Japanese school achievement, 56
Jefferson, Thomas, 33–34, 43
Job opportunities for rural students, 226
Junior high schools, 229

K

Kentucky Education Reform Act, 54
"Kid watchers," 213
K–W–L, 194–195

L

Lab activities in units, 208
Ladson-Billings, Gloria, 262–263
Land Grant College Act of 1862, 37
Language differences in students, 87, 153
Latchkey children, 225
Latin grammar schools, 33
Law and education, 73
Leadership, 243–247
    classroom activities, 247
    communication skills, 246
    multiple views, 244
    school, 230
    school-university partnerships, 243
    students in cooperative learning, 206
    teachers, 244–245
Learning, 112, 127
    disabilities, 91
    objectives, 206–207
    repetition and practice, 128
    strategies, 135–136

Learning problems in urban schools, 223
Learning specialists, 92
Learning to teach, 18
Lesson planning, 163, 206–211
Lesson plans
    example, 210–211
    outline, 209
Locke, John, 31, 43
Long-range instructional planning, 193
Low achievement in rural schools, 226
Low test scores, 71
Luther, Martin, 31

M

Magazines as instructional resources, 177
Males, classroom responses, 91
Management style of teachers, 150
Mann, Horace, 35, 43
Mathematics skills, 199
Memory
    long-term, 133–136
    modeling strategies, 133
    short-term, 133–136
Mental structures, 129, 131
Metacognition, 139
Mexican War of 1854, 37
Middle-class families, 225
Middle schools, 228–229
Minority groups
    critical philosophy, 46
    mismatch with schools, 89
    special education placement, 88
Minority parents, 88
    school involvement, 256
Minority teachers, 89
Misbehavior, 122
Mnemonics, 139
Modeling, 122, 205
Moslems, 87
Motivation, 161–162, 190, 207

Multimedia, 177–178, 197
Multistore model and cognition, 131
Murder rate, 93
Murray, Madeline, 74

N

NAACP, 266
Nation at Risk, 51–53
National Board for Professional Teaching Standards (NBPTS), 254
National Council for Improving Science Education, 191
National Council of Social Studies, 191
National Council of Teachers of English, 59, 191, 233
National Council for Teachers of Mathematics, 59, 191
National Education Association (NEA), 232
National education goals, 19, 52–53, 254
National education standards , 65
National Science Foundation, 69
National tests, 56
Needs assessment, 193
Negative reinforcement, 115–116
New Right, 71
Newspapers as instructional resources, 177
Nietzsche, 44
Normal Schools, 38
Nutrition, 99

O

Oberlin College, 36
Objectives for learning, 206
Observational learning, 121–122
Ogbu, James, 87
Old Deluder Satan Act, 33
Old Testament curriculum, 72

On-task behavior, 160–161
Operant conditioning, 114–121

P

Parent involvement, 101, 278
  beginning teachers, 278–279
  Comer's model, 69
  flexible arrangements, 259
  middle and high school, 255
  school conferences, 262
  successful educational programs, 70
Parents
  attitudes toward school, 264
  communication, 264–265
  first teachers, 254
  social services, 271
Parker, Francis, 38–39
Pavlov, 112–113
Pedagogical knowledge, 9–10
Peer
  coaching in learning to teach, 213
  conferences, 172
  relationships of students, 160
  pressure, 229
Pestalozzi, 35, 39–43
Philosophy and education, 41–46
Piaget, 129
Plato, 42–43
Plessy v. *Ferguson*, 73
Poor communities, 83
Portfolios and student learning, 208
Poverty, 83–86, 151
  ethnicity, 84–85
  experiences related to school, 85
  family structure, 85
  instructional impact, 86, 152
  large cities, 84
  mobility rate, 85
  public assistance, 85

race, 85
rural settings, 84, 226
school achievement, 83
teachers' beliefs, 85
urban schools, 223
Pragmatism, 43, 44
Premack principle, 115
Prenatal care, 98
Preschool, 228
Preservice teachers, 12–13
Principal, 237–241
decision-making processes, 241
influence on teachers, 240–241
leadership roles, 239
Prior knowledge, 138
Private educational companies, 224
Problem solving, 191, 205
Professional development schools (PDS),
20–21
Professional development of teachers, 54
Professional organizations, 231–233
Progressive education, 43
Progressive era, 38
Public law, 94–142, 92, 154,
Public schools, 35
Punishment, 116–117, 181

R

Race, 87–89
Racism, 46
Reading curriculum, 200
Realism, 42–43
Reagan, Ronald, 52, 71, 254
Referral and Information Network
(RAIN), 274
Reflection in teaching, 23, 125
Reflective teachers, 212
Reflexive behavior, 113
Reform efforts, 55

Reinforcement, 116–118
Religion, 46, 74
Religious study, 32
Remediation plan, 198
Resources
support for classroom activities, 196
urban schools, 224
Rogoff, 142
Role models, 266
Rosenshine, Barak, 123
Rosseau, Jean-Jacques, 31
Rote learning, 130
Rural schools, 225–227

S

Sadker and Sadker, 91
Sandia National Laboratory, 70
Sartre, 44
Scaffolding, 142
Scheduling, 174–175
Schema, 136
School
achievement, 82
administration, 237–241
"bashing", 71
boards, 234–235
choice, 59, 64
commonalities, 221–222
contexts, 156
critics, 71
district curriculum guides, 192
goals, 258
management, 240
prayer, 72, 74
size, 221
vision, 239–240
vouchers, 71
School Families, 275–276
School power, 69

Teacher stress, 15, 17
    classroom management, 159
    urban settings, 224
Teacher-student conferences, 171–173
Teachers
    career changes, 16
    career cycle, 13
    career development, 12
    career exit, 16–17
    career states, 14
    central office administration relation-
        ships, 236
    characteristics of good, 7–11
    competency building, 15
    cultures, 81
    cultural understandings, 79
    decision making, 10
    diversity, 79
    educational reform, 75
    enthusiasm, 15
    expectations, 155–156, 162, 256
    frustrations, 17
    induction into the profession, 14–15
    leadership, 244–245, 247
    life-long learners, 10, 12
    members of learning communities, 10
    minority, 79
    models for learning, 164
    motivators of students, 164
    personal philosophy, 23–24
    preservice education, 122
    professional organization, 233
    reflection, 11
    role models, 2
    roles as mentors, 15
    satisfaction, 17
    socialization processes, 18
    stability in profession, 16
    strikes, 233
    unions, 231–233

Teaching
    as art or science, 108
    commitment, 9
    knowledge of subject areas, 9
    professionalization, 65
Technology, 40, 196–197
Teen pregnancy, 99, 272
Telecommunications, 197
Test scores, 56
Testing, 56–57
Texas Assessment of Academic Skills,
    191–192
Texas language debates, 73
Textbooks, 176
    concerns, 176–177
    cultural diversity, 204
    learners' prior knowledge, 177
    publishers, 176
    supplemental materials, 176
Thematic instructional approach,
    203–204
Theory and practice links, 19
"Think aloud"
    protocol, 144
    strategies, 205
Thinking skills, 191
Time on task, 205
Traditional family unit, 96
Tuskegee Institute, 36

U

Unconditioned stimulus, 113
Unemployed parents, 84
Uninsured children, 98
Units, instructional, 203
Universal education, 32
University professors, 21–22
Upper grade schools, 228–229
Urban schools, 223, 224

U.S. Department of Education minority report, 87

V

Values, 44
Vicarious conditioning, 121
Violence, 93, 151
Vocational and agricultural programs, 227
Volunteers and community involvement, 266
Vouchers, 64
Vygotsky, 140

W

Washington, Booker T., 36
Weapons, 93

Whole class instruction
  activities, 175
  grouping, 169
"Withitness," 158
Women and critical philosophy, 46
Working parents, 97, 225
World War I, 44
World War II, 40
Writing skills, 200

Y

Young adult literature, 177

Z

Zone of proximal development, 140